CHILDREN AT PLAY

A *Cul de Sac* Collection

by Richard Thompson

Andrews McMeel
Publishing, LLC

Kansas City • Sydney • London

Cul de Sac is distributed internationally by Universal Press Syndicate.

Children at Play copyright © 2009 by Richard Thompson. Introduction by Mo Willems. Copyright © 2009 by Mo Willems. Used with permission. All rights reserved. Printed in China. No part of this book may be used or reproduced in any manner whatsoever without written permission except in the case of reprints in the context of reviews. For information, write Andrews McMeel Publishing, LLC, an Andrews McMeel Universal company, 1130 Walnut, Kansas City, Missouri 64106.

09 10 11 12 13 TEN 10 9 8 7 6 5 4 3 2 1

ISBN-13: 978-0-7407-8987-8
ISBN-10: 0-7407-8987-2

Library of Congress Control Number: 2009926281

www.andrewsmcmeel.com

─── **ATTENTION: SCHOOLS AND BUSINESSES** ───

Andrews McMeel books are available at quantity discounts with bulk purchase for educational, business, or sales promotional use. For information, please write to: Special Sales Department, Andrews McMeel Publishing, LLC, 1130 Walnut Street, Kansas City, Missouri 64106.

For Anne and Carol Sue,

who would have loved this.

Foreword

Richard Thompson is no friend to jealous cartoonists.[1] Speaking as someone who has had a long and varied career as both a cartoonist and a jealousian, I take Mr. Thompson's uniquely exquisite work as a personal affront.

Although other cartoonists' rough sketches invariably have more life than their finished drawings, we don't show them because, well, frankly, they're indecipherable blobs. Unfortunately, Mr. Thompson's loose, kinetic line work not only makes perfect sense, it also transforms each panel of his strip into a tiny jewel of draftsmanship.

Every cartoonist worth his or her salt[2] knows that after Schulz's *Peanuts* and Watterson's *Calvin and Hobbes*, there is nothing new that can be done with the suburban kid strip. Every cartoonist except Mr. Thompson, apparently, who breaks new ground by pairing a precocious spitfire and a paranoid misanthrope[3] in a realistically surreal world. Grrrr . . .

I won't even get into the gags that meander around the panels, unfixed, transmutable, yet consistently hilarious, or the innovative compositions, lettering, and coloring.

It is just not done. Or, at least, it hasn't been done until now.

Worst of all, *Cul de Sac*[4] is so addictively entertaining, it forces even us jealous cartoonists to put down our pencils, stop earning our salt, and get lost in a joyful, loopy, fully realized, half-baked reality.

Which is, for the record, Mr. Thompson's sole redeeming quality.

Mo Willems

---

1. The "jealous" category constitutes 87.5 percent of all cartoonists, the remaining percentage falling under either "seethingly jealous" or "Jules Feiffer."

2. Cartoonists actually work for salt, which in this economy is only slightly better than being a banker.

3. "Misanthrope" is Greek for "cartoonist." Look it up. Or don't. See if I care.

4. Is that supposed to be German or something?

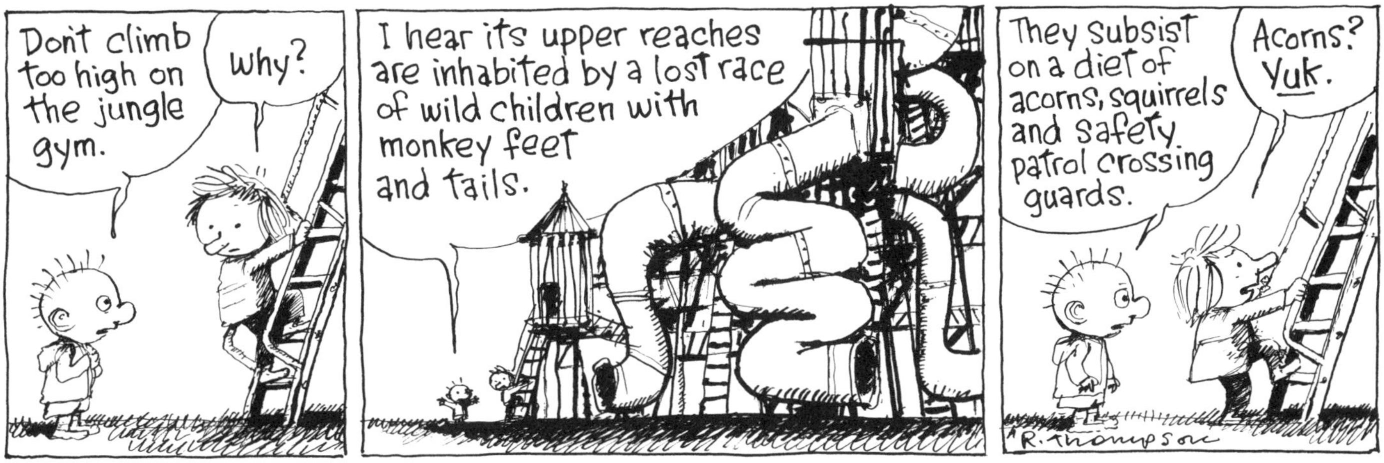
Don't climb too high on the jungle gym.
Why?
I hear its upper reaches are inhabited by a lost race of wild children with monkey feet and tails.
They subsist on a diet of acorns, squirrels and safety patrol crossing guards.
Acorns? Yuk.
R. Thompson

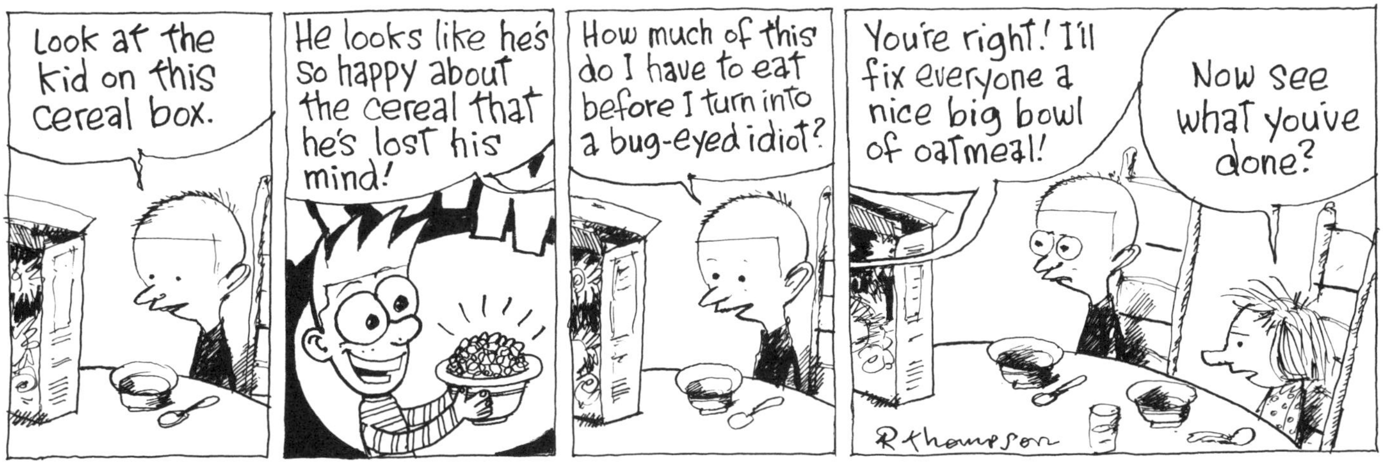
Look at the kid on this cereal box.
He looks like he's so happy about the cereal that he's lost his mind!
How much of this do I have to eat before I turn into a bug-eyed idiot?
You're right! I'll fix everyone a nice big bowl of oatmeal!
Now see what you've done?
R. Thompson

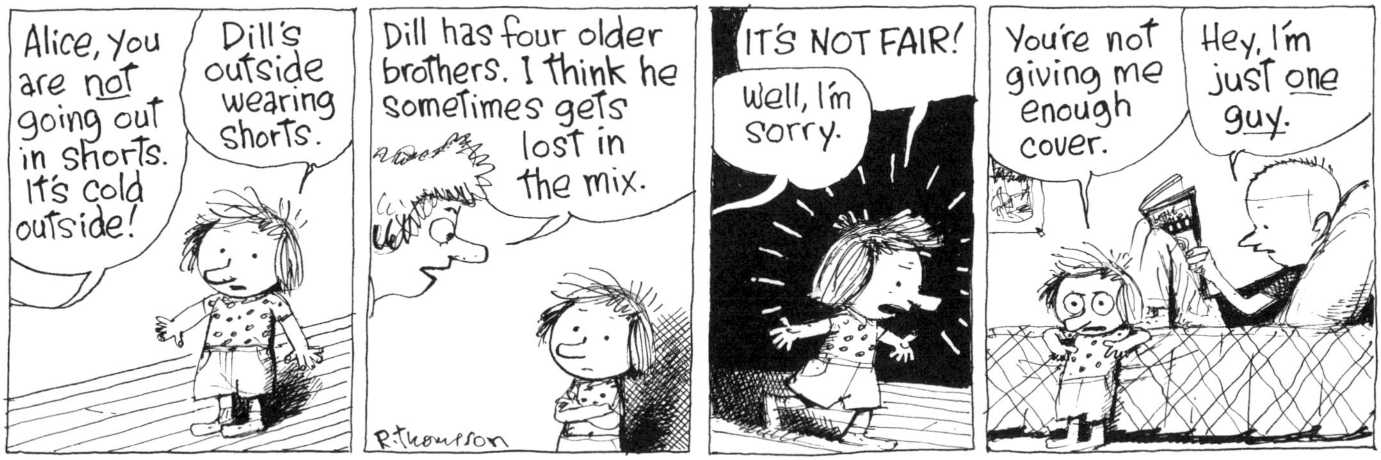
Alice, you are not going out in shorts. It's cold outside!
Dill's outside wearing shorts.
Dill has four older brothers. I think he sometimes gets lost in the mix.
R. Thompson
IT'S NOT FAIR!
Well, I'm sorry.
You're not giving me enough cover.
Hey, I'm just one guy.

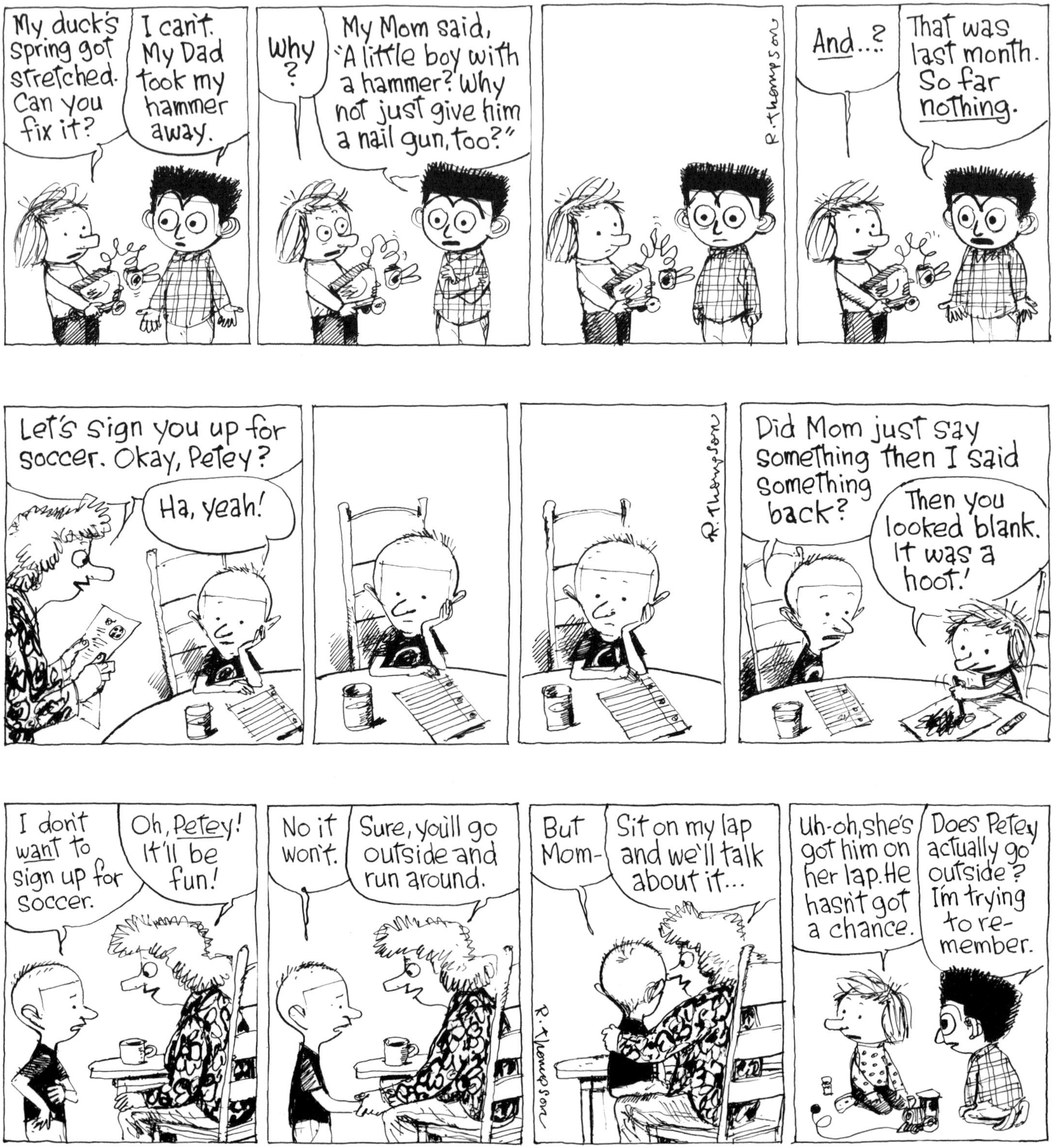
My duck's spring got stretched. Can you fix it?
I can't. My Dad took my hammer away.
Why?
My Mom said, "A little boy with a hammer? Why not just give him a nail gun, too?"
R. Thompson
And...?
That was last month. So far nothing.
Let's sign you up for soccer. Okay, Petey?
Ha, yeah!
R. Thompson
Did Mom just say something then I said something back?
Then you looked blank. It was a hoot.'
I don't want to sign up for soccer.
Oh, Petey! It'll be fun!
No it won't.
Sure, you'll go outside and run around.
But Mom-
Sit on my lap and we'll talk about it...
R. Thompson
Uh-oh, she's got him on her lap. He hasn't got a chance.
Does Petey actually go outside? I'm trying to re-member.

Hello? Alice? Where's Mommy? Would you tell her something?

Tell her there's lots of traffic and Daddy'll be late. What song?

No, I don't want to hear the song on TV. Tell Mom I'll be la—

No. Tell Mom— What dance? I can't see you dancing, can I?

Is Petey there? I know Petey can't sing or dance.

Alice! Stop singing along with the TV! Turn it DOWN!

There are ten billion cars out here—YES, that's a lot.

No, don't start counting—HELLO? HELLO? ALICE?

#@★ CELL PHONE

You know that job thing Daddy does? I think it makes him grouchy.

Where is he anyway? I made his favorite five-bean salad.

FIVE beans? I separated them into only four piles. Now I have to start all over.

R. O Thompson

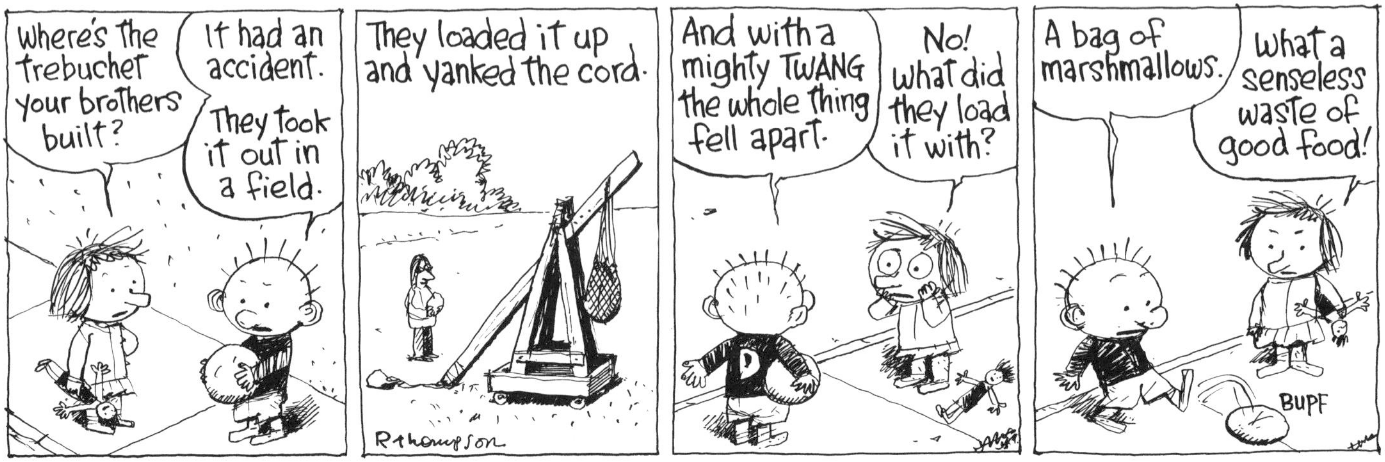
Where's the trebuchet your brothers built?
It had an accident.
They took it out in a field.
They loaded it up and yanked the cord.
And with a mighty TWANG the whole thing fell apart.
No! what did they load it with?
A bag of marshmallows.
What a senseless waste of good food!
BUPF

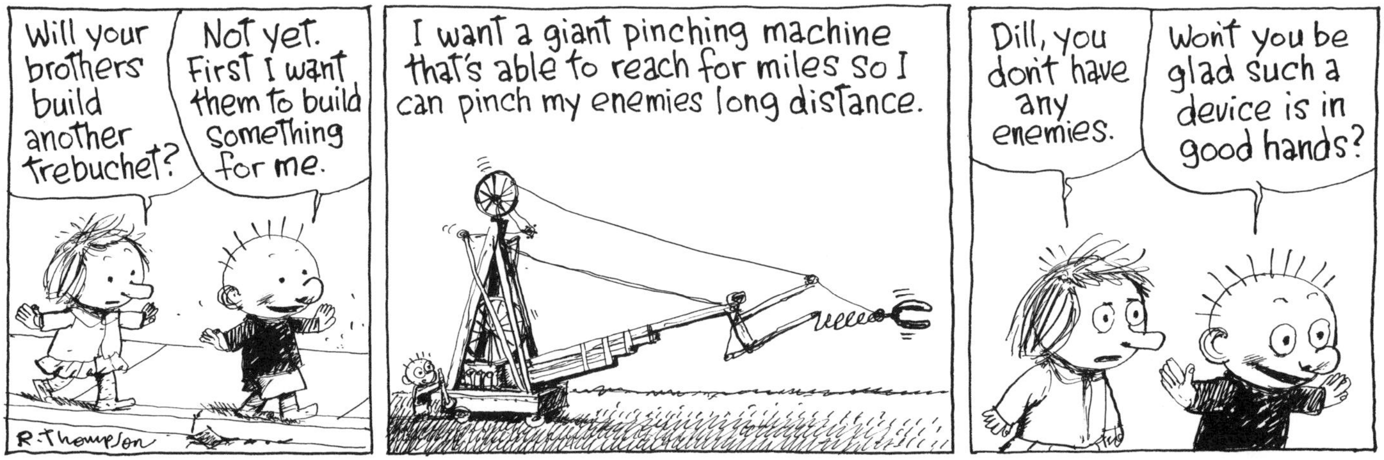
Will your brothers build another trebuchet?
Not yet. First I want them to build something for me.
I want a giant pinching machine that's able to reach for miles so I can pinch my enemies long distance.
Dill, you don't have any enemies.
Won't you be glad such a device is in good hands?

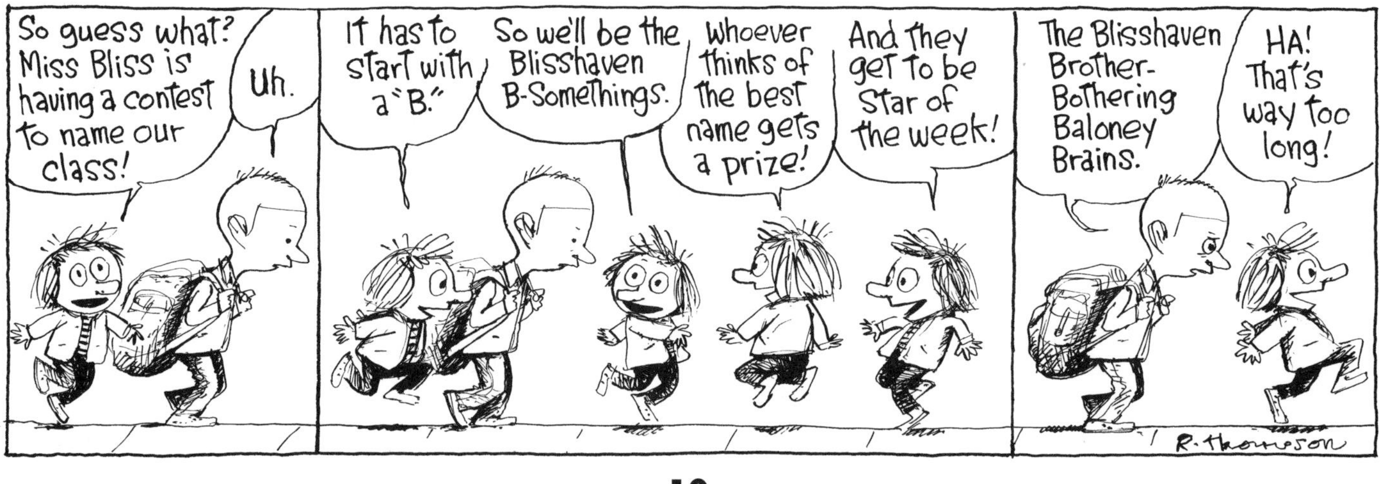
So guess what? Miss Bliss is having a contest to name our class!
Uh.
It has to start with a "B."
So we'll be the Blisshaven B-Somethings.
Whoever thinks of the best name gets a prize!
And they get to be Star of the week!
The Blisshaven Brother-Bothering Baloney Brains.
HA! That's way too long!

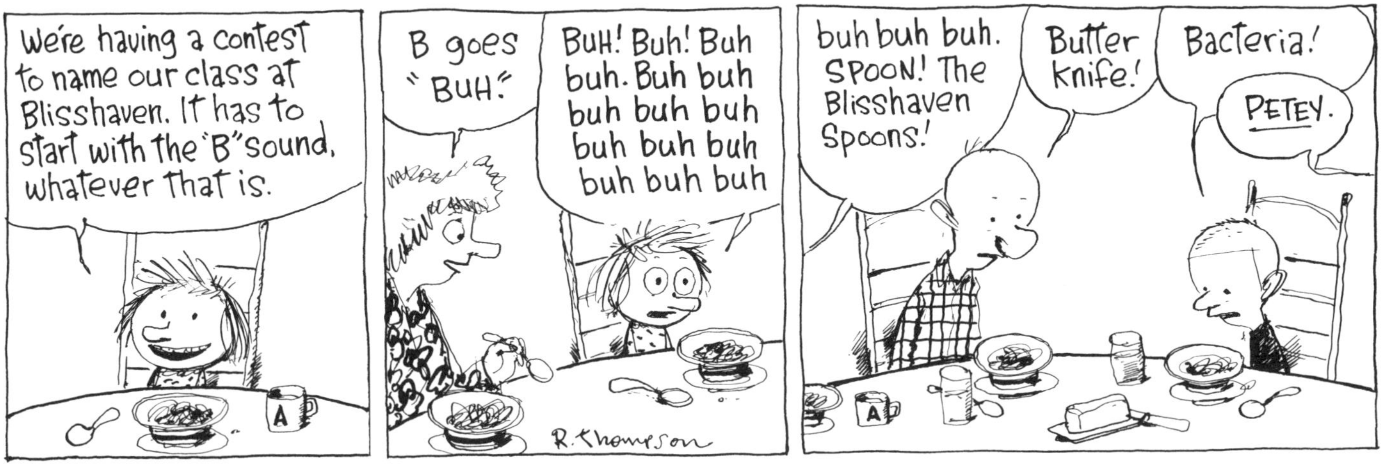
We're having a contest to name our class at Blisshaven. It has to start with the "B" sound, whatever that is.
B goes "BUH."
BUH! Buh! Buh buh. Buh buh buh buh buh buh buh buh buh buh buh
buh buh buh. SPOON! The Blisshaven Spoons!
Butter knife!
Bacteria!
PETEY.
R. Thompson

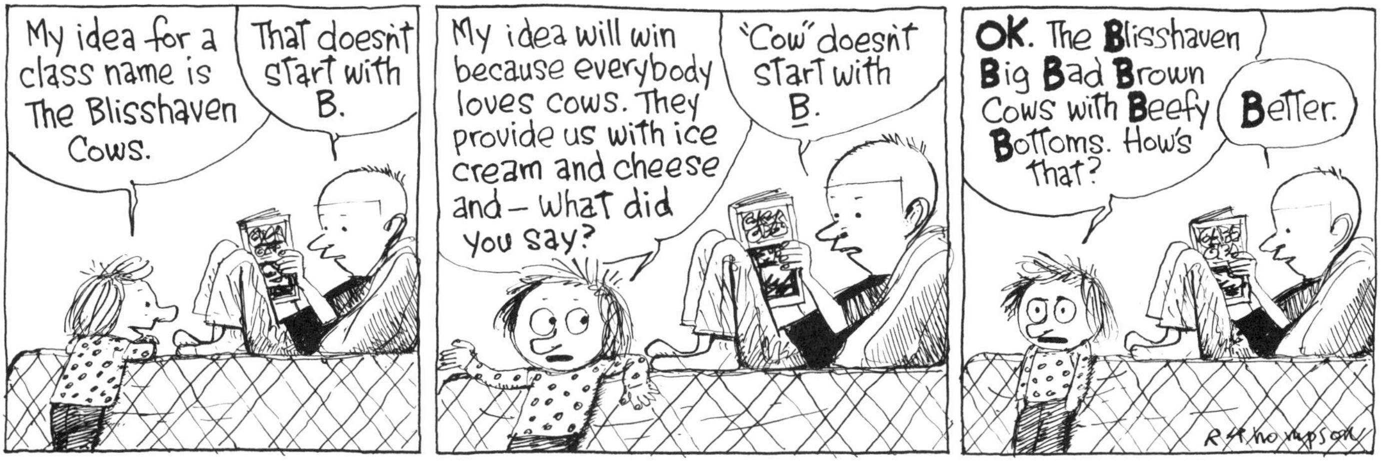
My idea for a class name is The Blisshaven Cows.
That doesn't start with B.
My idea will win because everybody loves cows. They provide us with ice cream and cheese and — what did you say?
"Cow" doesn't start with B.
OK. The Blisshaven Big Bad Brown Cows with Beefy Bottoms. How's that?
Better.

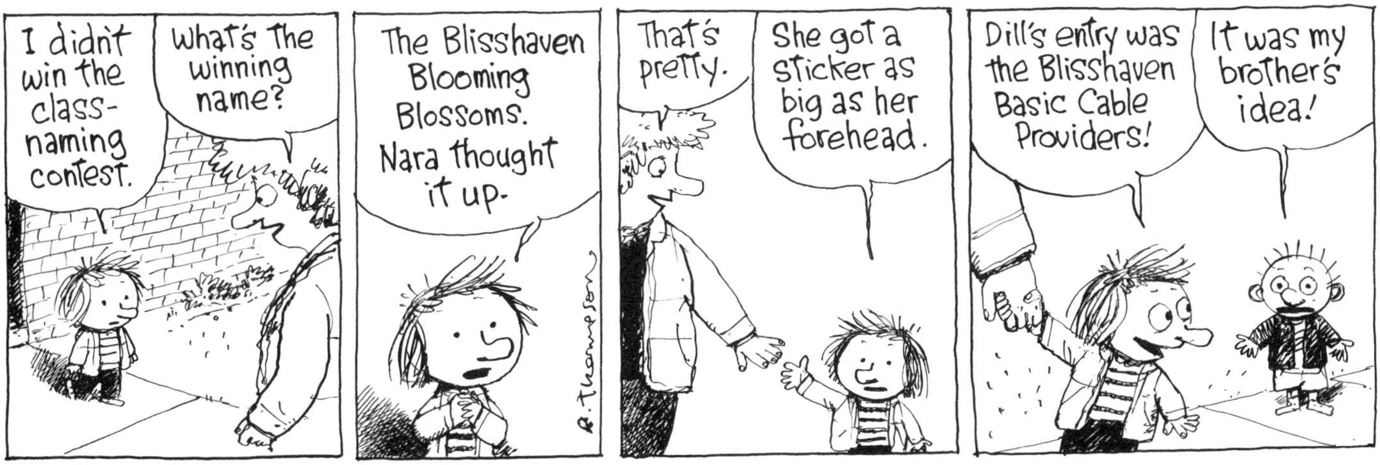
I didn't win the class-naming contest.
What's the winning name?
The Blisshaven Blooming Blossoms. Nara thought it up.
R. Thompson
That's pretty.
She got a sticker as big as her forehead.
Dill's entry was the Blisshaven Basic Cable Providers!
It was my brother's idea!

Petey, what's that?

It's an oral report for my Social Studies Interactive Verbal Skill Acquisition Learning Module on Ancient Egypt.

Oh! Read it to me!

AHEM. "Ancient Egypt," an oral report by Peter Otterloop. In Ancient Egypt there were many deities.

Like Ray, the Sun God, who had a head like a falcon.

And Hokh-Ptui, the Water God, whose drooling created the Nile.

Ancient Egyptians were rightly proud of their mummies, which were made by taking one high-ranking dead person, extracting his brains through his nose with a buttonhook, and stuffing him with mayonnaise and garlic, plus some expensive trinkets to impress the other mummies.

That was gr**eat**. Hey, do we have a buttonhook around the house?

No, and I've looked everywhere.

R. Thompson

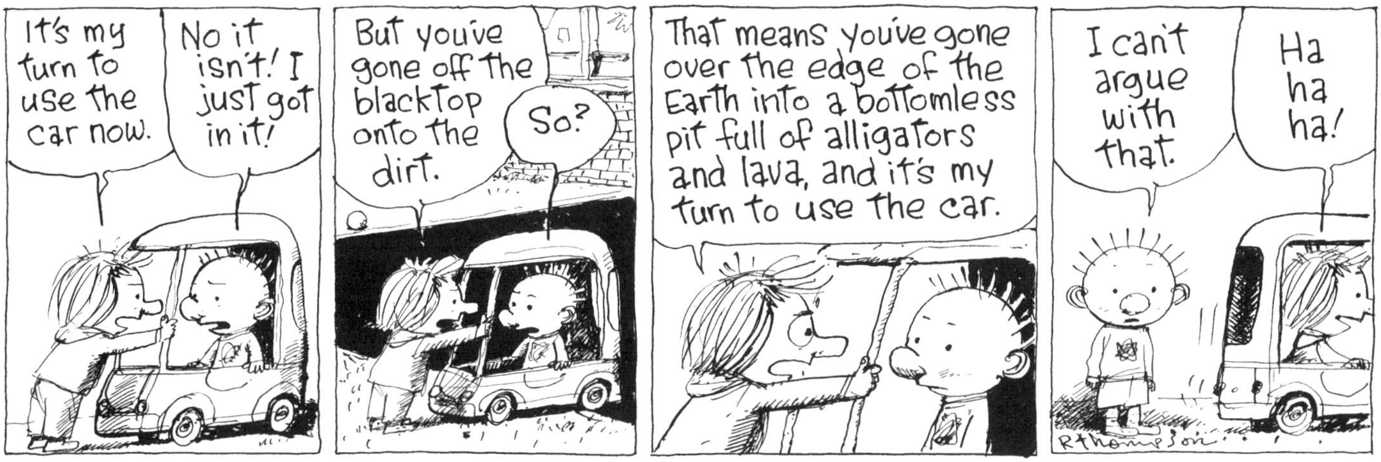
It's my turn to use the car now.
No it isn't! I just got in it!
But you've gone off the blacktop onto the dirt.
So?
That means you've gone over the edge of the Earth into a bottomless pit full of alligators and lava, and it's my turn to use the car.
I can't argue with that.
Ha ha ha!
RThompson

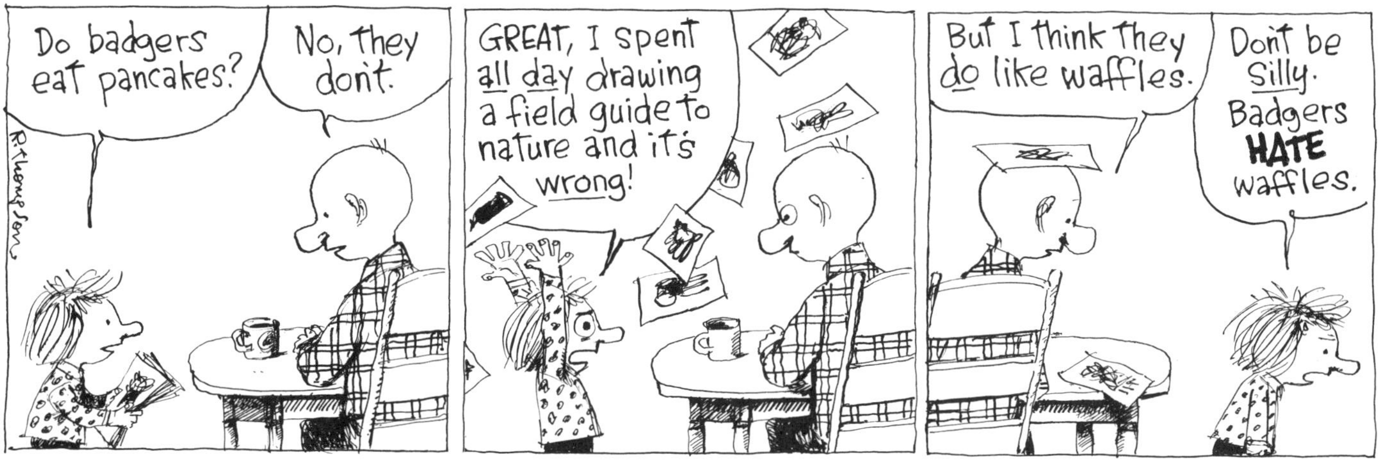
RThompson
Do badgers eat pancakes?
No, they don't.
GREAT, I spent all day drawing a field guide to nature and it's wrong!
But I think they do like waffles.
Don't be Silly. Badgers HATE waffles.

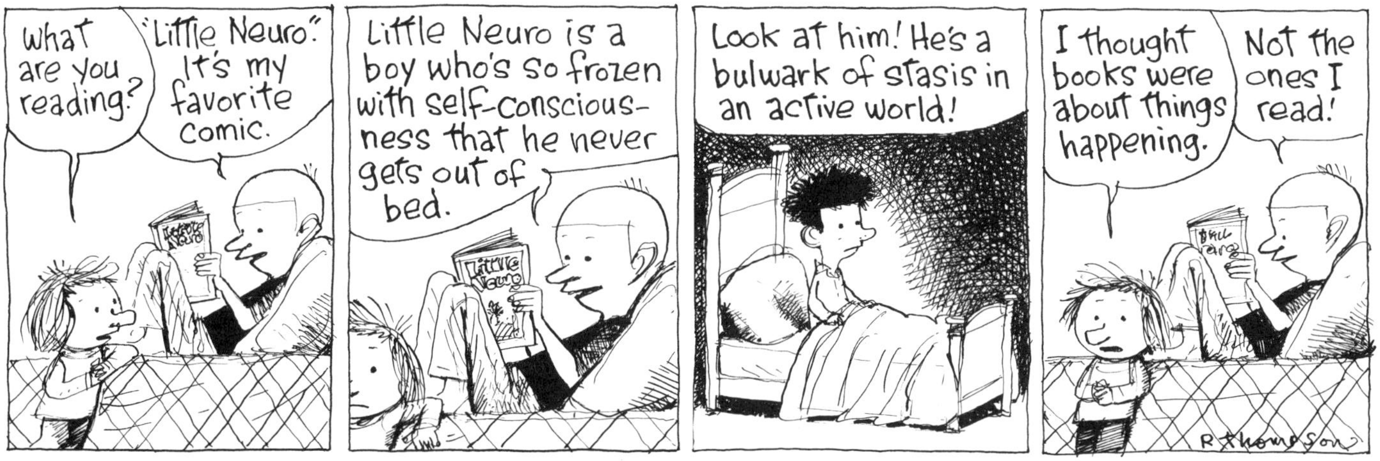
What are you reading?
"Little Neuro." It's my favorite comic.
Little Neuro is a boy who's so frozen with self-conscious-ness that he never gets out of bed.
Little Neuro
Look at him! He's a bulwark of stasis in an active world!
I thought books were about things happening.
Not the ones I read!
RThompson

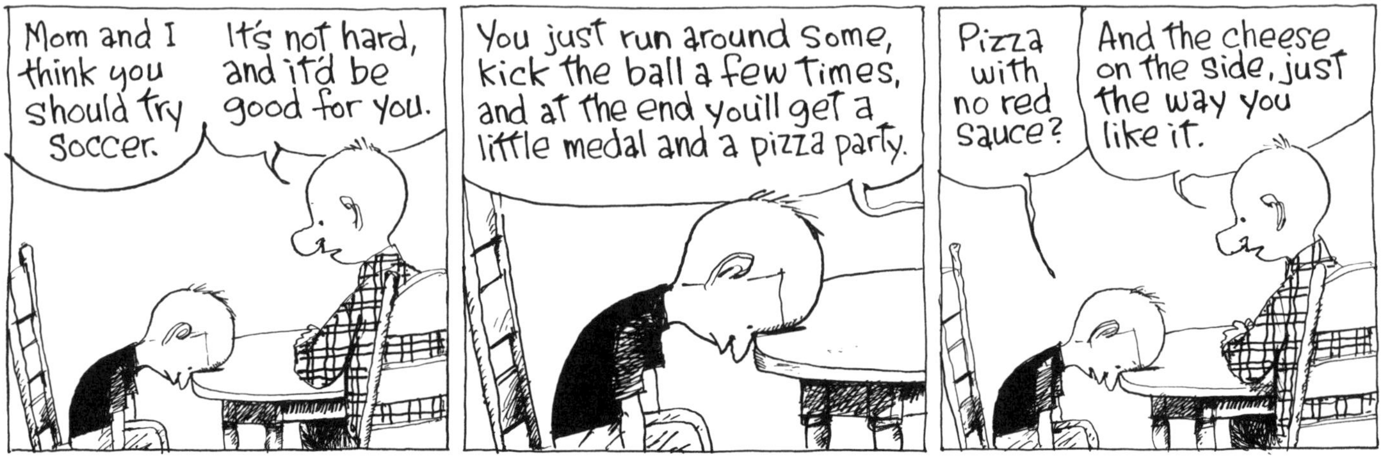
Mom and I think you should try soccer.
It's not hard, and it'd be good for you.
You just run around some, kick the ball a few times, and at the end you'll get a little medal and a pizza party.
Pizza with no red sauce?
And the cheese on the side, just the way you like it.

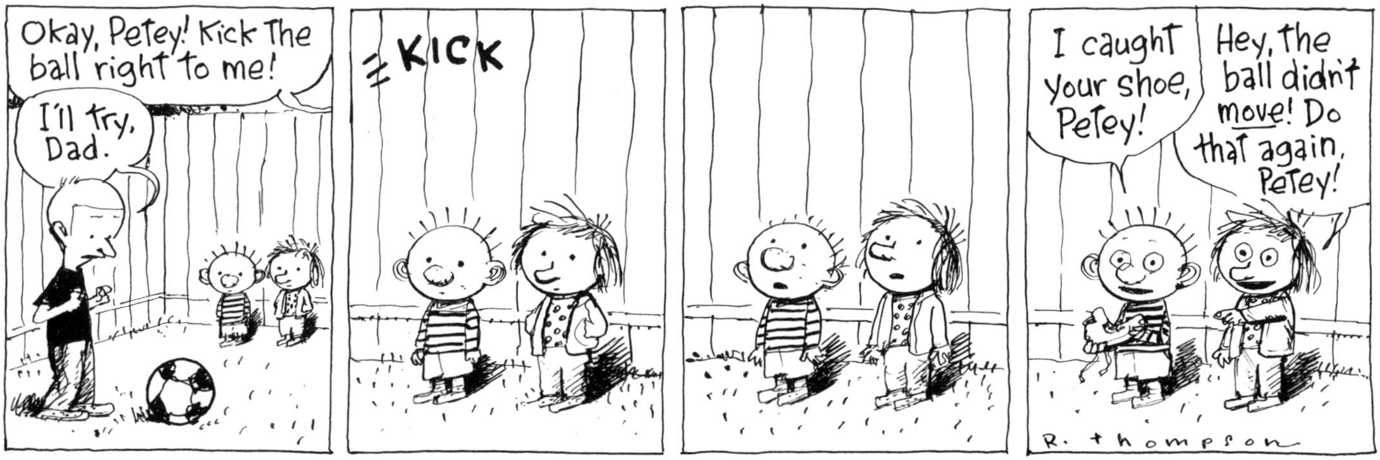
Okay, Petey! Kick the ball right to me!
I'll try, Dad.
KICK
I caught your shoe, Petey!
Hey, the ball didn't move! Do that again, Petey!
R. thompson

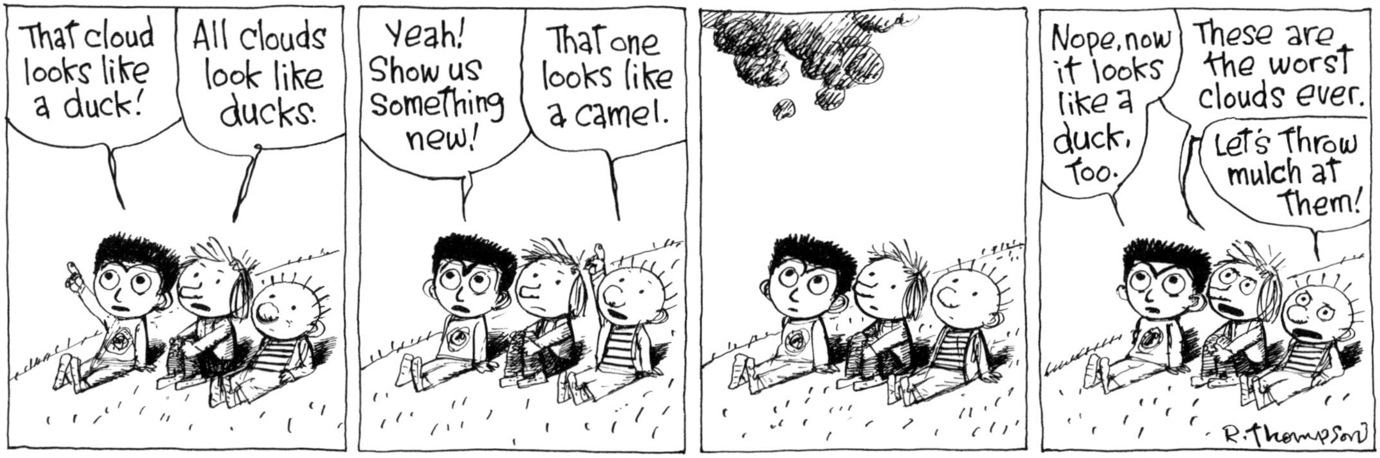
That cloud looks like a duck!
All clouds look like ducks.
Yeah! Show us something new!
That one looks like a camel.
Nope, now it looks like a duck, too.
These are the worst clouds ever.
Let's throw mulch at them!
R. Thompson

Alice?

What are you staring at?

I'm wondering what your hair looked like.

Then he said he has hair— it's just scalp-colored.

Sounds like something on a T-shirt you'd give to an old person.

15

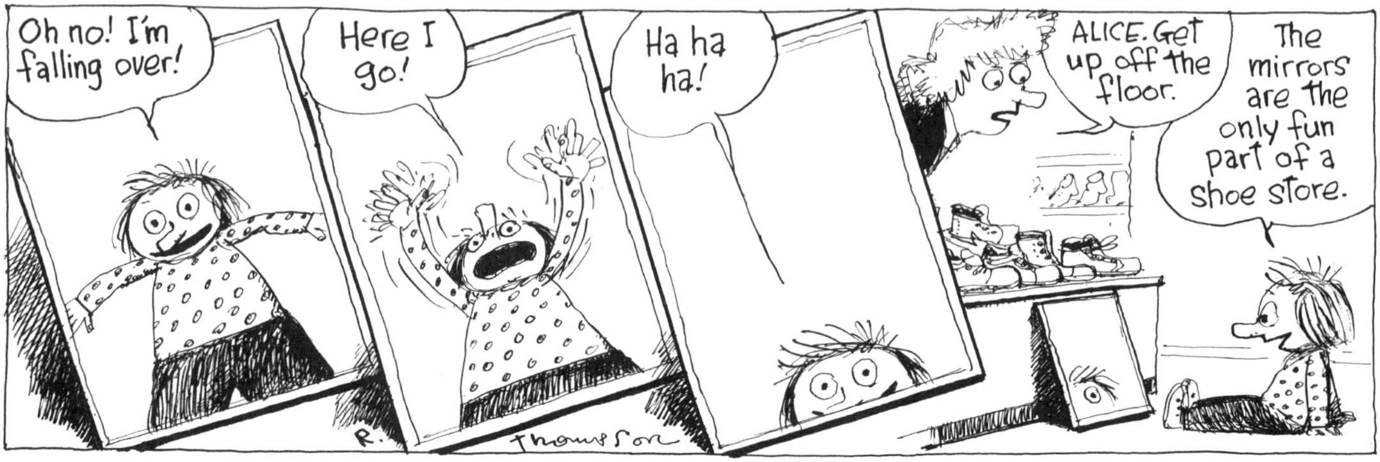
Oh no! I'm falling over!
Here I go!
Ha ha ha!
ALICE. Get up off the floor.
The mirrors are the only fun part of a shoe store.
R. Thompson

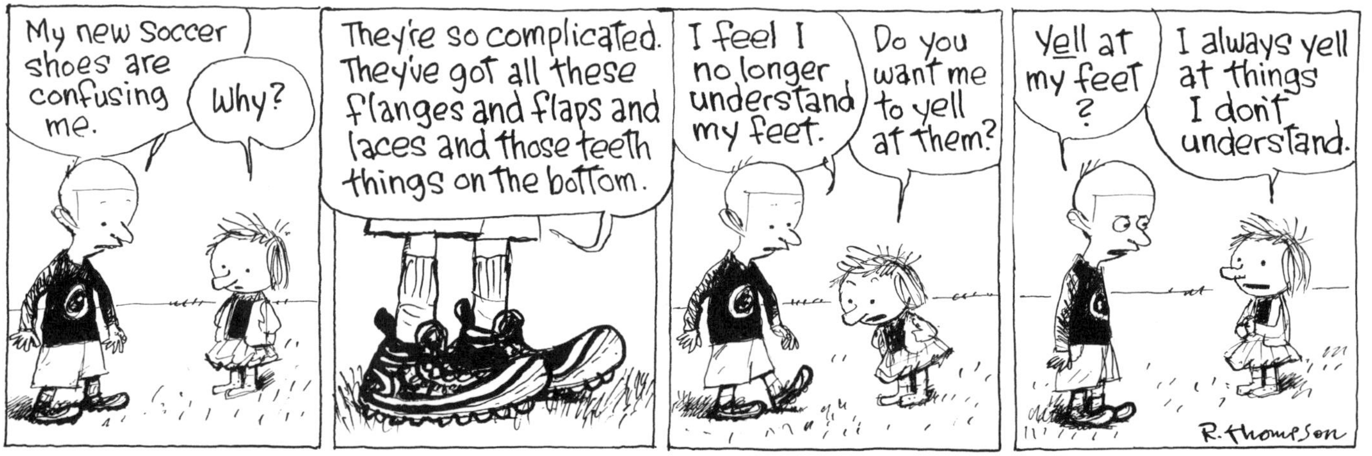
My new soccer shoes are confusing me.
Why?
They're so complicated. They've got all these flanges and flaps and laces and those teeth things on the bottom.
I feel I no longer understand my feet.
Do you want me to yell at them?
Yell at my feet?
I always yell at things I don't understand.
R. Thompson

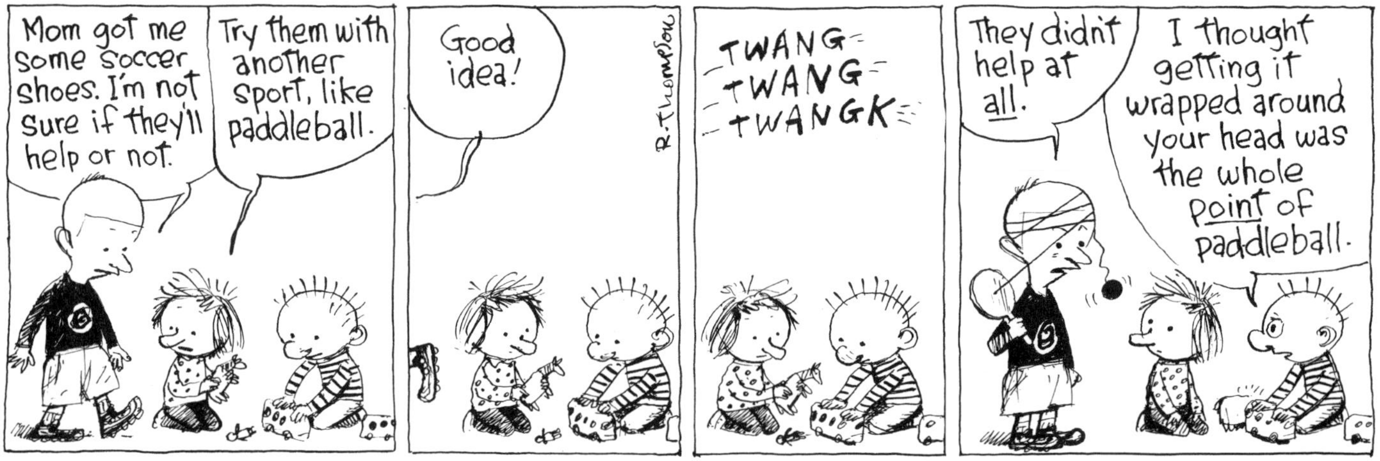
Mom got me some soccer shoes. I'm not sure if they'll help or not.
Try them with another sport, like paddleball.
Good idea!
R. Thompson
TWANG
TWANG
TWANGK
They didn't help at all.
I thought getting it wrapped around your head was the whole point of paddleball.

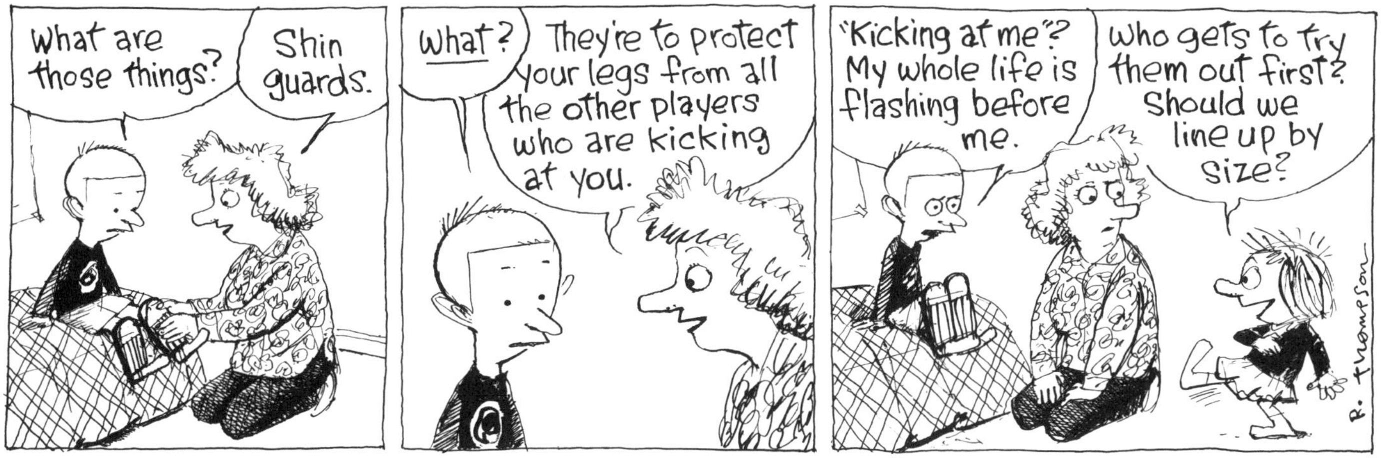
What are those things?
Shin guards.
What?
They're to protect your legs from all the other players who are kicking at you.
"Kicking at me"? My whole life is flashing before me.
Who gets to try them out first? Should we line up by size?
R. Thompson

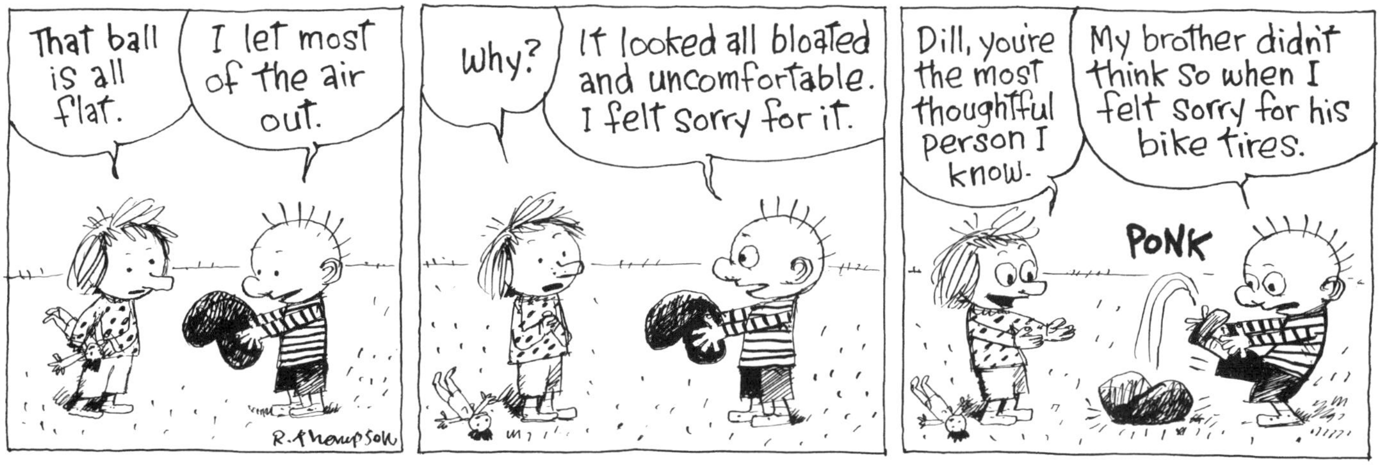
That ball is all flat.
I let most of the air out.
R. Thompson
Why?
It looked all bloated and uncomfortable. I felt sorry for it.
Dill, you're the most thoughtful person I know.
My brother didn't think so when I felt sorry for his bike tires.
PONK

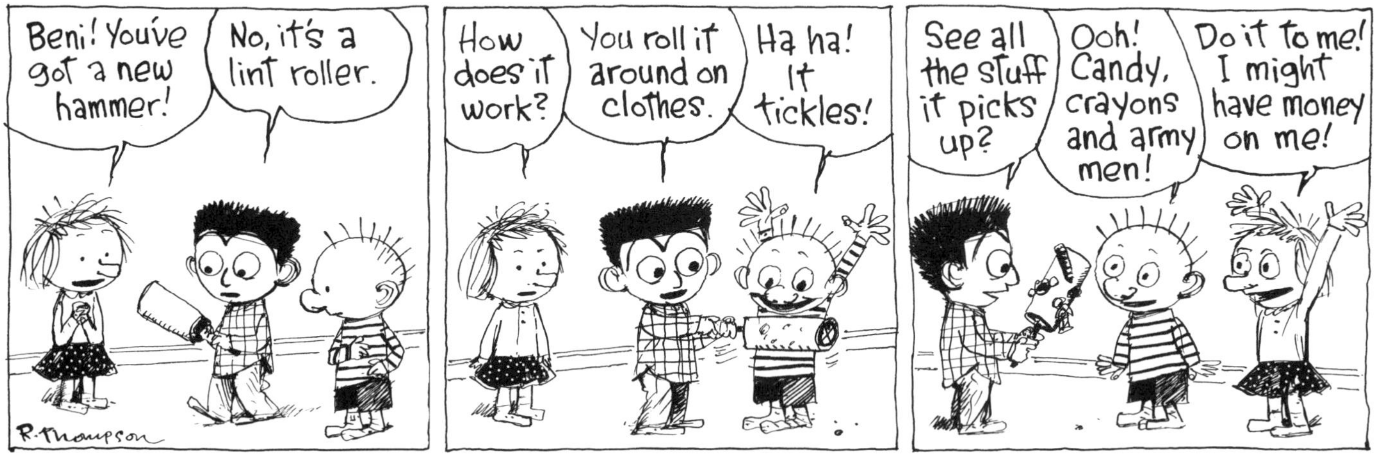
Beni! You've got a new hammer!
No, it's a lint roller.
R. Thompson
How does it work?
You roll it around on clothes.
Ha ha! It tickles!
See all the stuff it picks up?
Ooh! Candy, crayons and army men!
Do it to me! I might have money on me!

I hope the ball doesn't come this way.
If it does, I'll have an out-of-body experience.
R. Thompson
Why?
Because I can see myself failing to kick the ball.
Oh, yeah.
You need to be more supportive of yourself.
Huh?
Yeah!
Huh?
What?
You need a cheering section!
YEAH! YEAH! YAY!
PETEY, PETEY, HE'S OUR GUY! IF HE CAN'T DO IT, I DON'T KNOW—
PETEY OTTERLOOP! HEADS UP!
Huh?
Who?
What?
Why?
WHAM
Mom, was that a strike?
Was it? Shoot, I missed it.

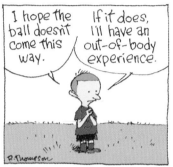

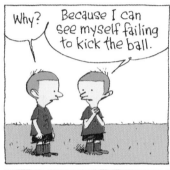

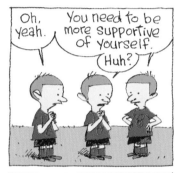

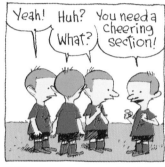

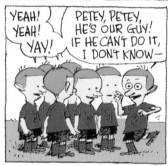

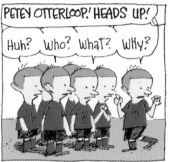

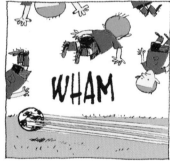

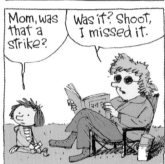

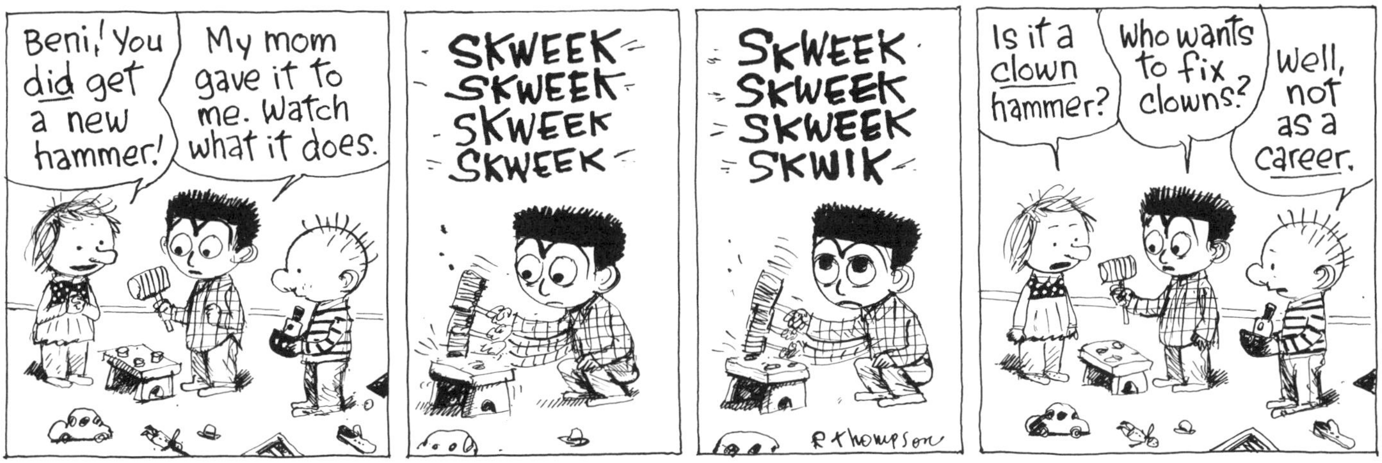
Beni! You did get a new hammer!
My mom gave it to me. Watch what it does.
SKWEEK SKWEEK SKWEEK SKWEEK
SKWEEK SKWEEK SKWEEK SKWIK
R. Thompson
Is it a clown hammer?
Who wants to fix clowns?
Well, not as a career.

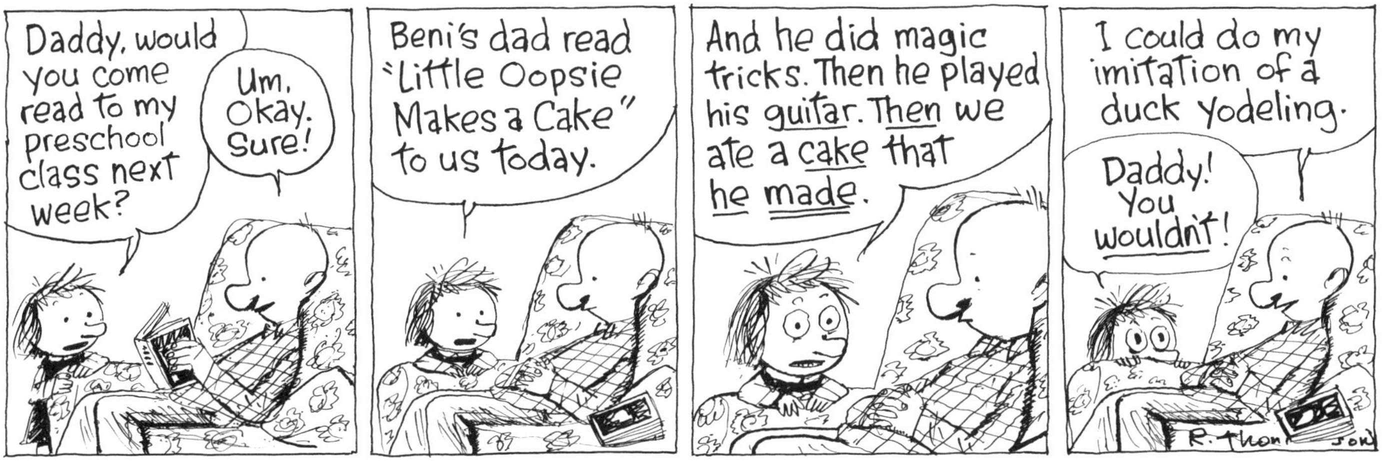
Daddy, would you come read to my preschool class next week?
Um. Okay. Sure!
Beni's dad read "Little Oopsie Makes a Cake" to us today.
And he did magic tricks. Then he played his guitar. Then we ate a cake that he made.
I could do my imitation of a duck yodeling.
Daddy! You wouldn't!

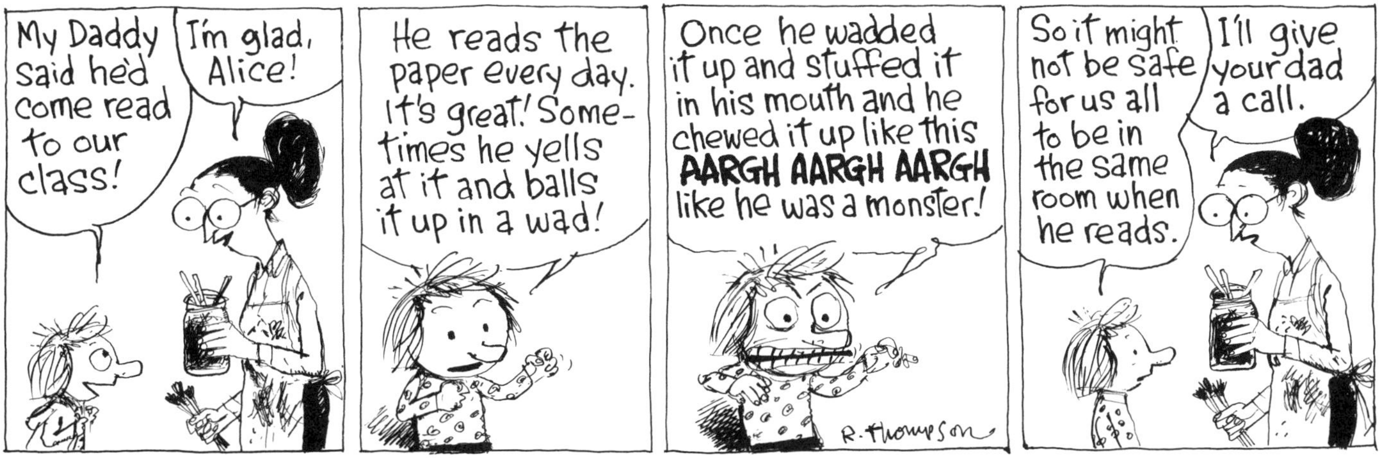
My Daddy said he'd come read to our class!
I'm glad, Alice!
He reads the paper every day. It's great! Sometimes he yells at it and balls it up in a wad!
Once he wadded it up and stuffed it in his mouth and he chewed it up like this AARGH AARGH AARGH like he was a monster!
R. Thompson
So it might not be safe for us all to be in the same room when he reads.
I'll give your dad a call.

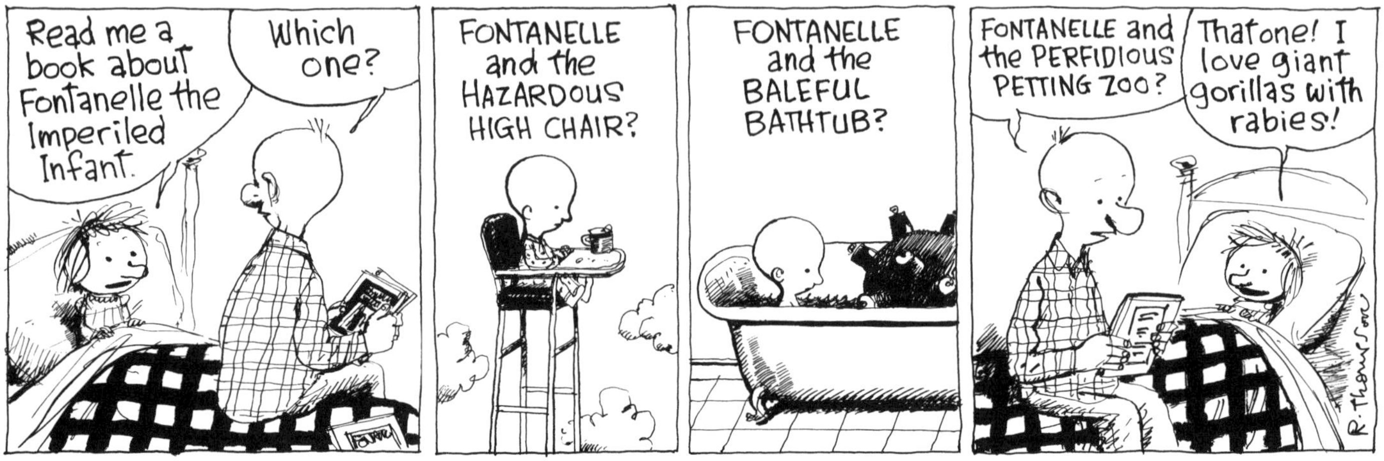
Read me a book about Fontanelle the Imperiled Infant.
Which one?
FONTANELLE and the HAZARDOUS HIGH CHAIR?
FONTANELLE and the BALEFUL BATHTUB?
FONTANELLE and the PERFIDIOUS PETTING ZOO?
That one! I love giant gorillas with rabies!
R Thompson

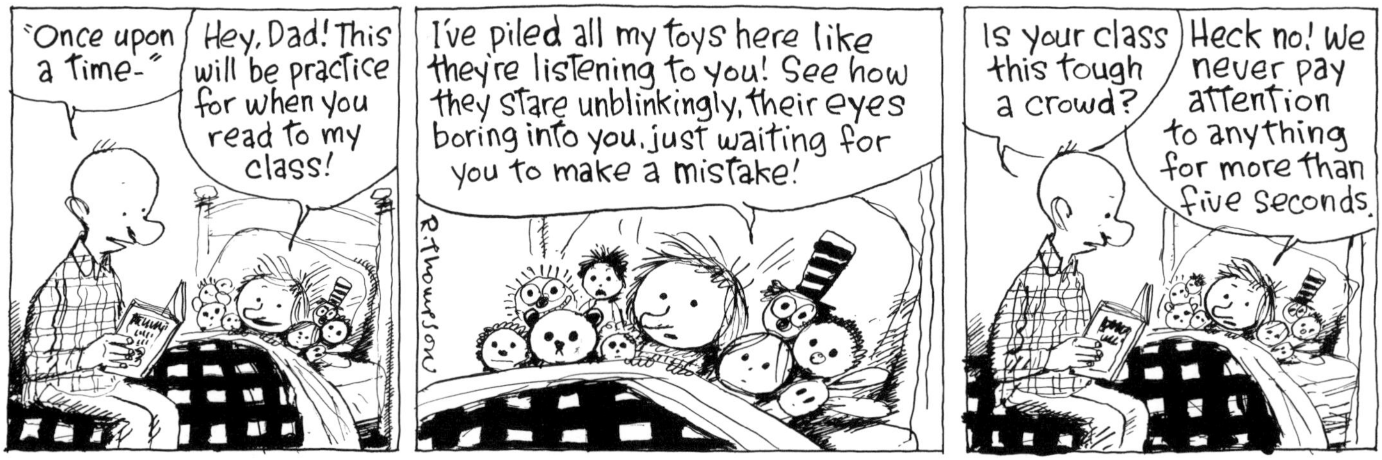
"Once upon a time-"
Hey, Dad! This will be practice for when you read to my class!
R Thompson
I've piled all my toys here like they're listening to you! See how they stare unblinkingly, their eyes boring into you, just waiting for you to make a mistake!
Is your class this tough a crowd?
Heck no! We never pay attention to anything for more than five seconds.

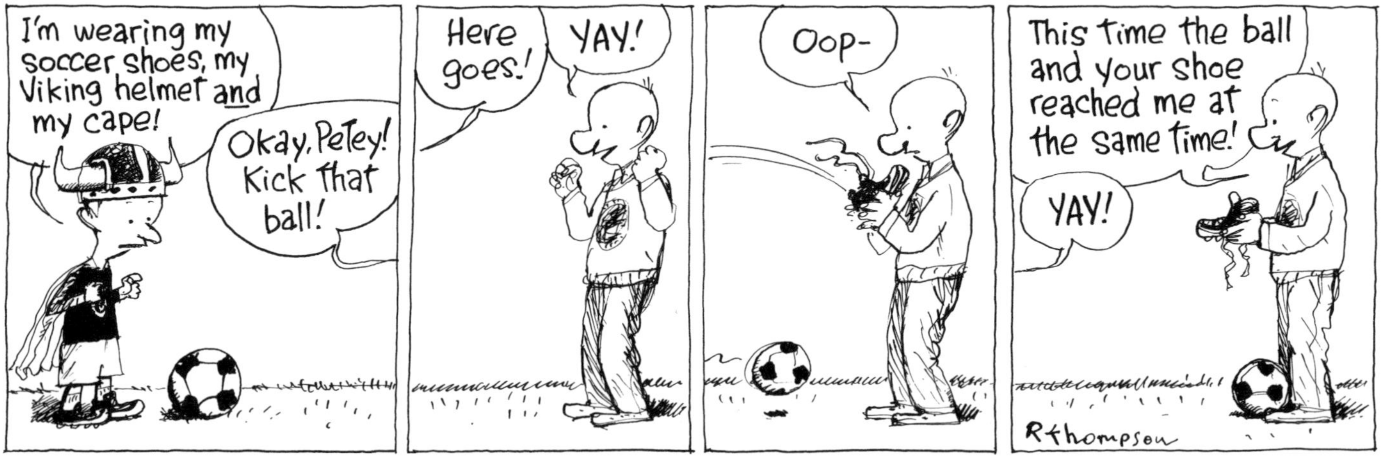
I'm wearing my soccer shoes, my Viking helmet and my cape!
Okay, Petey! Kick that ball!
Here goes!
YAY!
Oop-
This time the ball and your shoe reached me at the same time!
YAY!
R Thompson

That cloud looks like a TV set.
That one looks like a computer monitor.
That one looks like a monkey with a banjo.
Where?
There. Oops, now his head is drifting away.
I don't see–
Now it's growing a new head. And the banjo's turned into a club.
Where? Where?
It's got a dragon head! And tentacles! And look! Great big bat wings!
I still don't—
SEE? FLAMES BILLOW FROM ITS JAWS AS IT DESCENDS IN AWFUL MAJESTY!
NO! AAAGH.
R. Thompson
Now it looks like a guy eating soup.
Oh, thank God.

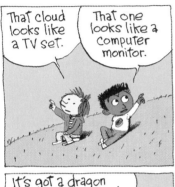

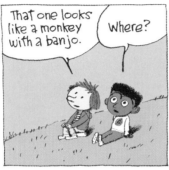

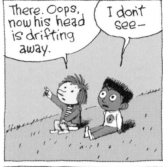

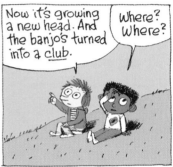

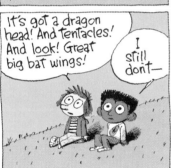

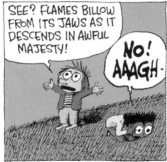

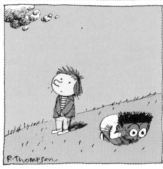

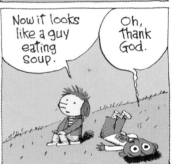

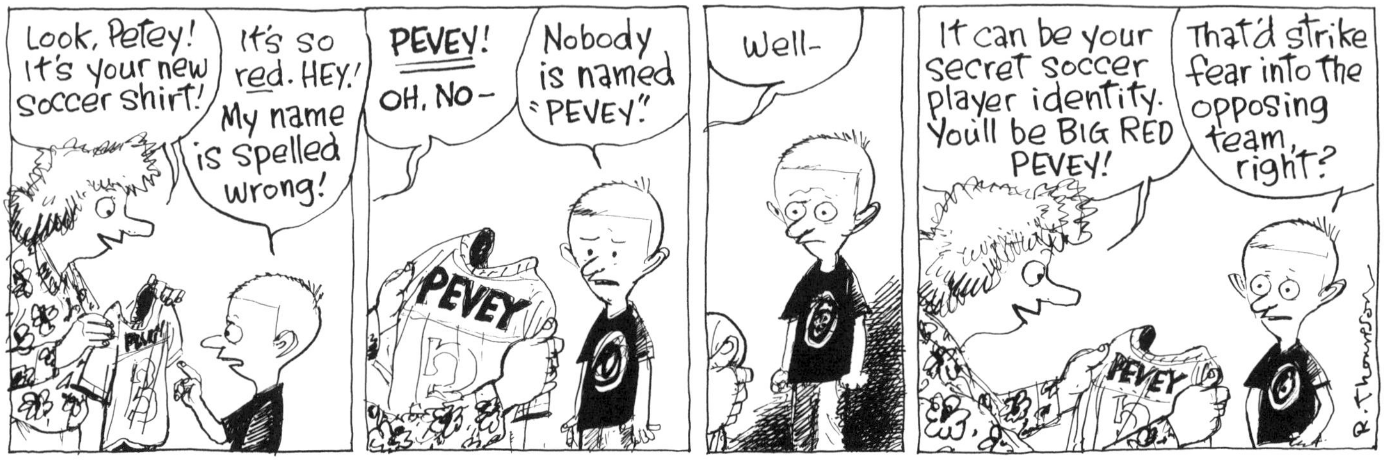
Look, Petey! It's your new soccer shirt!
It's so red. HEY! My name is spelled wrong!
PEVEY! OH, NO-
Nobody is named "PEVEY."
PEVEY
Well-
It can be your secret soccer player identity. You'll be BIG RED PEVEY!
That'd strike fear into the opposing team, right?
R. Thompson

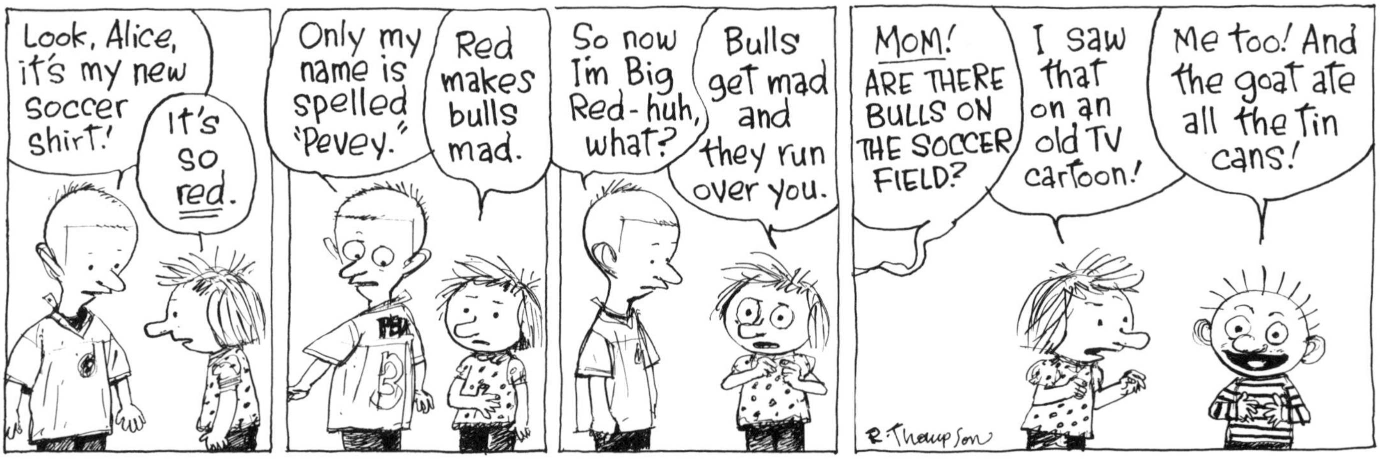
Look, Alice, it's my new soccer shirt!
It's so red.
Only my name is spelled "Pevey."
Red makes bulls mad.
So now I'm Big Red-huh, what?
Bulls get mad and they run over you.
MOM! ARE THERE BULLS ON THE SOCCER FIELD?
I saw that on an old TV cartoon!
Me too! And the goat ate all the tin cans!
R. Thompson

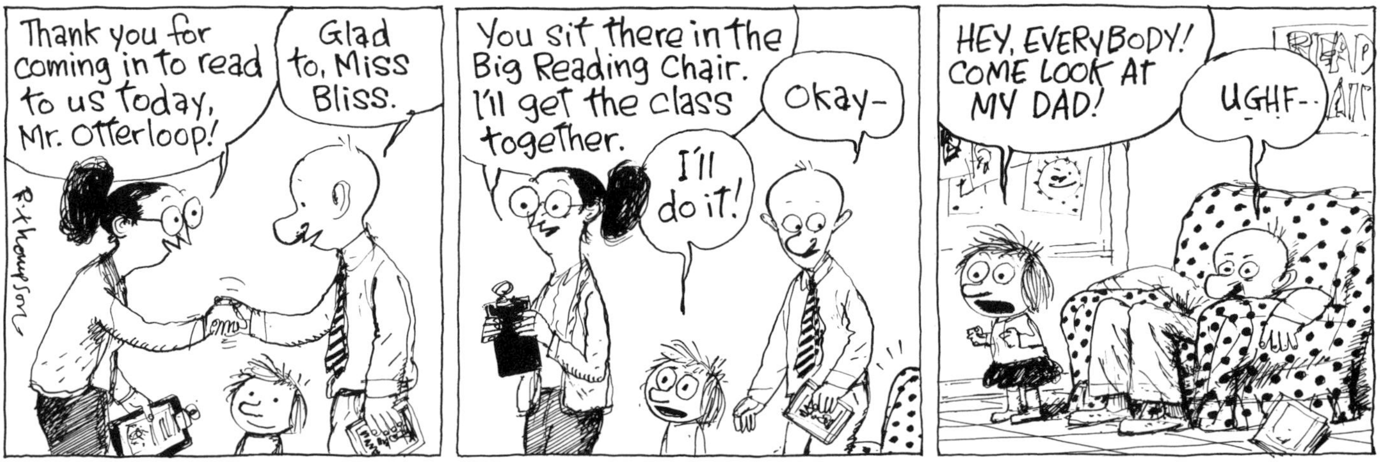
Thank you for coming in to read to us today, Mr. Otterloop!
Glad to, Miss Bliss.
R. Thompson
You sit there in the Big Reading Chair. I'll get the class together.
Okay-
I'll do it!
HEY, EVERYBODY! COME LOOK AT MY DAD!
UGHF--

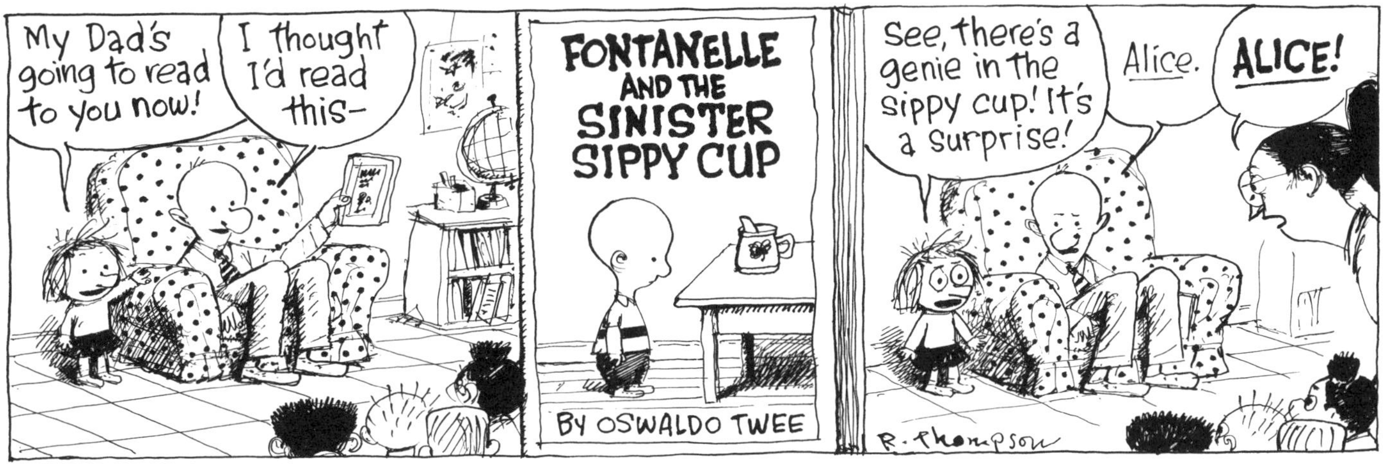
My Dad's going to read to you now!
I thought I'd read this-
FONTANELLE AND THE SINISTER SIPPY CUP
BY OSWALDO TWEE
See, there's a genie in the sippy cup! It's a surprise!
Alice.
ALICE!
R. Thompson

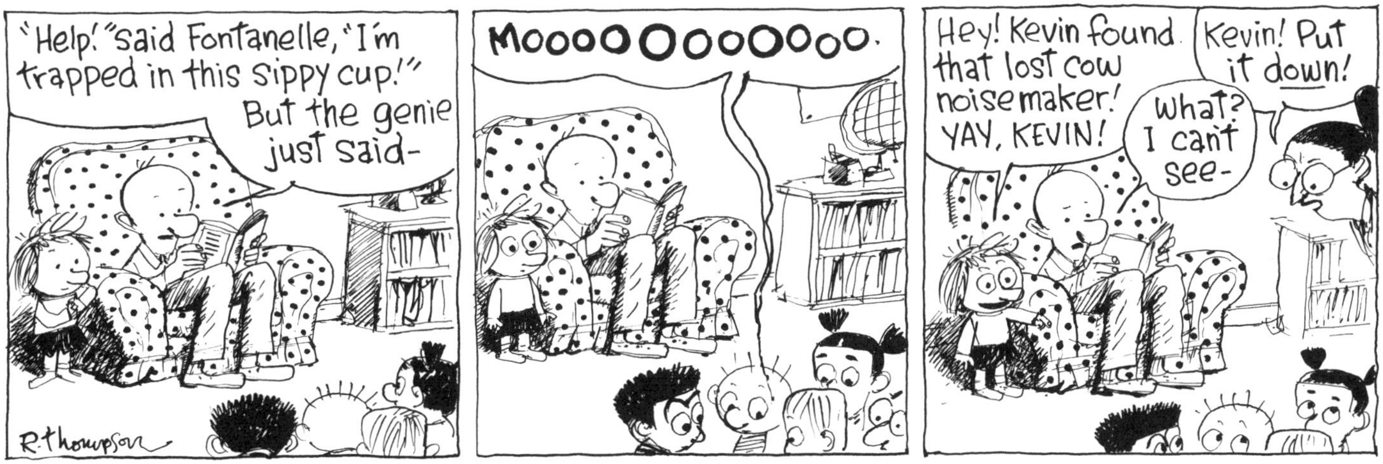
"Help!" said Fontanelle, "I'm trapped in this sippy cup!"
But the genie just said-
R. Thompson
MOOOOOOOOOOo.
Hey! Kevin found that lost cow noisemaker! YAY, KEVIN!
Kevin! Put it down!
What? I can't see-

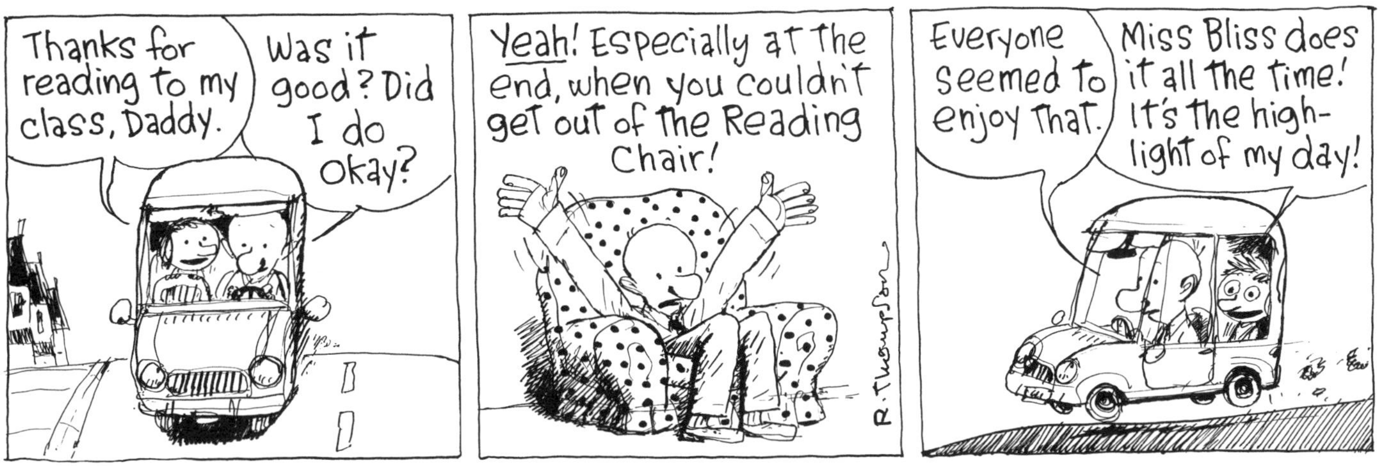
Thanks for reading to my class, Daddy.
Was it good? Did I do okay?
Yeah! Especially at the end, when you couldn't get out of the Reading Chair!
R. Thompson
Everyone seemed to enjoy that.
Miss Bliss does it all the time! It's the highlight of my day!

Let's see how fast we can get through the grocery store.
Can I ride in the cart shaped like a train?
Jeez, it's like pushing a truck!
Can we go to the deli counter to see if they have that cheese that smells like feet?
Alice, SIT DOWN!
I'm singing my Cheese Song. LET'S GO SMELL THE CHEESE.
If I step on a green square, I'll plunge to my doom!
PETEY! NOT SO LOUD!
DOOM, DOOM, DOOM AWAITS US FAR BELOW!
FRESH LOBSTERS
ALICE! SIT DOWN!
SMELL THE CHEESE, IT SMELLS LIKE FEET, STINKY, STINKY FEET!
DOOM DOOM DOOM
Pinch me to see if I'm dreaming.
I keep trying to.
FRESH LOBSTERS
R. Thompson

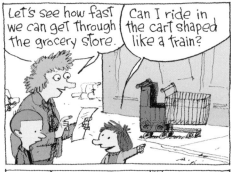

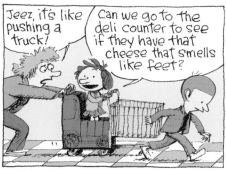

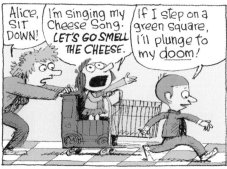

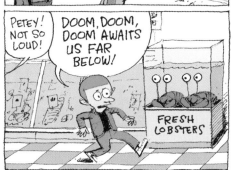

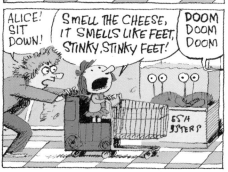

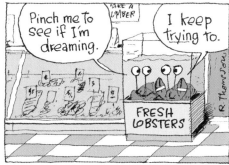

I'm reading a comic called 'Little Neuro and the Music of the Spheres.'

Uh-huh.

In it the Moon and planets come down to Little Neuro's window and sing close-harmony pop songs.

R. Thompson

What does he do?

Picks fuzz off his blanket and pretends he doesn't hear them! Ha! What a guy!

That's a good stick!

Thanks! I just found it.

It's not a great stick.

No, but it is a good stick.

Definitely a keeper though.

Yes. It's going into my stick collection.

R. Thompson

Maybe it's beavers?

Do beavers infest houses?

Here's a great stick.

That's bamboo, Alice!

You can make a fishing pole out of bamboo! Pandas love to eat it!

R. Thompson

Oh!

Alice, I don't care what Miss Bliss says. PANDAS DON'T GO FISHING!

She seemed pretty adamant about it.

25

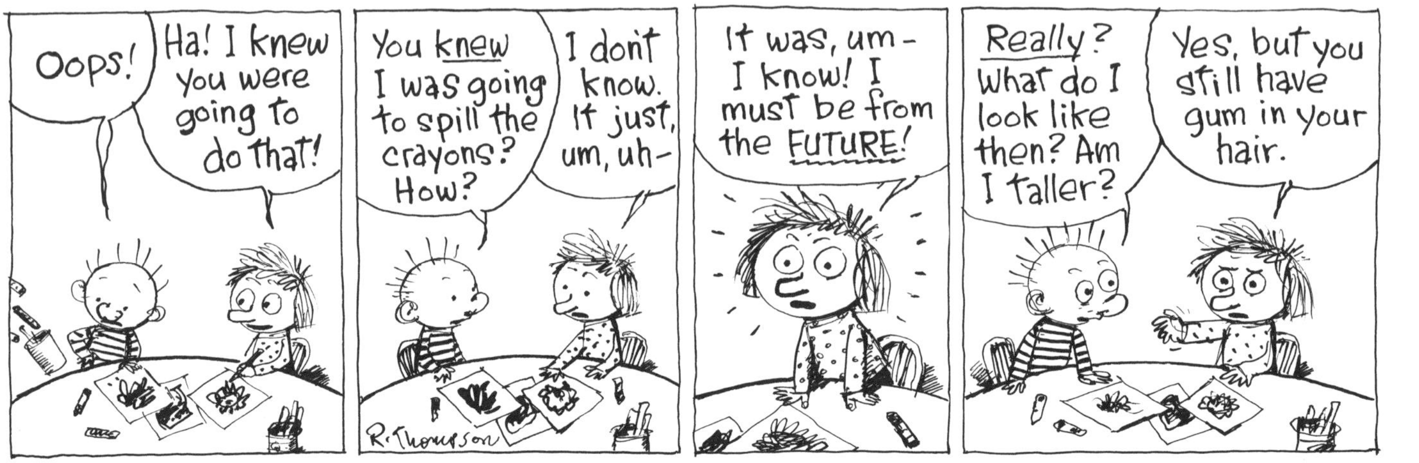
Oops!
Ha! I knew you were going to do that!
You knew I was going to spill the crayons? How?
I don't know. It just, um, uh-
It was, um- I know! I must be from the FUTURE!
Really? What do I look like then? Am I taller?
Yes, but you still have gum in your hair.

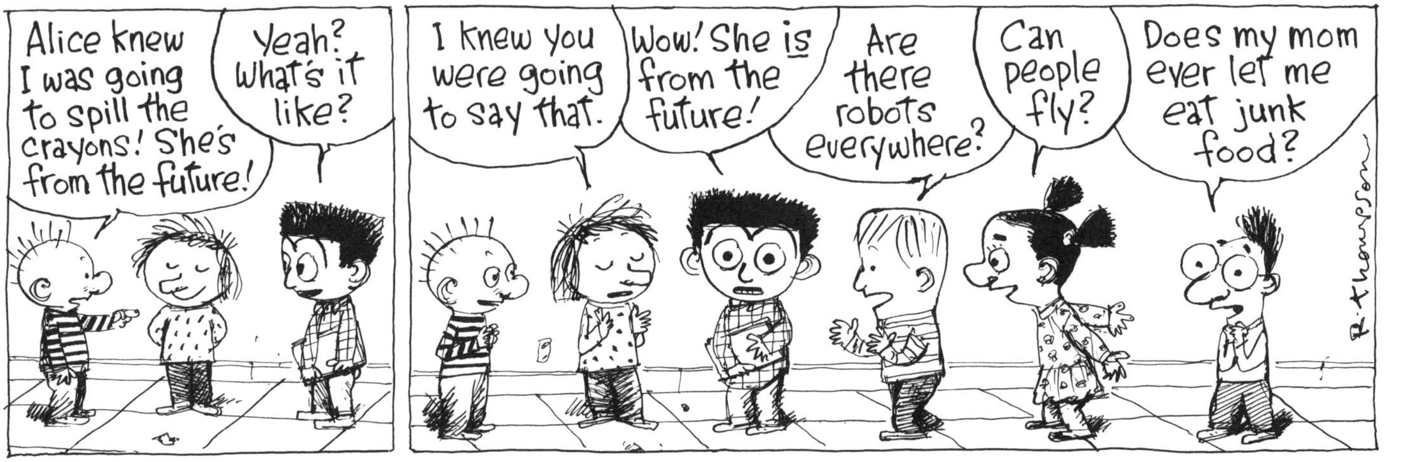
Alice knew I was going to spill the crayons! She's from the future!
Yeah? What's it like?
I knew you were going to say that.
Wow! She is from the future!
Are there robots everywhere?
Can people fly?
Does my mom ever let me eat junk food?

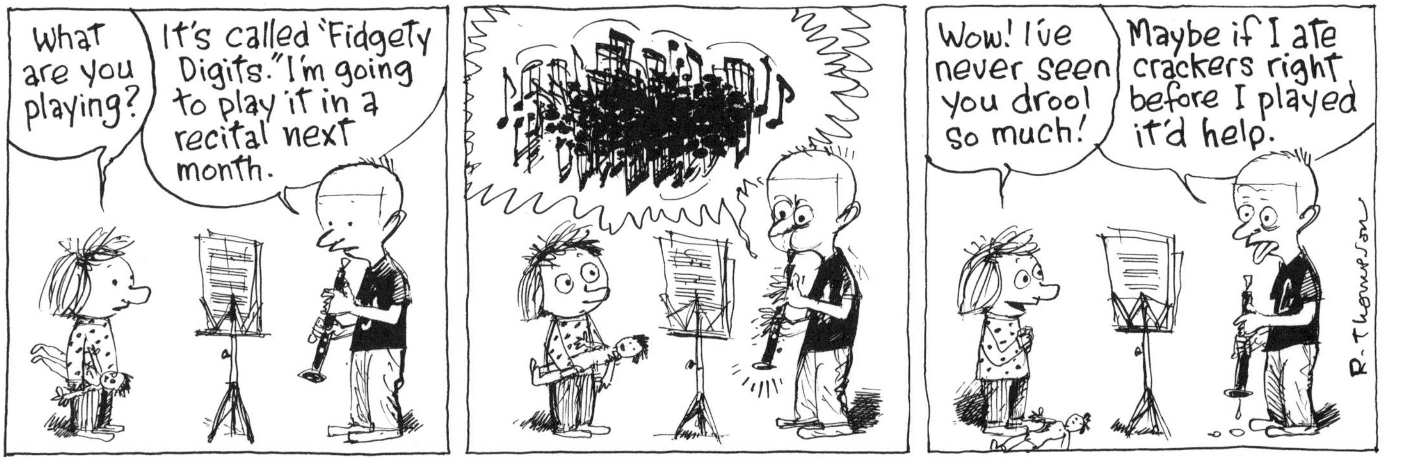
What are you playing?
It's called "Fidgety Digits." I'm going to play it in a recital next month.
Wow! I've never seen you drool so much!
Maybe if I ate crackers right before I played it'd help.

SPRING

POP

THERE HE IS! LET'S GET HIM! NO!

R. Thompson

NO! SPORES! POLLEN! GAH!

Petey'd get more respect if he was allergic to bears.

Or chipmunks.

Are we going to talk or are we going to tunnel to Disney World?

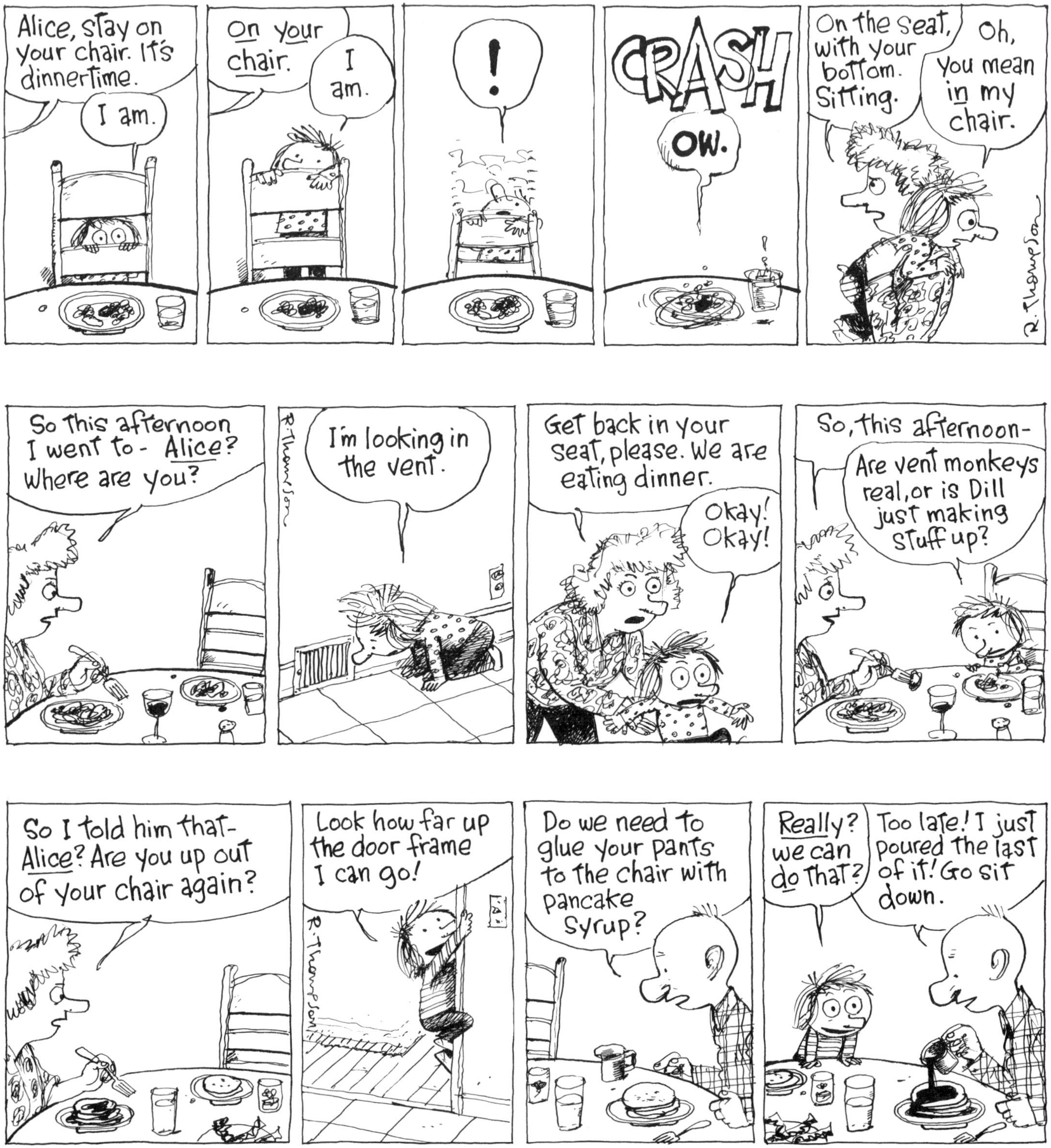
Alice, stay on your chair. It's dinnertime.
I am.
On your chair.
I am.
!
CRASH
OW.
On the seat, with your bottom. Sitting.
Oh, You mean in my chair.
R. Thompson
So this afternoon I went to - Alice? Where are you?
R. Thompson
I'm looking in the vent.
Get back in your seat, please. We are eating dinner.
Okay! Okay!
So, this afternoon-
Are vent monkeys real, or is Dill just making stuff up?
So I told him that- Alice? Are you up out of your chair again?
Look how far up the door frame I can go!
R. Thompson
Do we need to glue your pants to the chair with pancake syrup?
Really? we can do that?
Too late! I just poured the last of it! Go sit down.

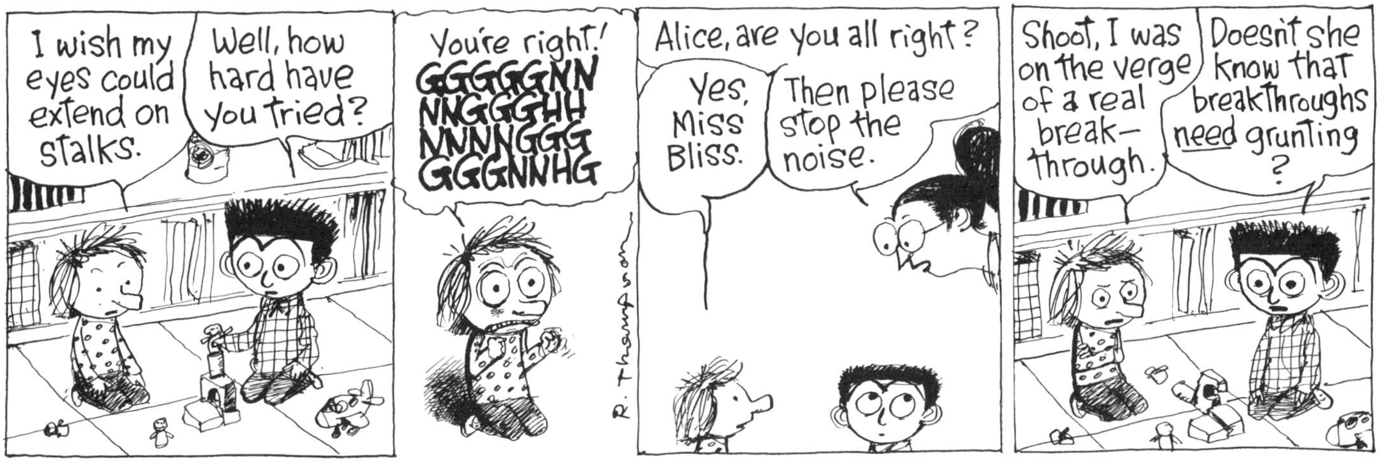
I wish my eyes could extend on stalks.
Well, how hard have you tried?
You're right! GGGGGNN NNGGGHH NNNNGGG GGGNNHG
R. Thompson
Alice, are you all right?
Yes, Miss Bliss.
Then please stop the noise.
Shoot, I was on the verge of a real break-through.
Doesn't she know that breakthroughs need grunting?

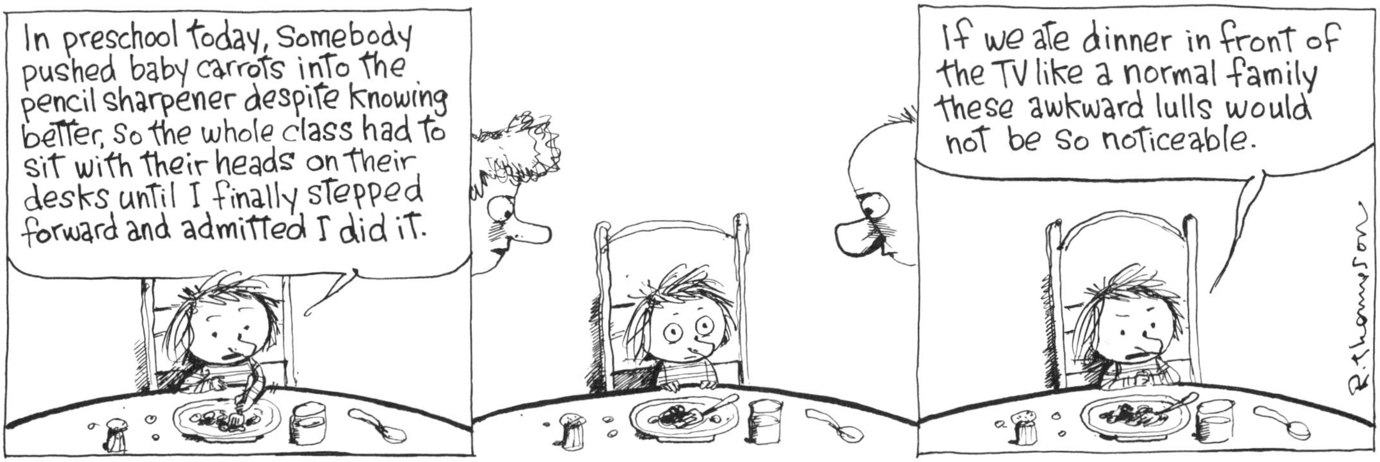
In preschool today, somebody pushed baby carrots into the pencil sharpener despite knowing better, so the whole class had to sit with their heads on their desks until I finally stepped forward and admitted I did it.
If we ate dinner in front of the TV like a normal family these awkward lulls would not be so noticeable.
R. Thompson

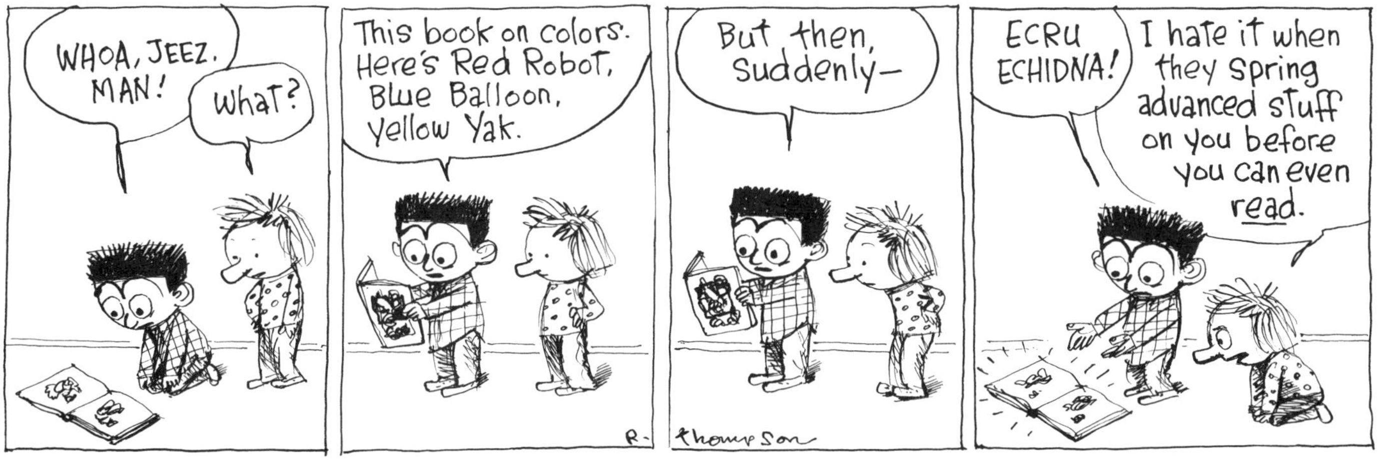
WHOA, JEEZ. MAN!
What?
This book on colors. Here's Red Robot, Blue Balloon, Yellow Yak.
But then, suddenly—
R. Thompson
ECRU ECHIDNA!
I hate it when they spring advanced stuff on you before you can even read.

Is your mom still scrap-booking your stuff?

Now she's saving everything I touch.

Last night I played tic-tac-toe on a children's menu at a pizza restaurant.

Mom took the menu home and put it in a scrapbook along with the napkin I used and a photo of me with the waiter.

My dad read her a magazine article about how parents today have fallen victim to the cult of the child.

About how they've fetishized their kids and worship them as miniature deities.

And yet no one will push me on this stupid swing.

Mom glued the article into a scrapbook. I feel like I'm being stalked by a deranged fan.

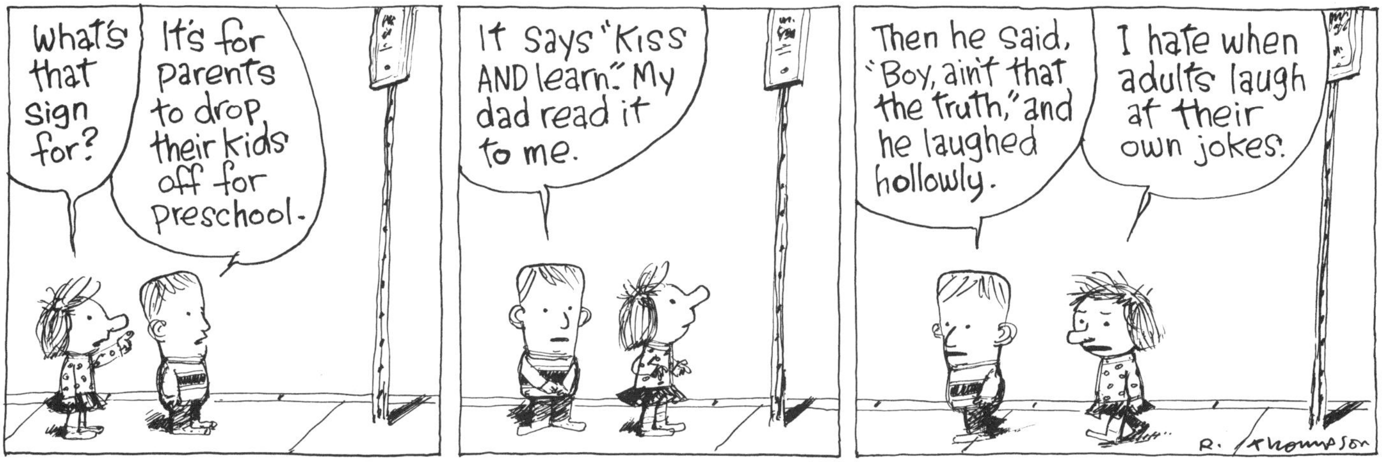
What's that sign for?
It's for parents to drop their kids off for preschool.
It says "KISS AND learn." My dad read it to me.
Then he said, "Boy, ain't that the truth," and he laughed hollowly.
I hate when adults laugh at their own jokes.
R. Thompson

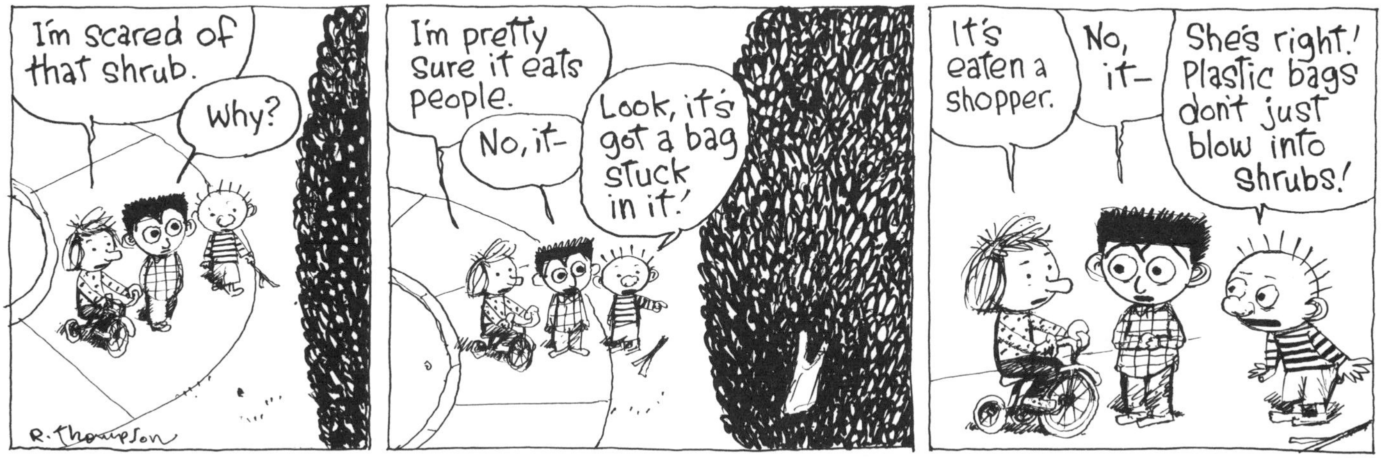
I'm scared of that shrub.
Why?
I'm pretty sure it eats people.
No, it-
Look, it's got a bag stuck in it!
It's eaten a shopper.
No, it-
She's right! Plastic bags don't just blow into shrubs!
R. Thompson

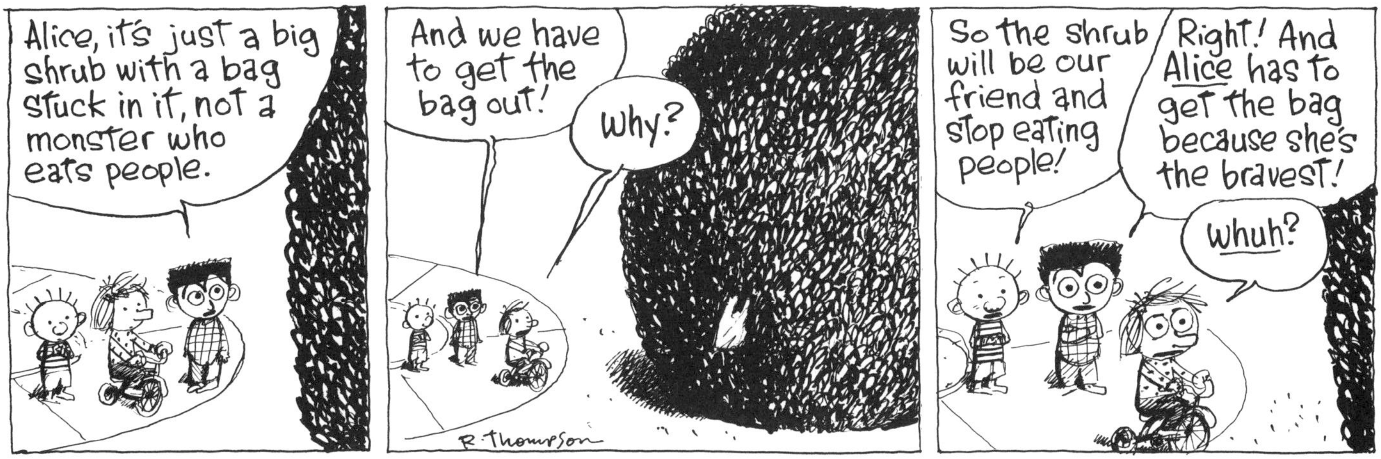
Alice, it's just a big shrub with a bag stuck in it, not a monster who eats people.
And we have to get the bag out!
Why?
So the shrub will be our friend and stop eating people!
Right! And Alice has to get the bag because she's the bravest!
Whuh?
R. Thompson

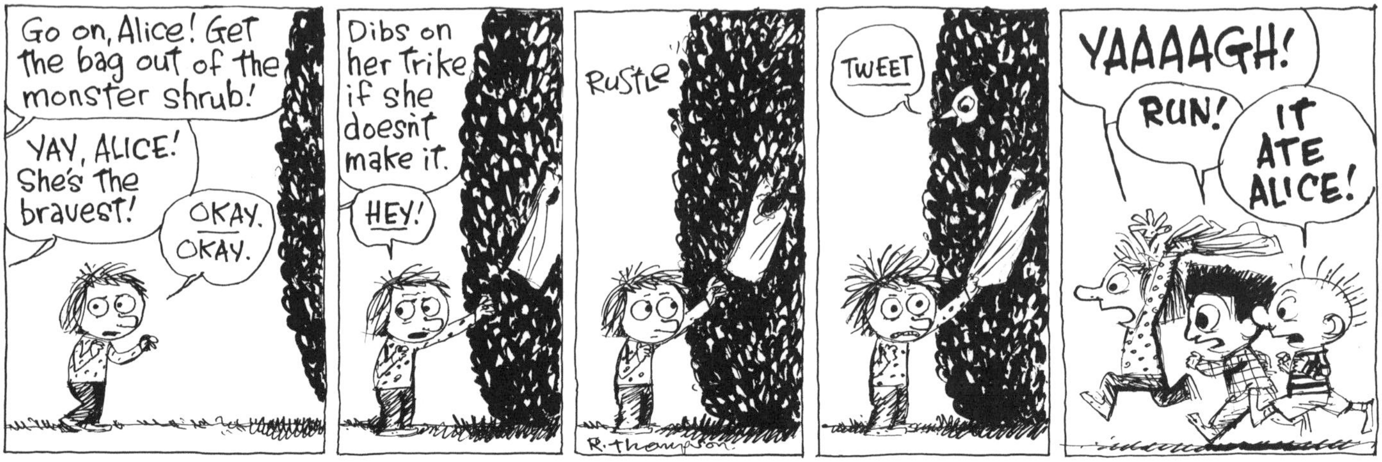
Go on, Alice! Get the bag out of the monster shrub!
YAY, ALICE! She's the bravest!
OKAY. OKAY.
Dibs on her trike if she doesn't make it.
HEY!
RUSTLE
TWEET
YAAAAGH!
RUN!
IT ATE ALICE!
R. Thompson

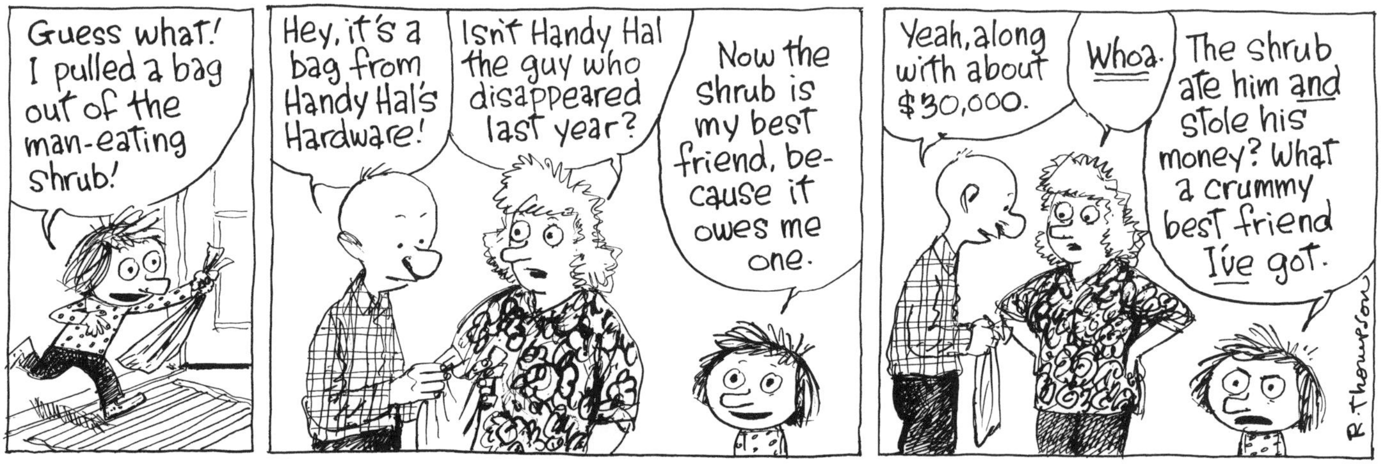
Guess what! I pulled a bag out of the man-eating shrub!
Hey, it's a bag from Handy Hal's Hardware!
Isn't Handy Hal the guy who disappeared last year?
Now the shrub is my best friend, because it owes me one.
Yeah, along with about $30,000.
Whoa.
The shrub ate him and stole his money? What a crummy best friend I've got.
R. Thompson

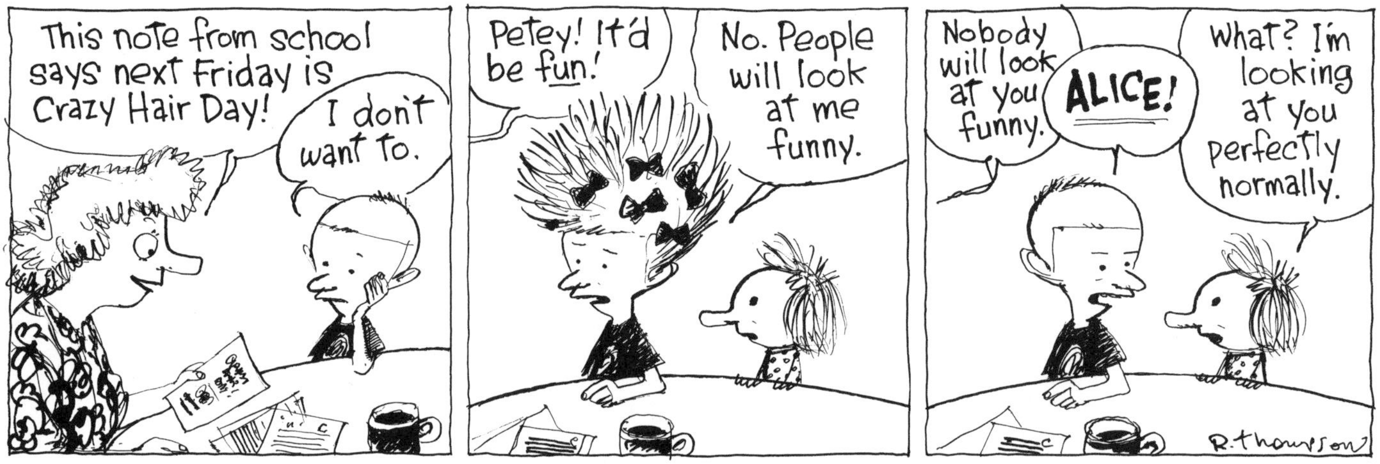
This note from school says next Friday is Crazy Hair Day!
I don't want to.
Petey! It'd be fun!
No. People will look at me funny.
Nobody will look at you funny.
ALICE!
What? I'm looking at you perfectly normally.
R. Thompson

My brother heard about a guy who'd lie on the sofa watching TV ALL THE TIME.

So?

So one day he dozed off in front of the TV.

And awoke to find a terrible transformation had taken place.

He'd become a Sofa Centaur, half man and half sofa!

I wish I was a Sofa Centaur! It'd be great!

No, it wouldn't. If Grandma came to visit you'd have to fold out for her to sleep on, and you know how Grandma snores.

He's right, you know.

I hate it when Petey's the voice of reason.

R. Thompson

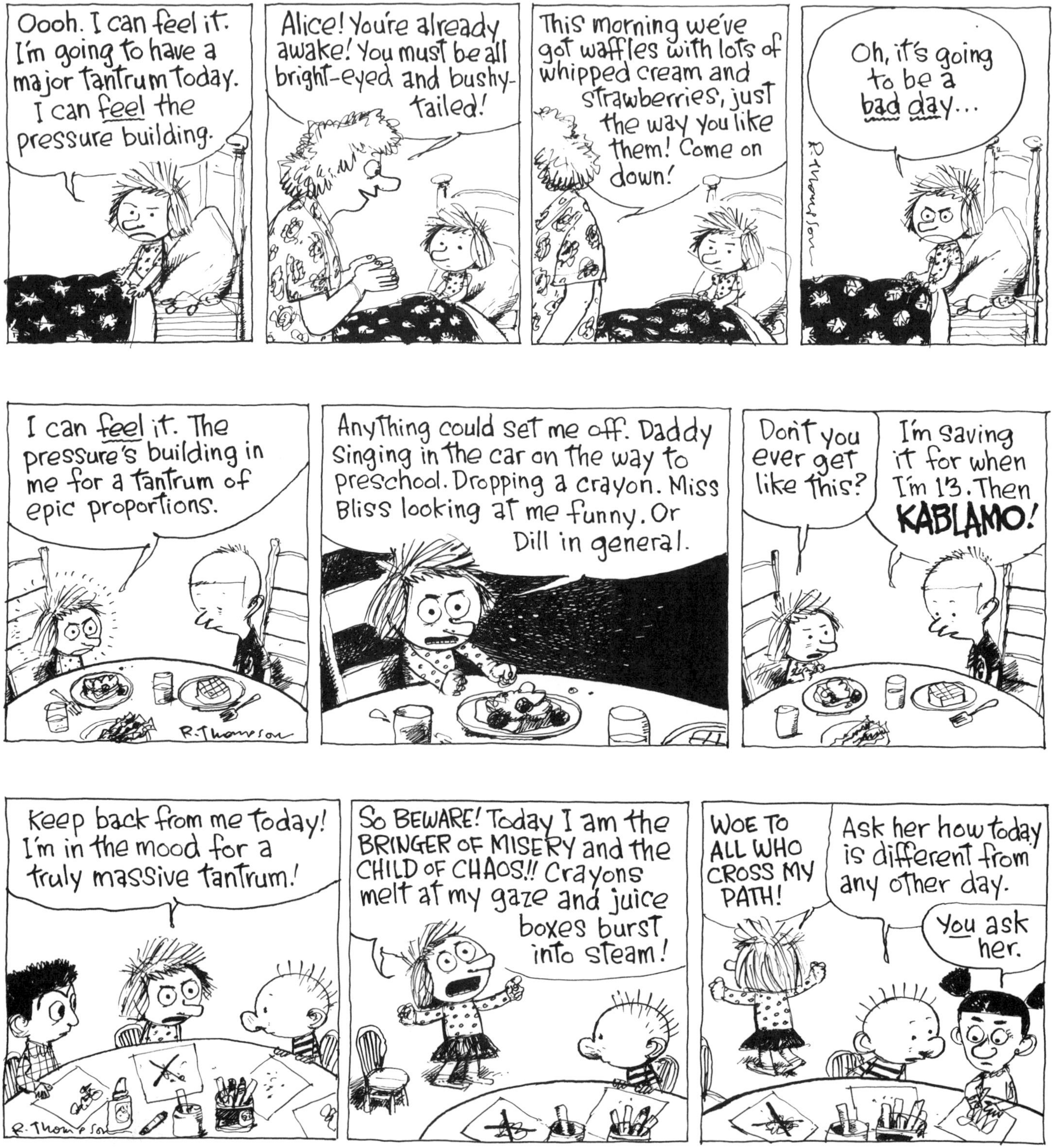
Oooh. I can feel it. I'm going to have a major tantrum today. I can feel the pressure building.
Alice! You're already awake! You must be all bright-eyed and bushy-tailed!
This morning we've got waffles with lots of whipped cream and strawberries, just the way you like them! Come on down!
Oh, it's going to be a bad day...
I can feel it. The pressure's building in me for a tantrum of epic proportions.
Anything could set me off. Daddy singing in the car on the way to preschool. Dropping a crayon. Miss Bliss looking at me funny. Or Dill in general.
Don't you ever get like this?
I'm saving it for when I'm 13. Then KABLAMO!
Keep back from me today! I'm in the mood for a truly massive tantrum!
So BEWARE! Today I am the BRINGER OF MISERY and the CHILD OF CHAOS!! Crayons melt at my gaze and juice boxes burst into steam!
WOE TO ALL WHO CROSS MY PATH!
Ask her how today is different from any other day.
You ask her.

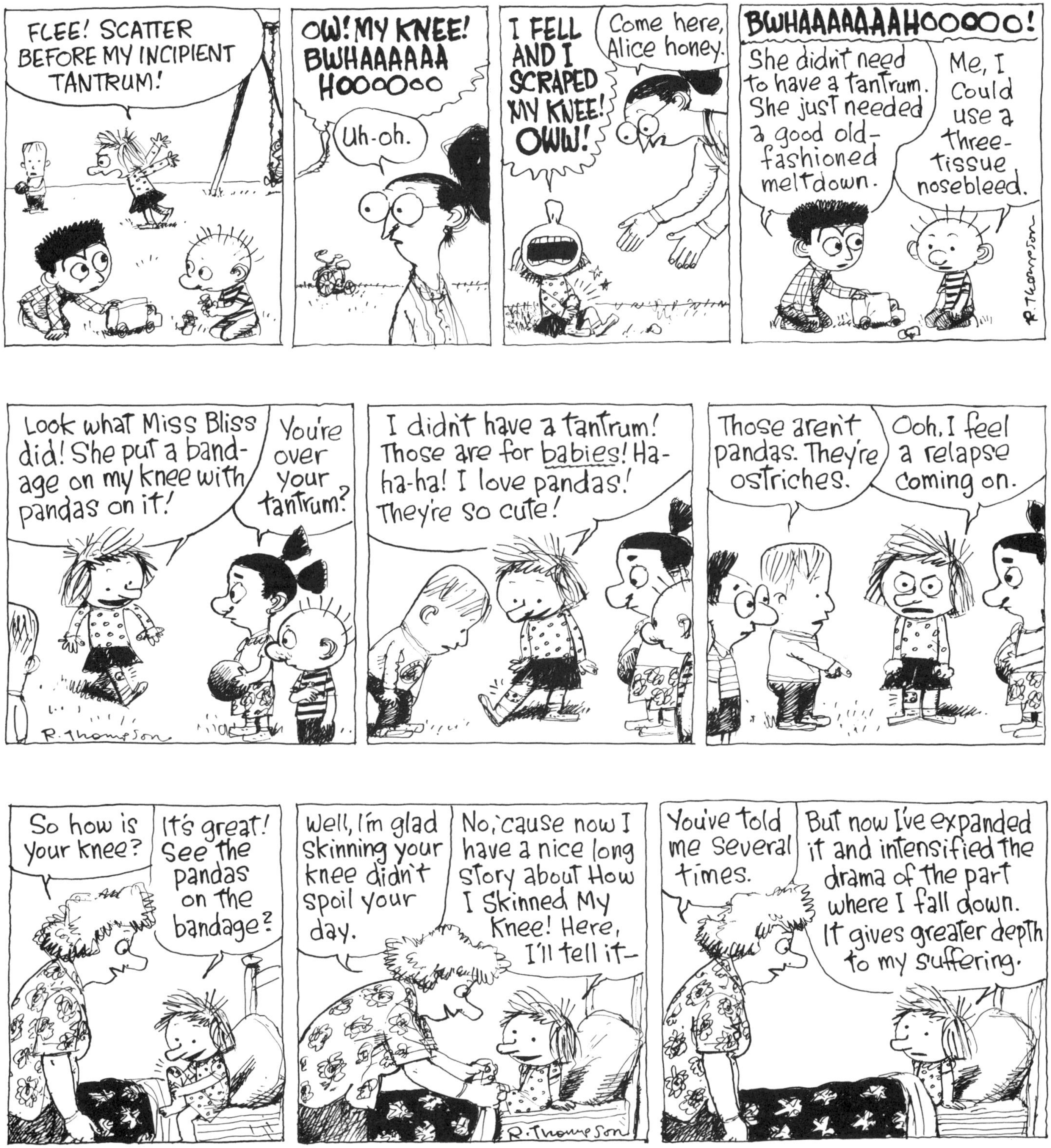
FLEE! SCATTER BEFORE MY INCIPIENT TANTRUM!
OW! MY KNEE! BWHAAAAAAA HOOOOoo
Uh-oh.
I FELL AND I SCRAPED MY KNEE! OWW!
Come here, Alice honey.
BWHAAAAAAAHOOOOO!
She didn't need to have a tantrum. She just needed a good old-fashioned meltdown.
Me, I could use a three-tissue nosebleed.
R. Thompson
Look what Miss Bliss did! She put a bandage on my knee with pandas on it!
You're over your tantrum?
R. Thompson
I didn't have a tantrum! Those are for babies! Ha-ha-ha! I love pandas! They're so cute!
Those aren't pandas. They're ostriches.
Ooh, I feel a relapse coming on.
So how is your knee?
It's great! See the pandas on the bandage?
Well, I'm glad skinning your knee didn't spoil your day.
No, 'cause now I have a nice long story about How I Skinned My Knee! Here, I'll tell it—
R. Thompson
You've told me several times.
But now I've expanded it and intensified the drama of the part where I fall down. It gives greater depth to my suffering.

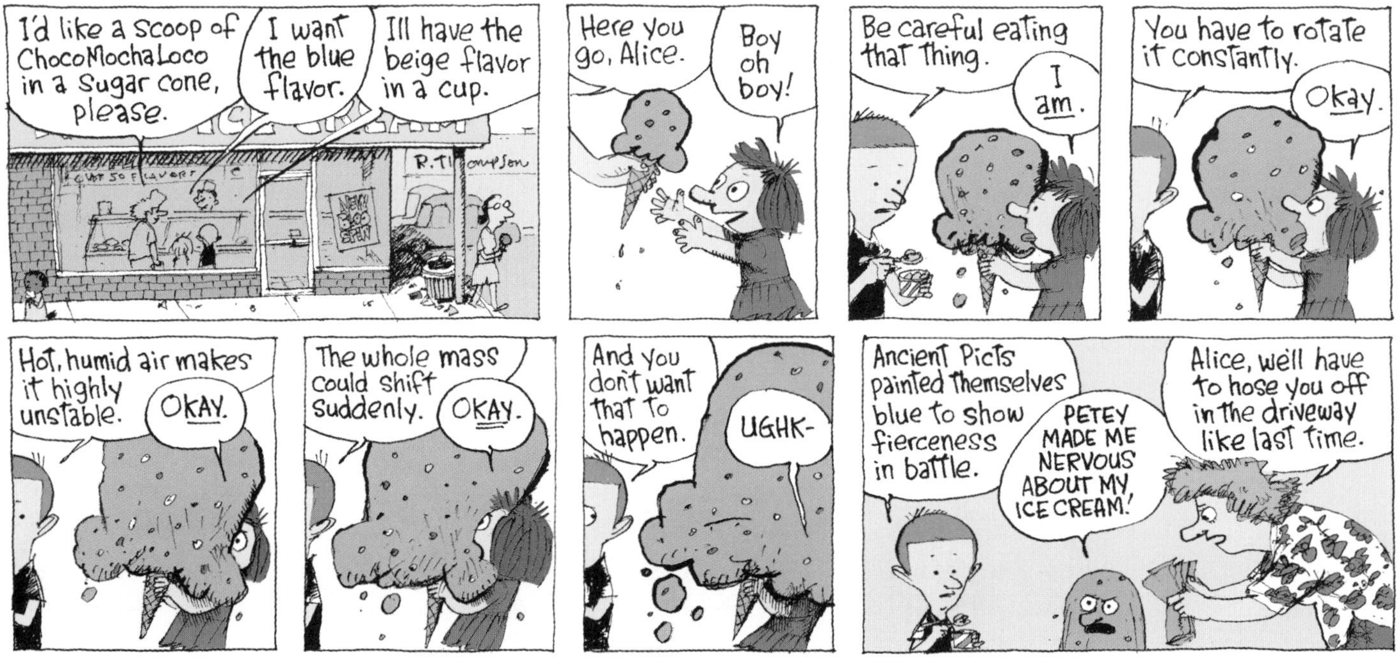
I'd like a scoop of ChocoMochaLoco in a sugar cone, please.
I want the blue flavor.
Ill have the beige flavor in a cup.
R. THOMPSON
Here you go, Alice.
Boy oh boy!
Be careful eating that thing.
I am.
You have to rotate it constantly.
Okay.
Hot, humid air makes it highly unstable.
OKAY.
The whole mass could shift suddenly.
OKAY.
And you don't want that to happen.
UGHK-
Ancient Picts painted themselves blue to show fierceness in battle.
PETEY MADE ME NERVOUS ABOUT MY ICE CREAM!
Alice, we'll have to hose you off in the driveway like last time.

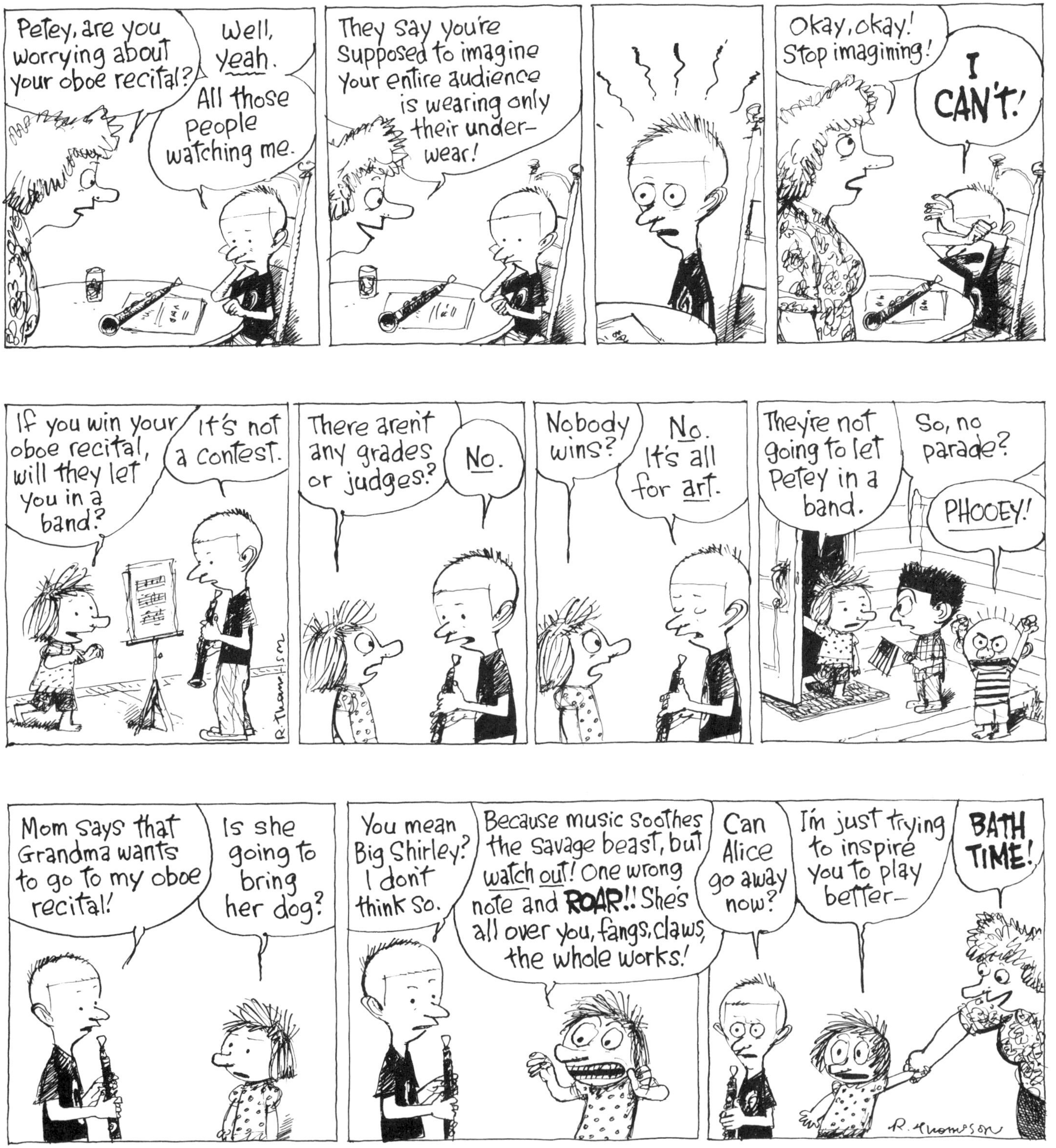
Petey, are you worrying about your oboe recital?
Well, yeah. All those people watching me.
They say you're supposed to imagine your entire audience is wearing only their under-wear!
Okay, okay! Stop imagining!
I CAN'T!
If you win your oboe recital, will they let you in a band?
It's not a contest.
There aren't any grades or judges?
No.
Nobody wins?
No. It's all for art.
They're not going to let Petey in a band.
So, no parade?
PHOOEY!
Mom says that Grandma wants to go to my oboe recital!
Is she going to bring her dog?
You mean Big Shirley? I don't think so.
Because music soothes the savage beast, but watch out! One wrong note and ROAR!! She's all over you, fangs, claws, the whole works!
Can Alice go away now?
I'm just trying to inspire you to play better—
BATH TIME!

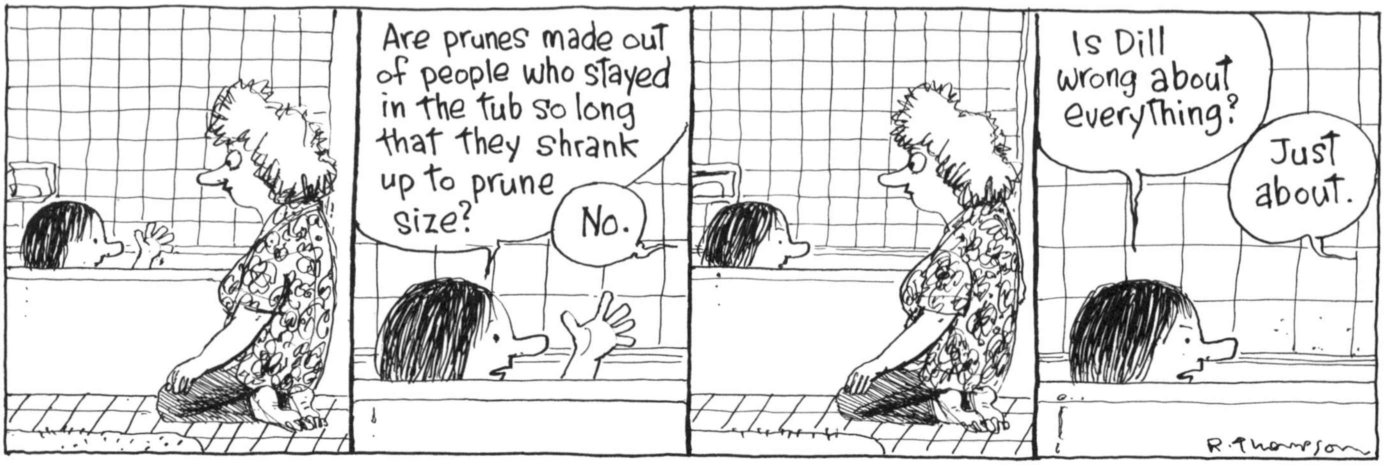
Are prunes made out of people who stayed in the tub so long that they shrank up to prune size?
No.
Is Dill wrong about everything?
Just about.
R. Thompson

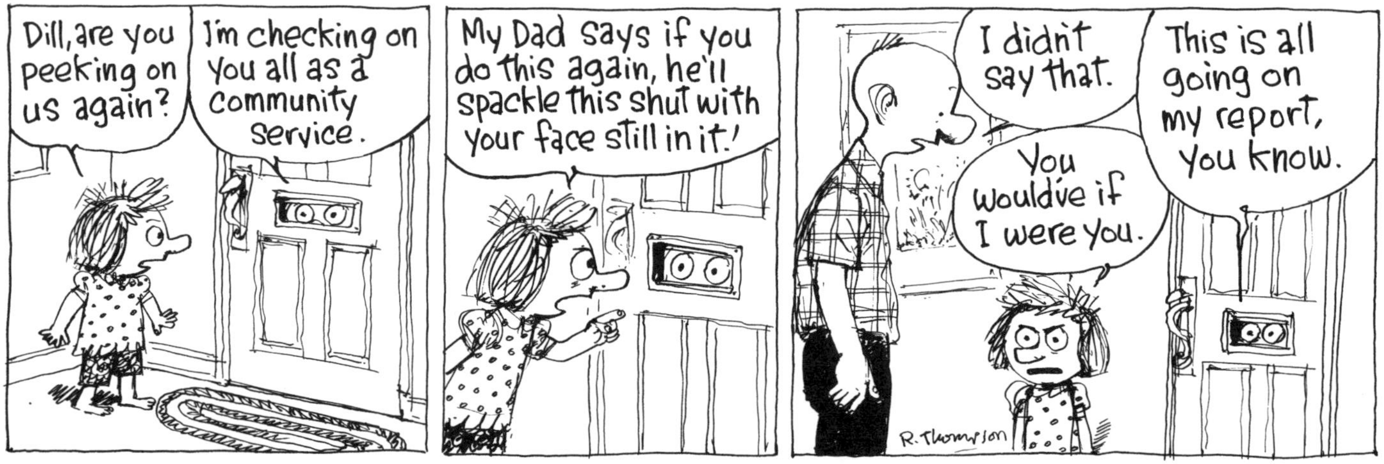
Dill, are you peeking on us again?
I'm checking on you all as a community service.
My Dad says if you do this again, he'll spackle this shut with your face still in it!
I didn't say that.
You would've if I were you.
This is all going on my report, you know.
R. Thompson

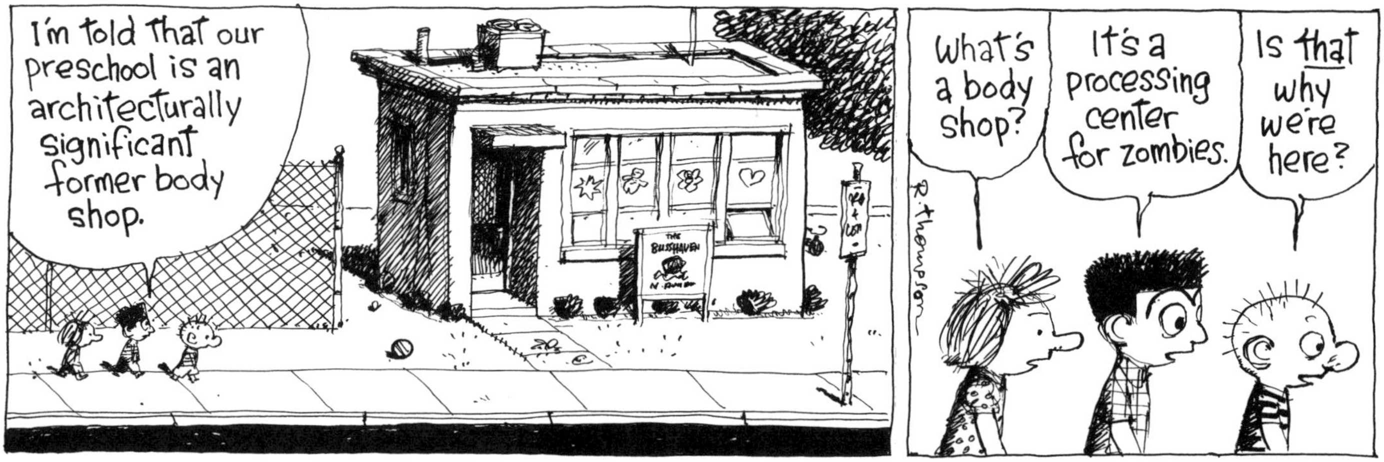
I'm told that our preschool is an architecturally significant former body shop.
What's a body shop?
It's a processing center for zombies.
Is that why we're here?
R. Thompson

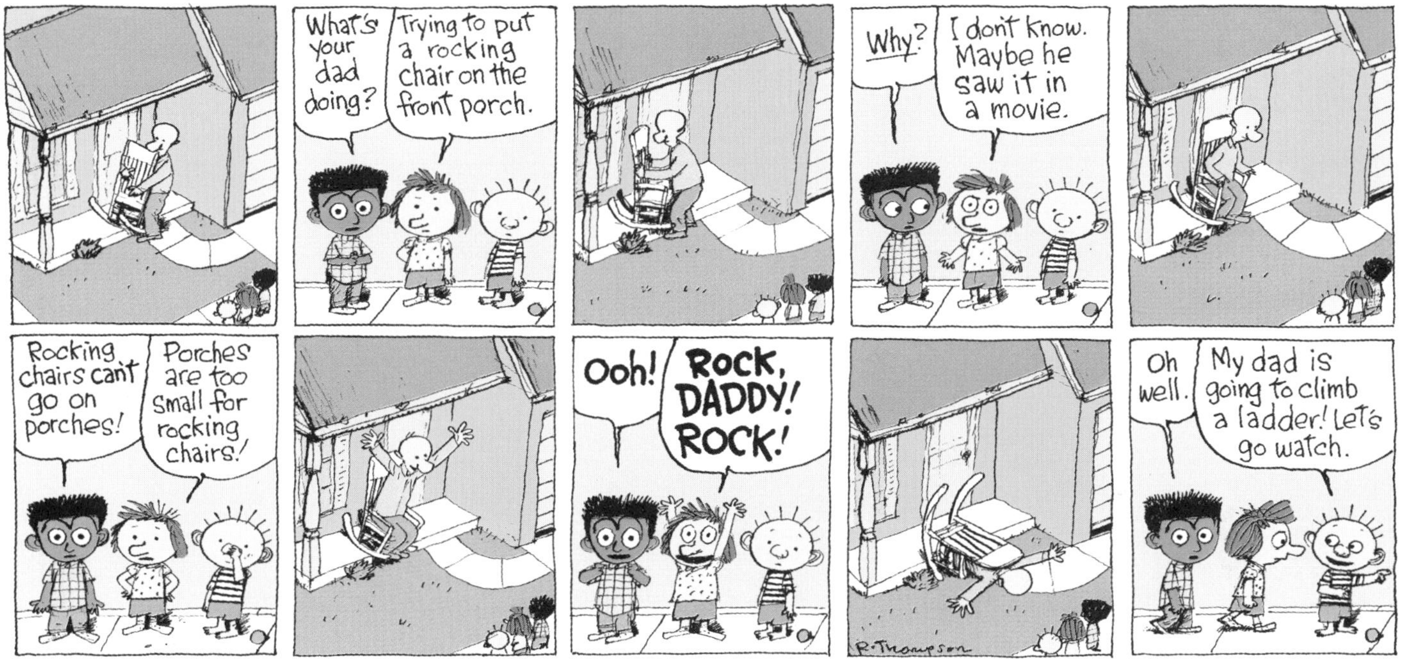
What's your dad doing?
Trying to put a rocking chair on the front porch.
Why?
I don't know. Maybe he saw it in a movie.
Rocking chairs can't go on porches!
Porches are too small for rocking chairs!
Ooh!
ROCK, DADDY! ROCK!
R. Thompson
Oh well.
My dad is going to climb a ladder! Let's go watch.

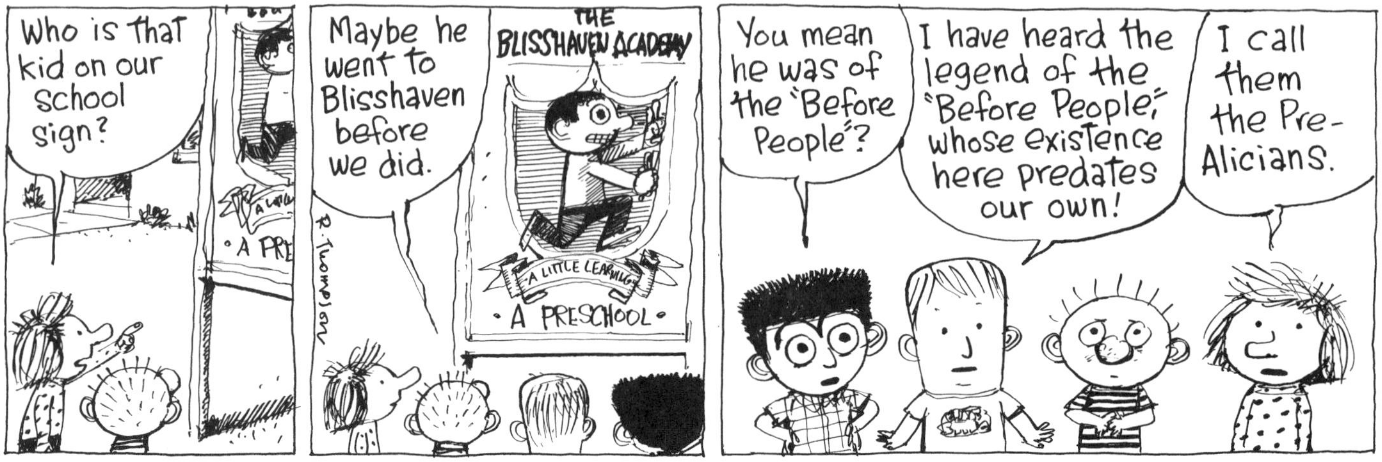
Who is that kid on our school sign?
Maybe he went to Blisshaven before we did.
THE BLISSHAVEN ACADEMY
A LITTLE LEARNING
A PRESCHOOL
R. Thompson
You mean he was of the "Before People"?
I have heard the legend of the "Before People," whose existence here predates our own!
I call them the Pre-Alicians.

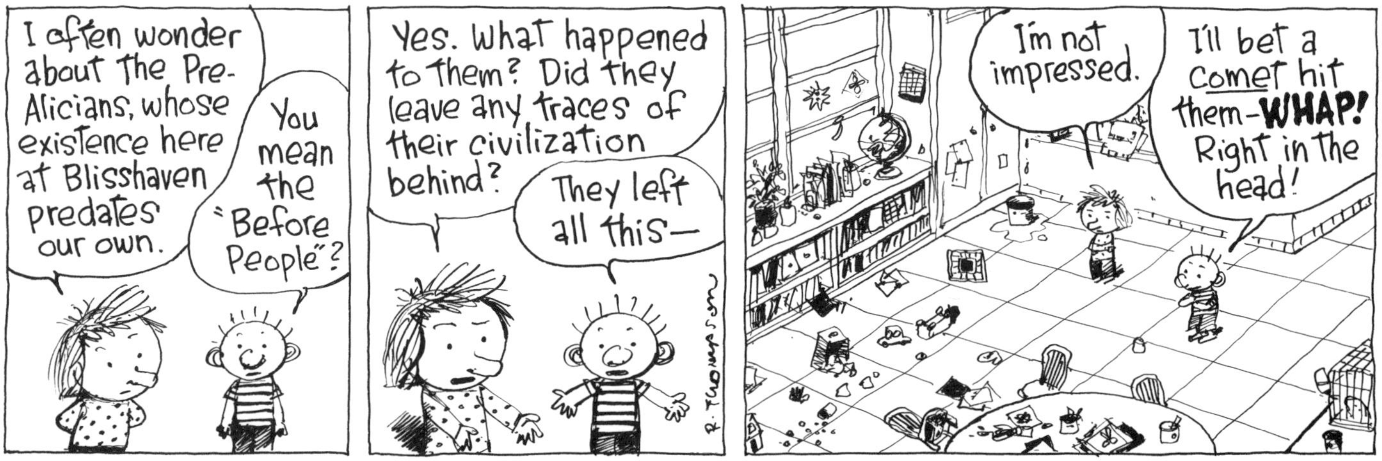
I often wonder about the Pre-Alicians, whose existence here at Blisshaven predates our own.
You mean the "Before People"?
Yes. What happened to them? Did they leave any traces of their civilization behind?
They left all this—
R. Thompson
I'm not impressed.
I'll bet a comet hit them—WHAP! Right in the head!

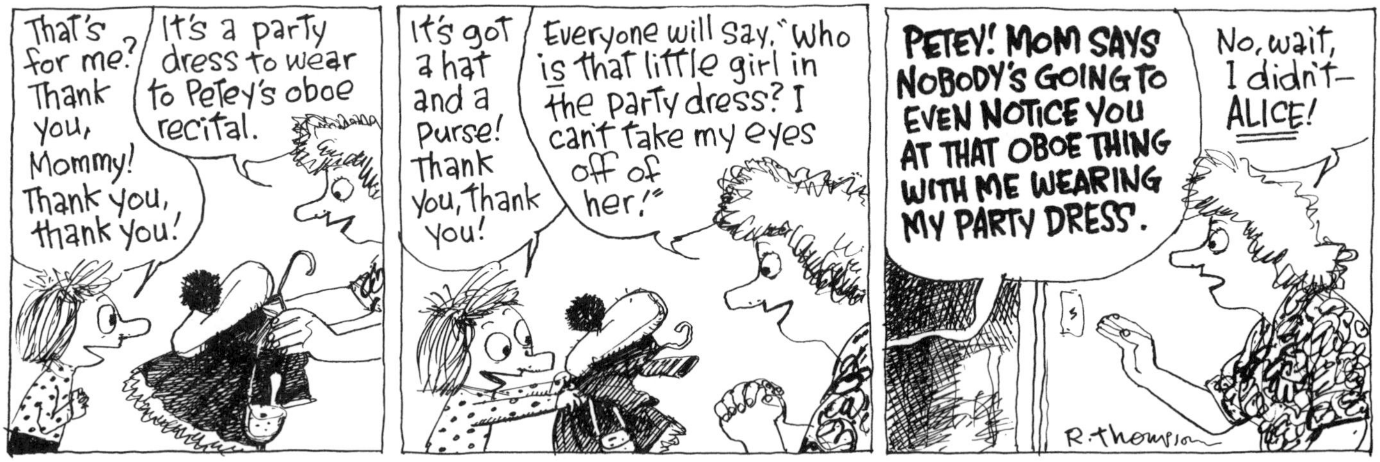
That's for me? Thank you, Mommy! Thank you, thank you!
It's a party dress to wear to Petey's oboe recital.
It's got a hat and a purse! Thank you, thank you!
Everyone will say, "Who is that little girl in the party dress? I can't take my eyes off of her!"
PETEY! MOM SAYS NOBODY'S GOING TO EVEN NOTICE YOU AT THAT OBOE THING WITH ME WEARING MY PARTY DRESS.
No, wait, I didn't— ALICE!
R. Thompson

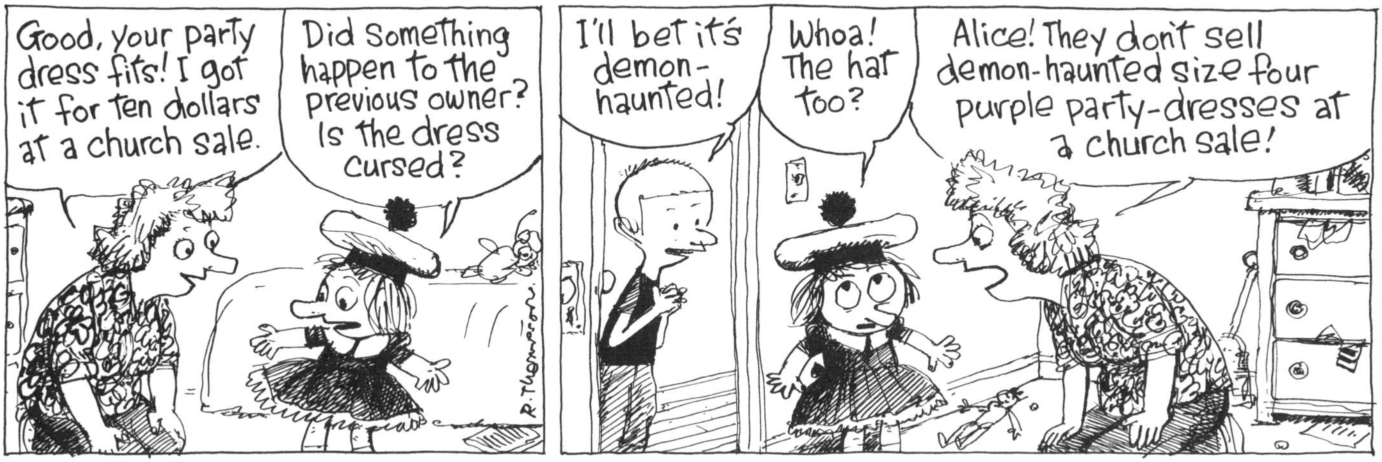
Good, your party dress fits! I got it for ten dollars at a church sale.
Did something happen to the previous owner? Is the dress cursed?
I'll bet it's demon-haunted!
Whoa! The hat too?
Alice! They don't sell demon-haunted size four purple party-dresses at a church sale!

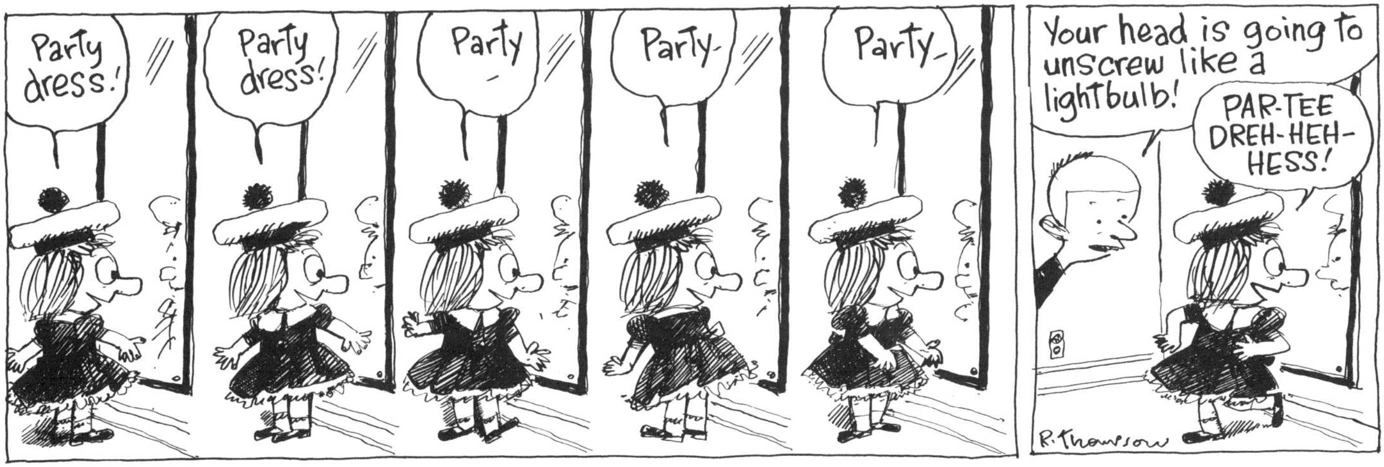
Party dress!
Party dress!
Party
Party
Party
Your head is going to unscrew like a lightbulb!
PAR-TEE DREH-HEH-HESS!

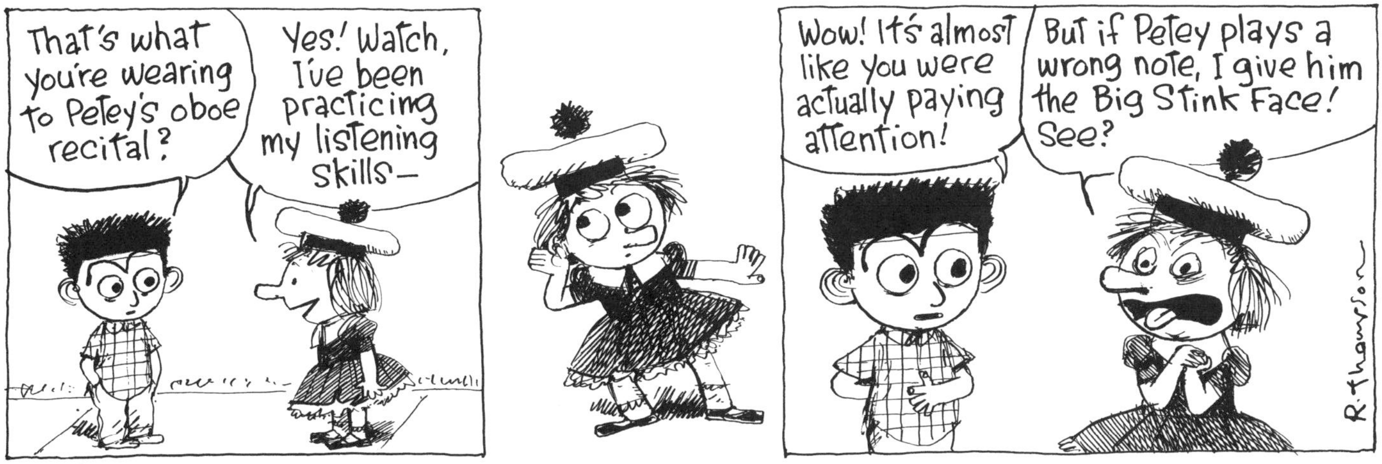
That's what you're wearing to Petey's oboe recital?
Yes! Watch, I've been practicing my listening skills—
Wow! It's almost like you were actually paying attention!
But if Petey plays a wrong note, I give him the Big Stink Face! See?

Petey, would you-
MOMMY!
What?
I'm not Petey!
Oh. You're not?
NO!
Lulu? Esmé? Muffin? Tootsie?
MOMMY!
What?
I'M ALICE!
Pleased to meet you, Alice!
AGH!
First I thought it was an accident, but then it was almost like she was doing it on purpose.
I mean, if Mommy had a real name, I'd try to remember it.
You should've told her your name was Mad Dog when you had the chance.
R. Thompson

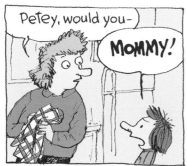

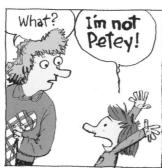

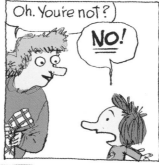

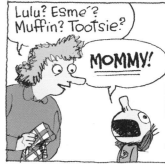

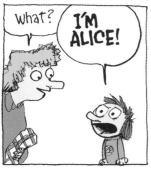

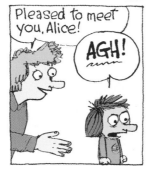

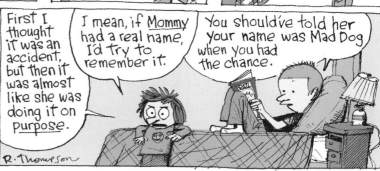

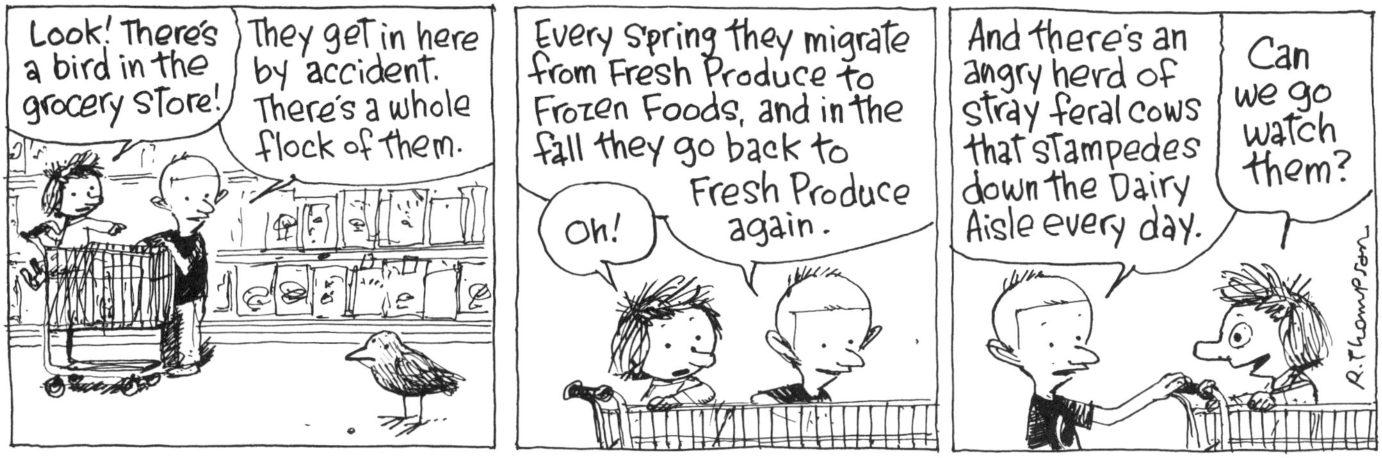
Look! There's a bird in the grocery store!
They get in here by accident. There's a whole flock of them.
Every spring they migrate from Fresh Produce to Frozen Foods, and in the fall they go back to Fresh Produce again.
Oh!
And there's an angry herd of stray feral cows that stampedes down the Dairy Aisle every day.
Can we go watch them?
R. Thompson

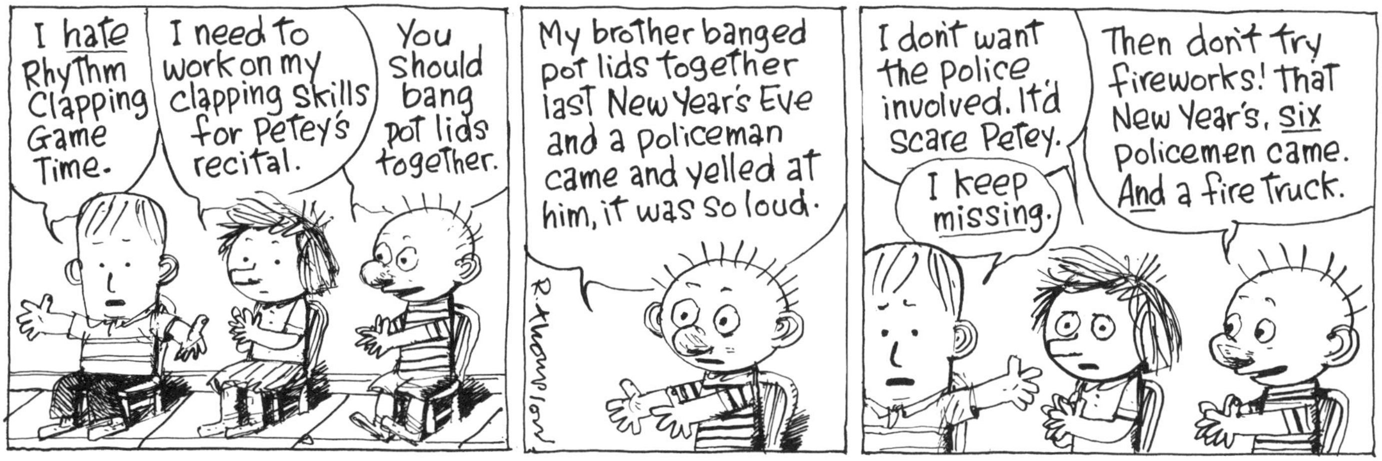
I hate Rhythm Clapping Game Time.
I need to work on my clapping skills for Petey's recital.
You should bang pot lids together.
R. Thompson
My brother banged pot lids together last New Year's Eve and a policeman came and yelled at him, it was so loud.
I don't want the police involved. It'd scare Petey.
I keep missing.
Then don't try fireworks! That New Year's, six policemen came. And a fire truck.

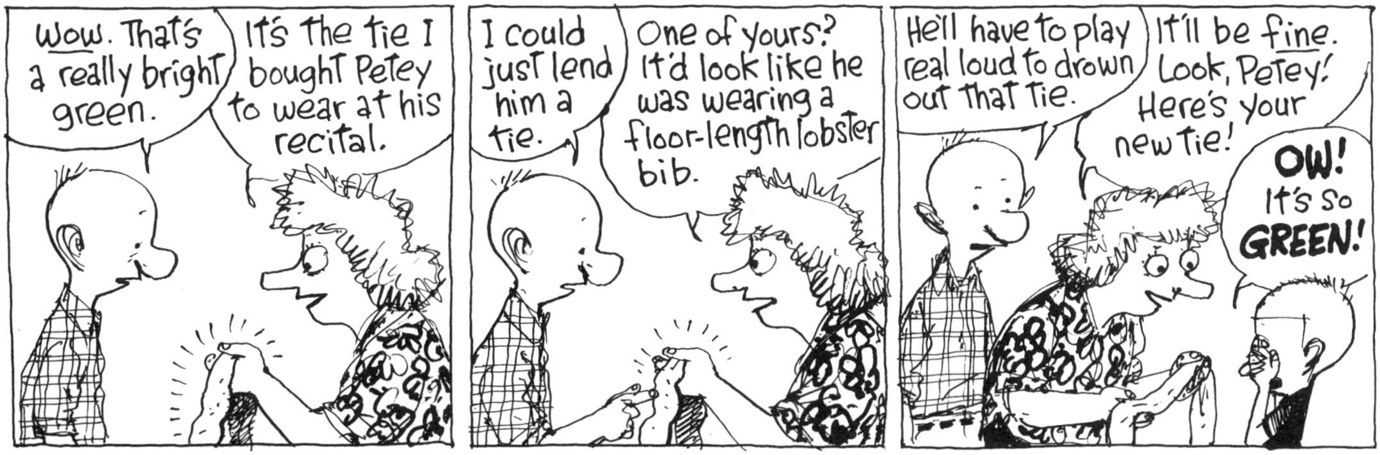
Wow. That's a really bright green.
It's the tie I bought Petey to wear at his recital.
I could just lend him a tie.
One of yours? It'd look like he was wearing a floor-length lobster bib.
He'll have to play real loud to drown out that tie.
It'll be fine. Look, Petey! Here's your new tie!
OW! It's so GREEN!

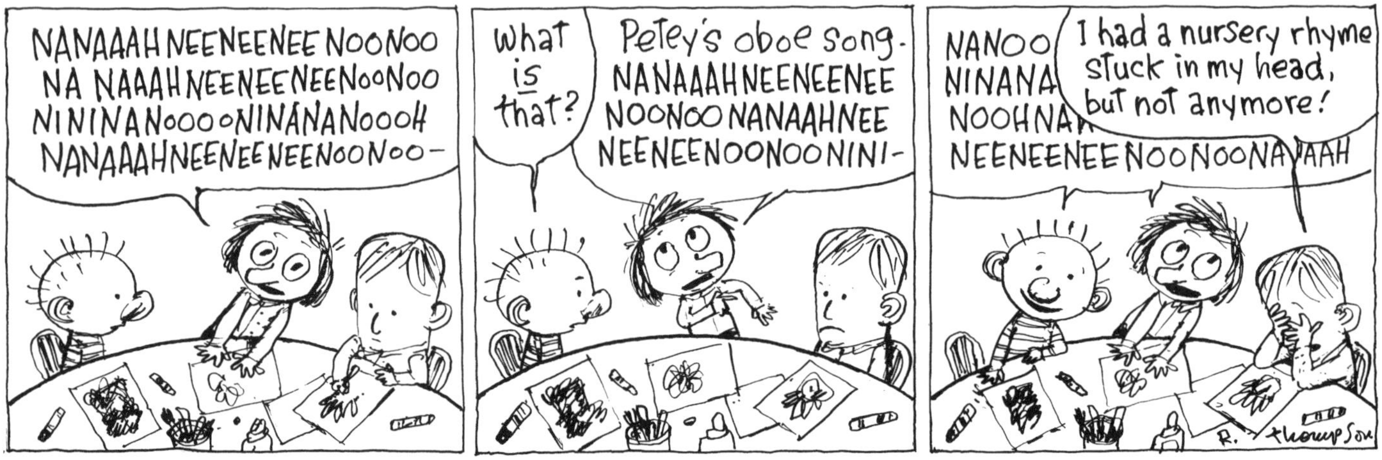
NANAAAH NEENEENEE NOONOO NA NAAAH NEENEENEENOONOO NININANOOOONINANANOOOH NANAAAHNEENEENEENOONOO-
What is that?
Petey's oboe song. NANAAAHNEENEENEE NOONOO NANAAHNEE NEENEENOONOONINI-
NANOO NINANA NOOHNA NEENEENEE NOONOONA AAH
I had a nursery rhyme stuck in my head, but not anymore!

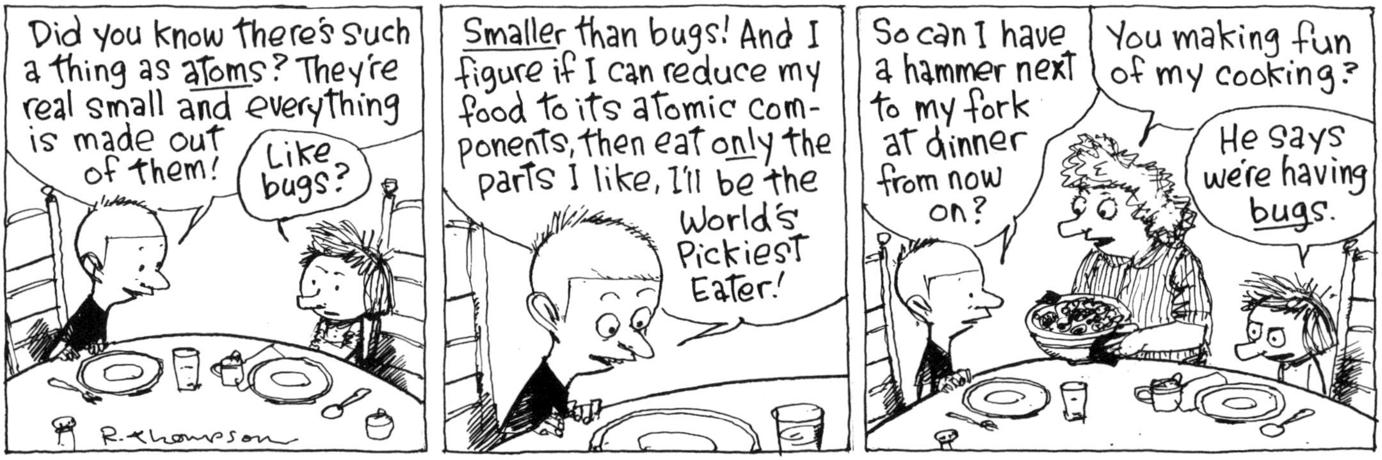
Did you know there's such a thing as atoms? They're real small and everything is made out of them!
Like bugs?
Smaller than bugs! And I figure if I can reduce my food to its atomic components, then eat only the parts I like, I'll be the World's Pickiest Eater!
So can I have a hammer next to my fork at dinner from now on?
You making fun of my cooking?
He says we're having bugs.

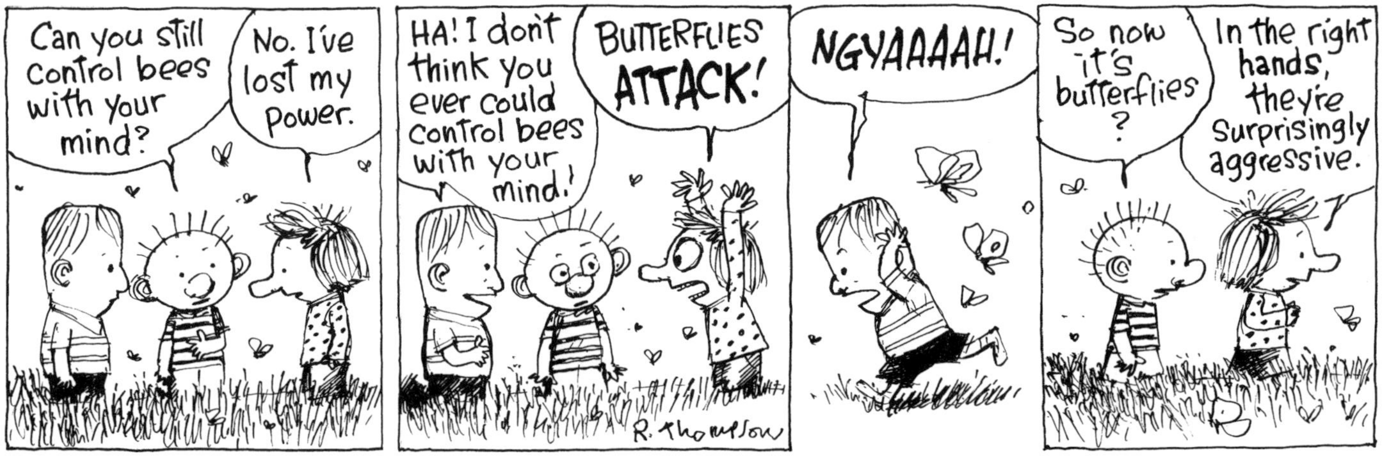
Can you still control bees with your mind?
No. I've lost my power.
HA! I don't think you ever could control bees with your mind!
BUTTERFLIES ATTACK!
NGYAAAAH!
So now it's butterflies?
In the right hands, they're surprisingly aggressive.

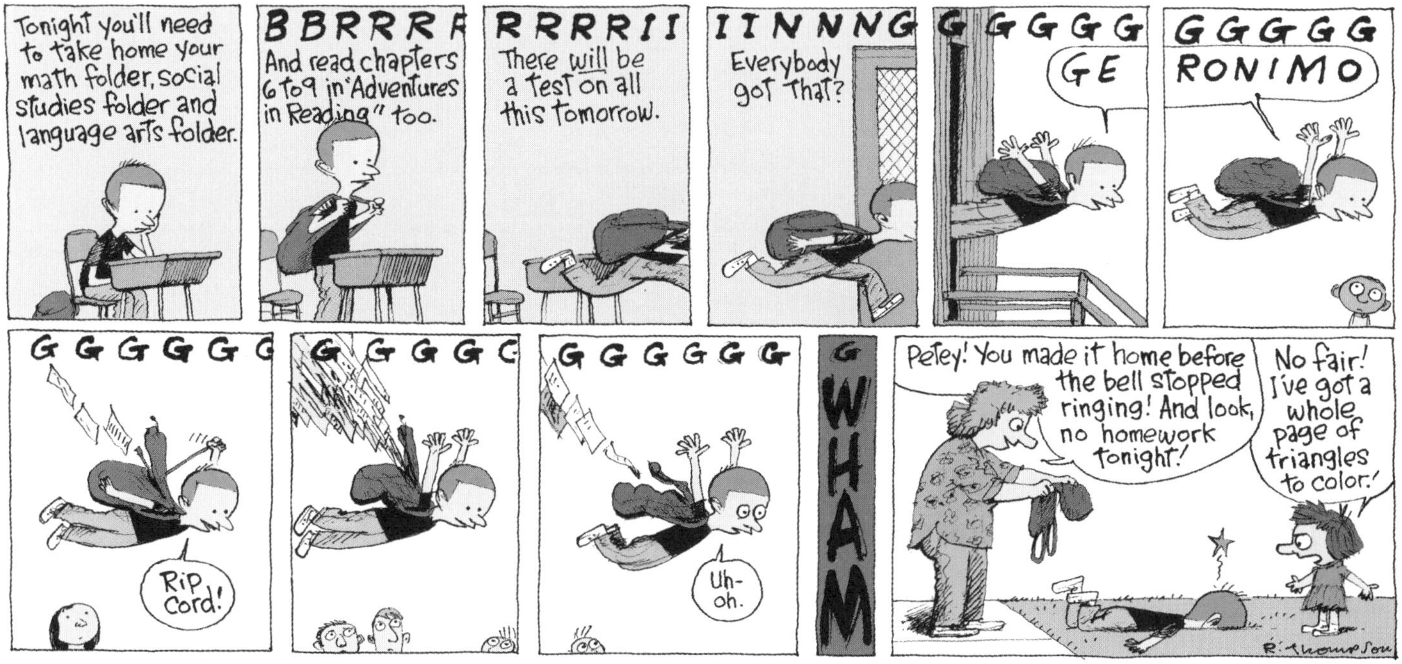
Tonight you'll need to take home your math folder, social studies folder and language arts folder.
BBRRRRR
And read chapters 6 to 9 in "Adventures in Reading" too.
RRRRRII
There will be a test on all this tomorrow.
IINNNG
Everybody got that?
GGGGGG
GE
GGGGG
RONIMO
GGGGGG
Rip cord!
GGGGG
GGGGGG
Uh-oh.
G
WHAM
Petey! You made it home before the bell stopped ringing! And look, no homework tonight!
No fair! I've got a whole page of triangles to color!
R. Thompson

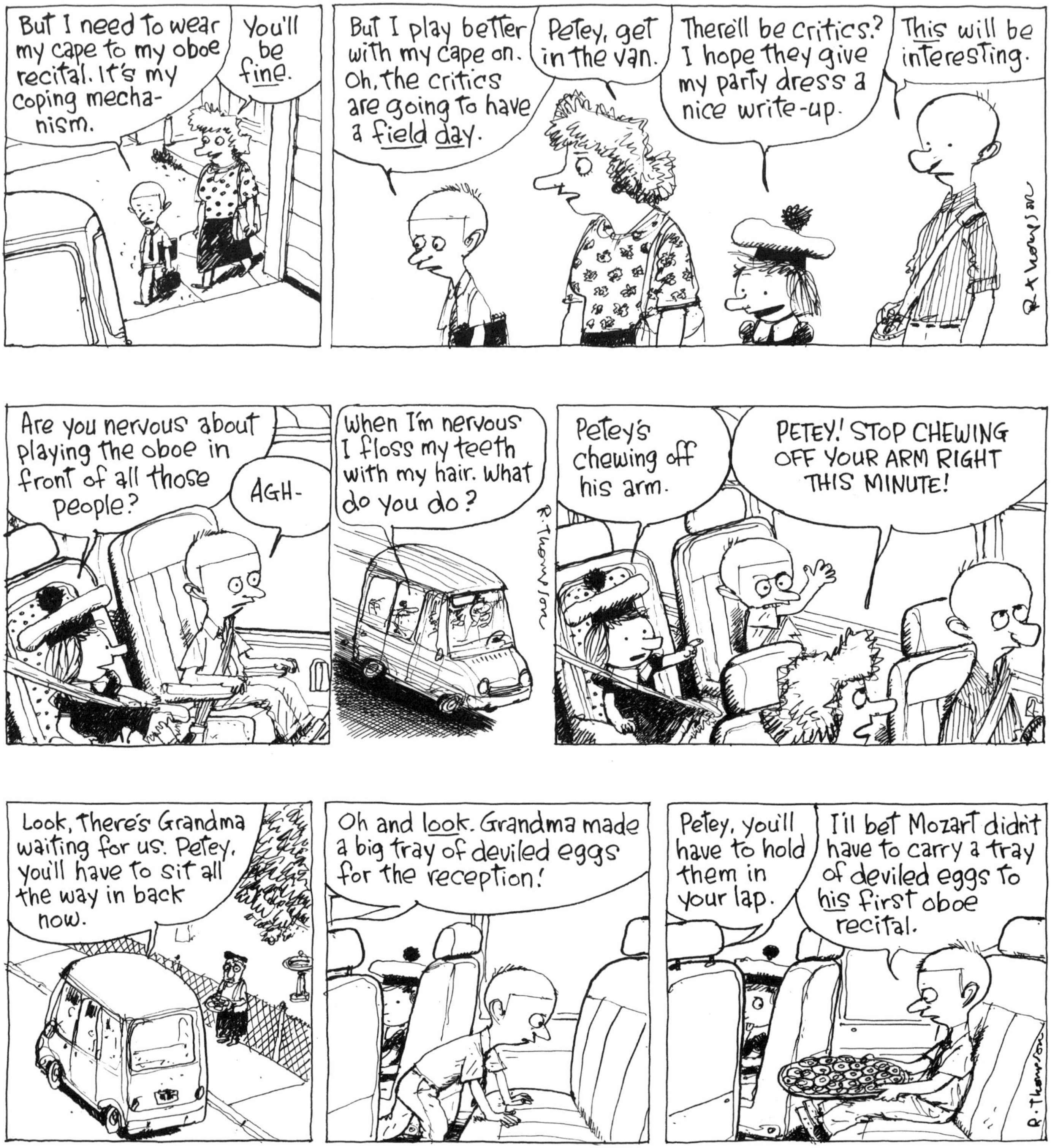

But I need to wear my cape to my oboe recital. It's my coping mechanism.
You'll be fine.
But I play better with my cape on. Oh, the critics are going to have a field day.
Petey, get in the van.
There'll be critics? I hope they give my party dress a nice write-up.
This will be interesting.
Are you nervous about playing the oboe in front of all those people?
AGH-
When I'm nervous I floss my teeth with my hair. What do you do?
Petey's chewing off his arm.
PETEY! STOP CHEWING OFF YOUR ARM RIGHT THIS MINUTE!
Look, there's Grandma waiting for us. Petey, you'll have to sit all the way in back now.
Oh and look. Grandma made a big tray of deviled eggs for the reception!
Petey, you'll have to hold them in your lap.
I'll bet Mozart didn't have to carry a tray of deviled eggs to his first oboe recital.

Okay! We're almost to the rec center for Petey's big recital! Petey, are you all right back there? You're not eating those deviled eggs, are you?

The deviled eggs are staring at me.

We're almost there!

Here's where Petey's recital is!

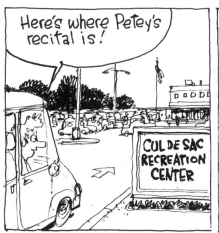

CUL DE SAC
RECREATION
CENTER

Look! A sign with balloons! Isn't this exciting!

WELCOME YOUNG MUSICIANS

There's a playground! Can I go on the swings?

When I was a girl, this whole place was a chicken farm. And WHOO-EE did it smell!

Here's the recital program.

My dress is the prettiest one here!

TODAYS PRGRM TAKE ONE

Petey, you'll be the second to last.

So we'll have lots of time to sit and enjoy the performances.

How long does this thing last? I have to walk Big Shirley at 3:30.

This dress is making me itchy. Can I take it off?

47

Look, Dad's home.
Hey, Dad! You're late.
We've finished our dinner.
Mom put yours in the fridge. It started to shrivel.
Gee, Dad, you look awful. Was there a fight at work?
Now I can do my song for you! And my dance!
Was there a road-rage incident?
I'll sing loud so you can hear it over the dancing.
Were the police involved?
SLAM
SLAM
You'd think an inspiring moment with the Arts would be a perfect end to a Dad's day. But No.
The repressive, boorish father is a standard figure in all artists' lives.
Yeah, and it sounds like the police are after him anyway.
R. Thompson

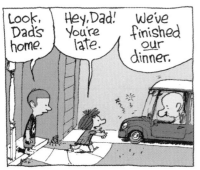

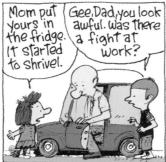

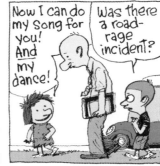

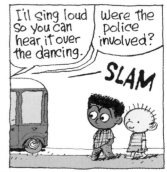

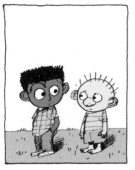

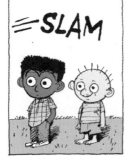

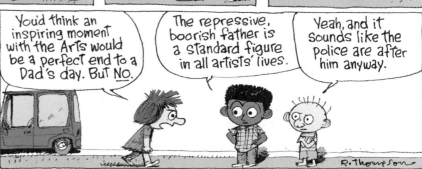

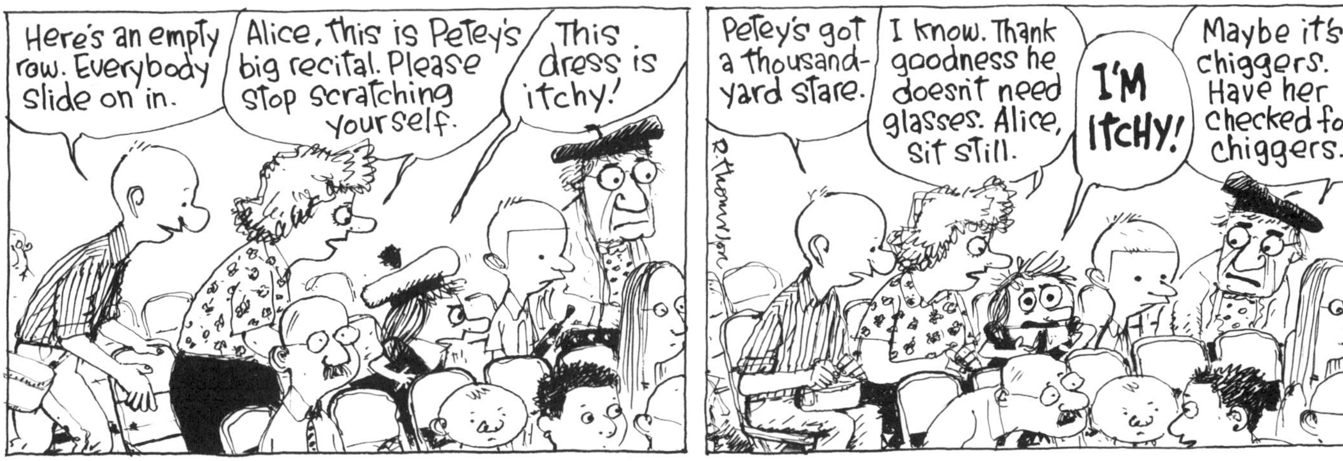
Here's an empty row. Everybody slide on in.
Alice, this is Petey's big recital. Please stop scratching yourself.
This dress is itchy!
R. Thompson
Petey's got a thousand-yard stare.
I know. Thank goodness he doesn't need glasses. Alice, sit still.
I'M ITCHY!
Maybe it's chiggers. Have her checked for chiggers.

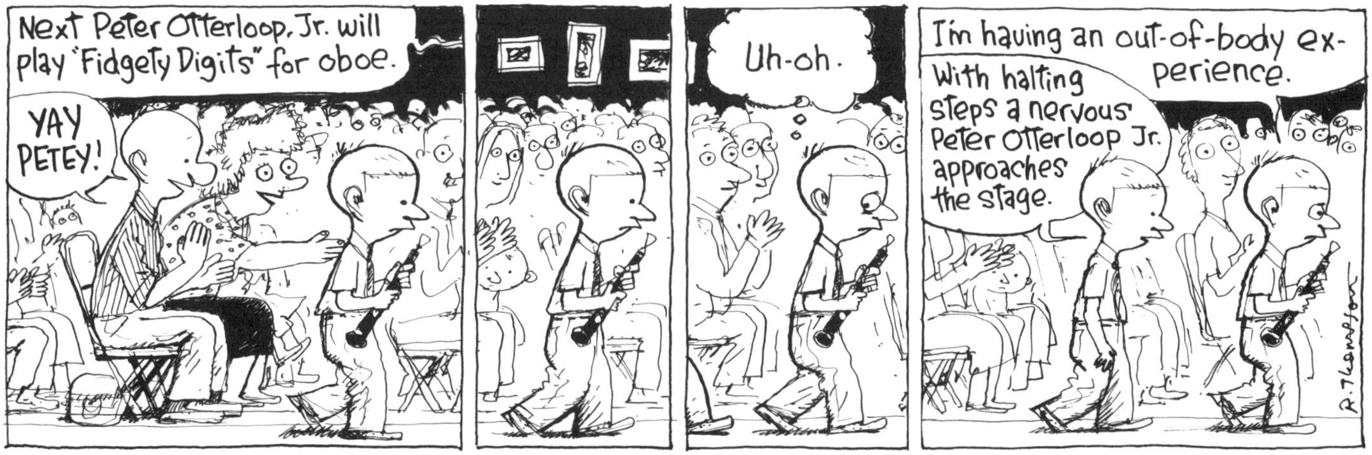
Next Peter Otterloop, Jr. will play "Fidgety Digits" for oboe.
YAY PETEY!
Uh-oh.
I'm having an out-of-body experience.
With halting steps a nervous Peter Otterloop Jr. approaches the stage.
R. Thompson

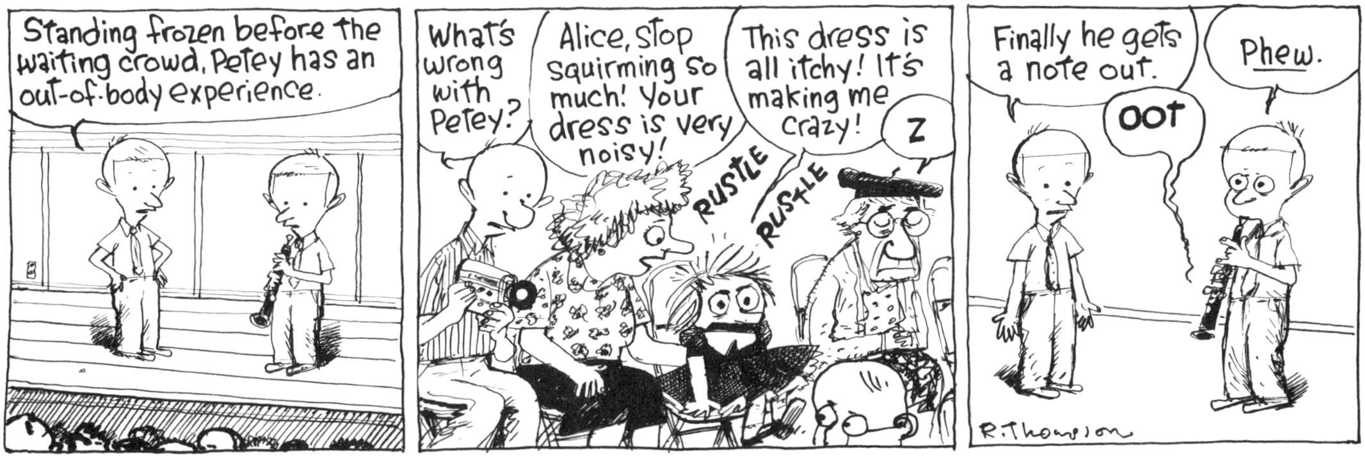
Standing frozen before the waiting crowd, Petey has an out-of-body experience.
What's wrong with Petey?
Alice, stop squirming so much! Your dress is very noisy!
This dress is all itchy! It's making me crazy!
Z
RUSTLE
RUSTLE
Finally he gets a note out.
OOT
Phew.
R. Thompson

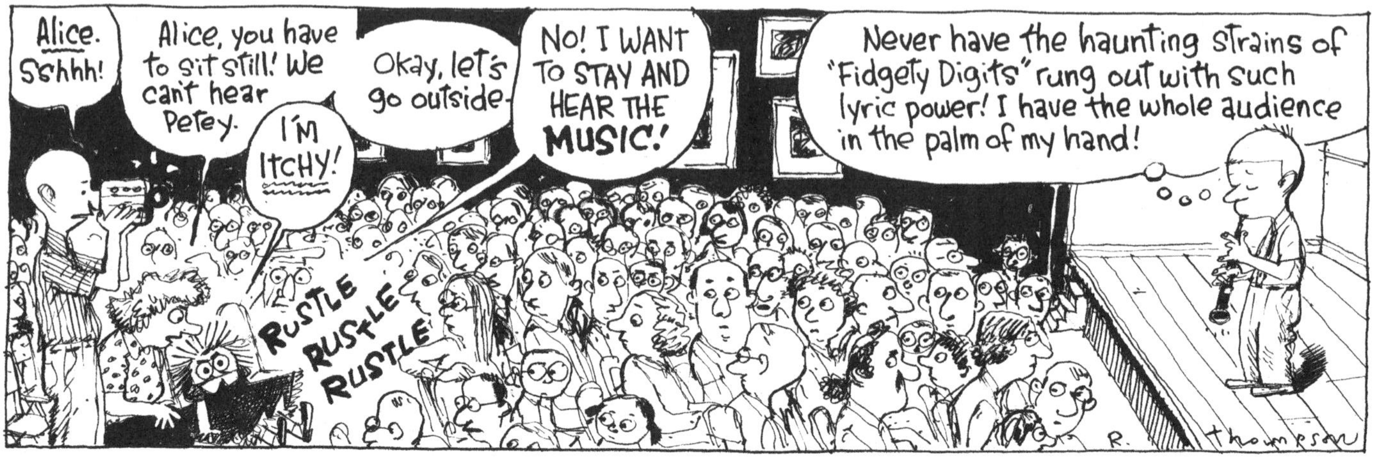
Alice. Sshhh!
Alice, you have to sit still! We can't hear Petey.
I'M ITCHY!
Okay, let's go outside-
NO! I WANT TO STAY AND HEAR THE MUSIC!
RUSTLE RUSTLE RUSTLE
Never have the haunting strains of "Fidgety Digits" rung out with such lyric power! I have the whole audience in the palm of my hand!
R. thompson

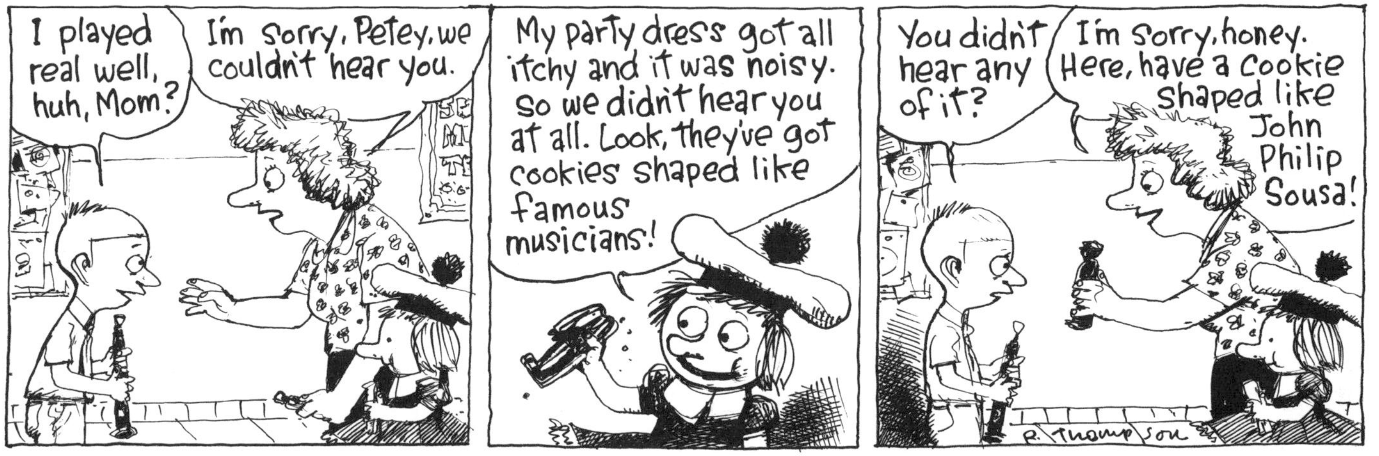
I played real well, huh, Mom?
I'm sorry, Petey, we couldn't hear you.
My party dress got all itchy and it was noisy. So we didn't hear you at all. Look, they've got cookies shaped like famous musicians!
You didn't hear any of it?
I'm sorry, honey. Here, have a cookie shaped like John Philip Sousa!
R. thompson

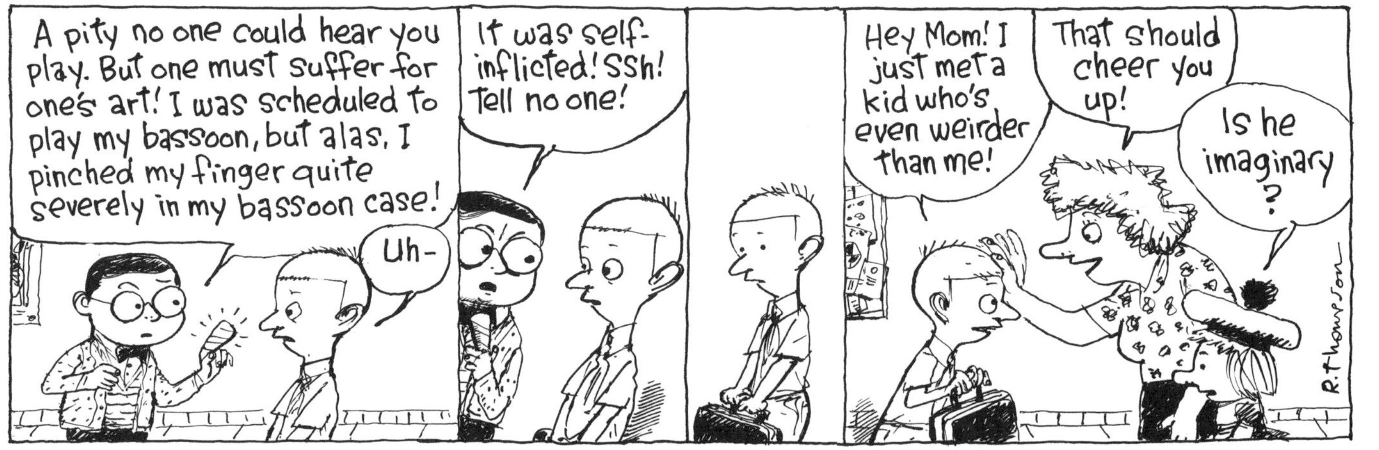
A pity no one could hear you play. But one must suffer for one's art! I was scheduled to play my bassoon, but alas, I pinched my finger quite severely in my bassoon case!
Uh-
It was self-inflicted! Ssh! Tell no one!
Hey Mom! I just met a kid who's even weirder than me!
That should cheer you up!
Is he imaginary?
R. thompson

There's stuff in my cubby I don't even remember.
Why do we have to clean out our cubbies anyway?
It's the last day of pre-school.
We've all been "let go."
Like where'd this dumb hat come from?
HA-HA! It's the dumbest hat ever!
You clean out your cubby, then security escorts you from the building.
HA-HA! I've got a dumb hat!
HA-HA! Hey, wait. That's MY hat!
We'll have to find positions at other preschools and take pay cuts!
You should thank me.
Your big fat head ruined my favorite hat!
LOOK AT ME!
MISS BLISS IS HUGGING PEOPLE! IF YOU VALUE YOUR DIGNITY, RUN!

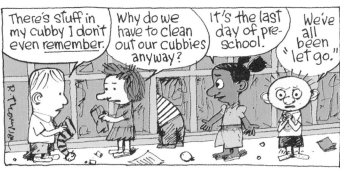

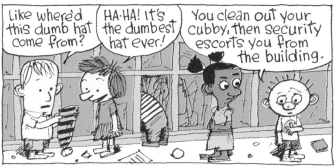

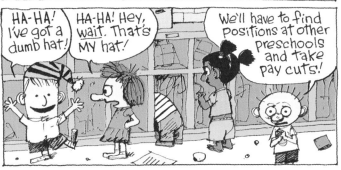

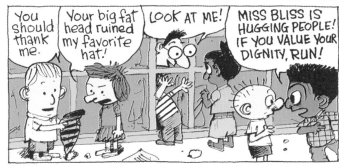

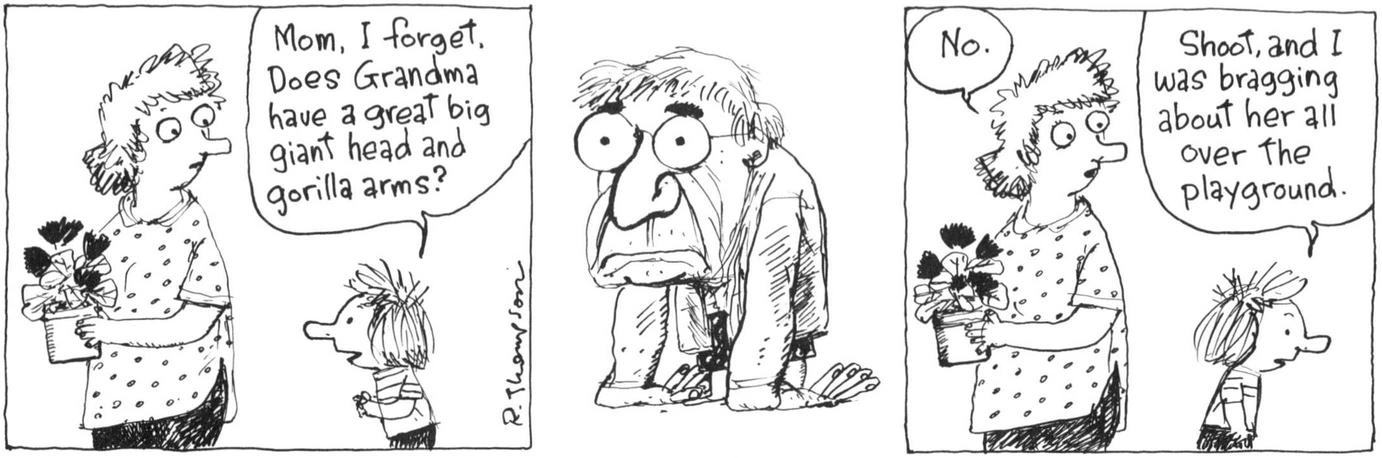
Mom, I forget. Does Grandma have a great big giant head and gorilla arms?
R. Thompson
No.
Shoot, and I was bragging about her all over the playground.

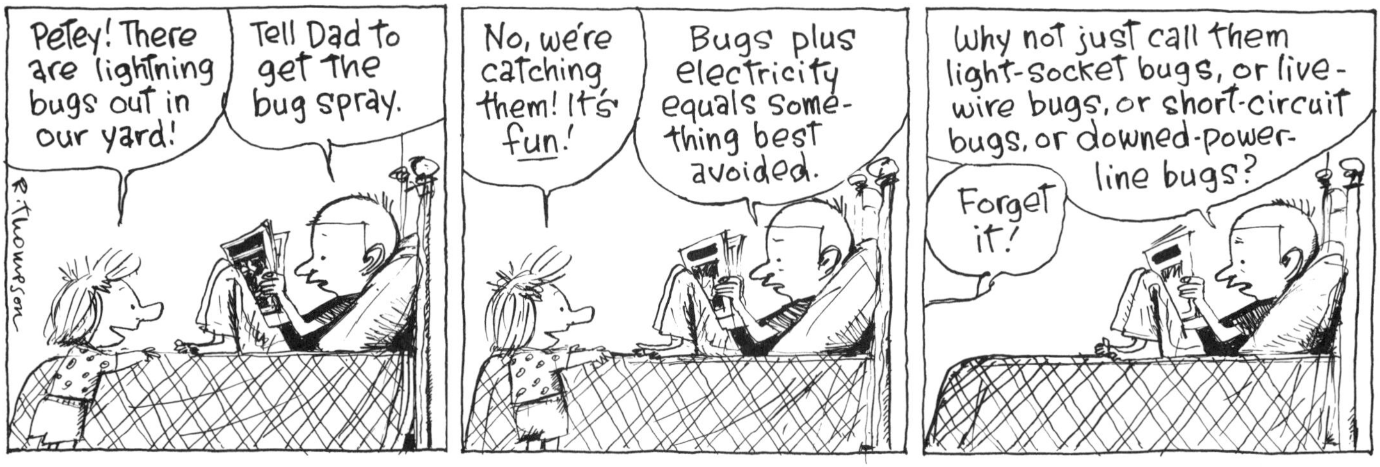
Petey! There are lightning bugs out in our yard!
Tell Dad to get the bug spray.
R. Thompson
No, we're catching them! It's fun!
Bugs plus electricity equals some-thing best avoided.
Why not just call them light-socket bugs, or live-wire bugs, or short-circuit bugs, or downed-power-line bugs?
Forget it!

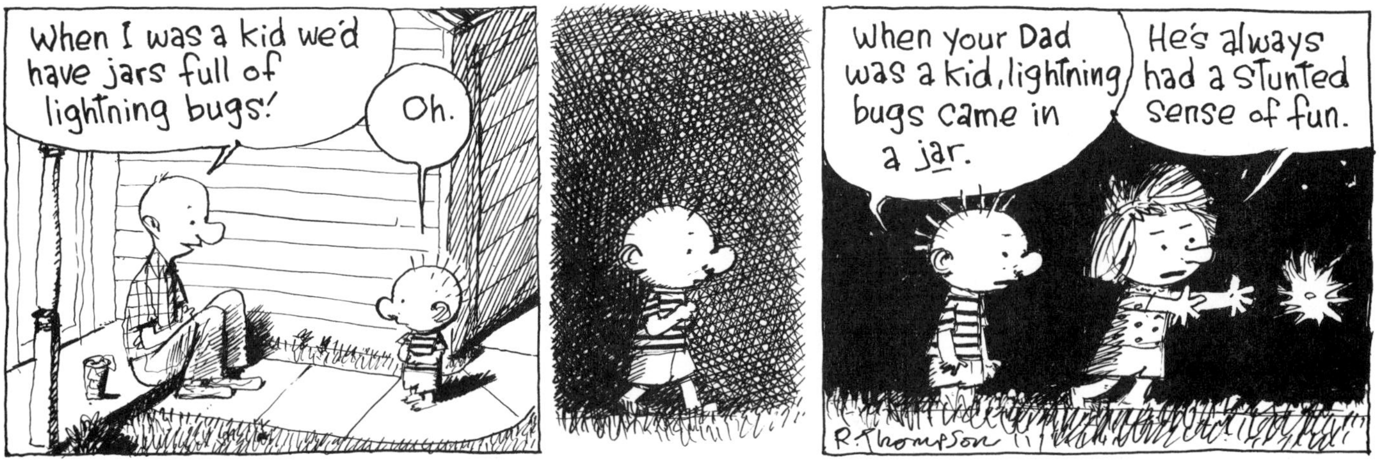
When I was a kid we'd have jars full of lightning bugs!
Oh.
When your Dad was a kid, lightning bugs came in a jar.
He's always had a stunted sense of fun.
R. Thompson

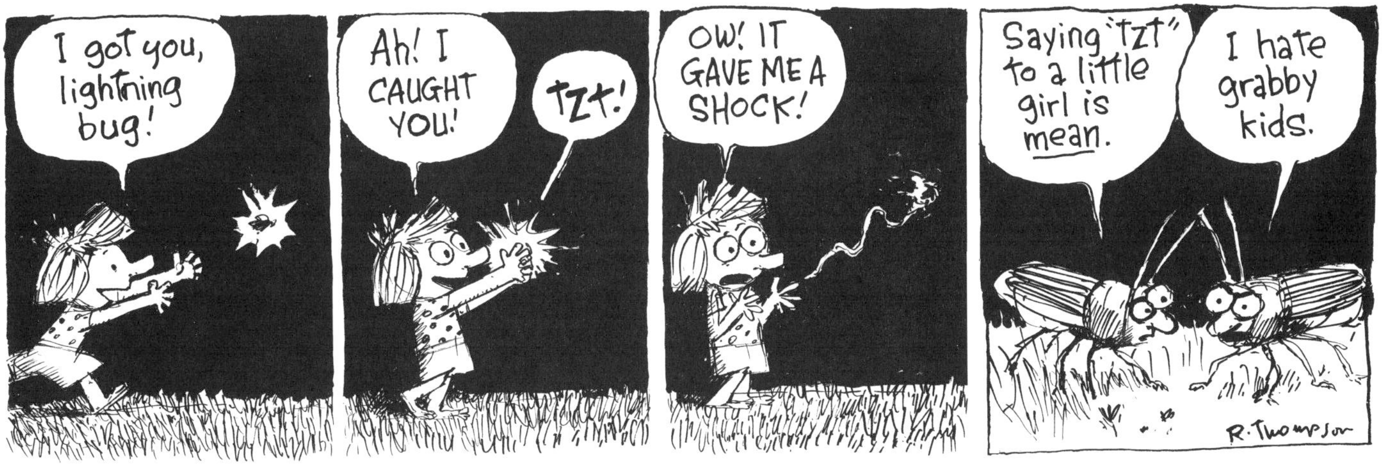
I got you, lightning bug!
Ah! I CAUGHT YOU!
TZT!
OW! IT GAVE ME A SHOCK!
Saying "TZT" to a little girl is mean.
I hate grabby kids.
R. Thompson

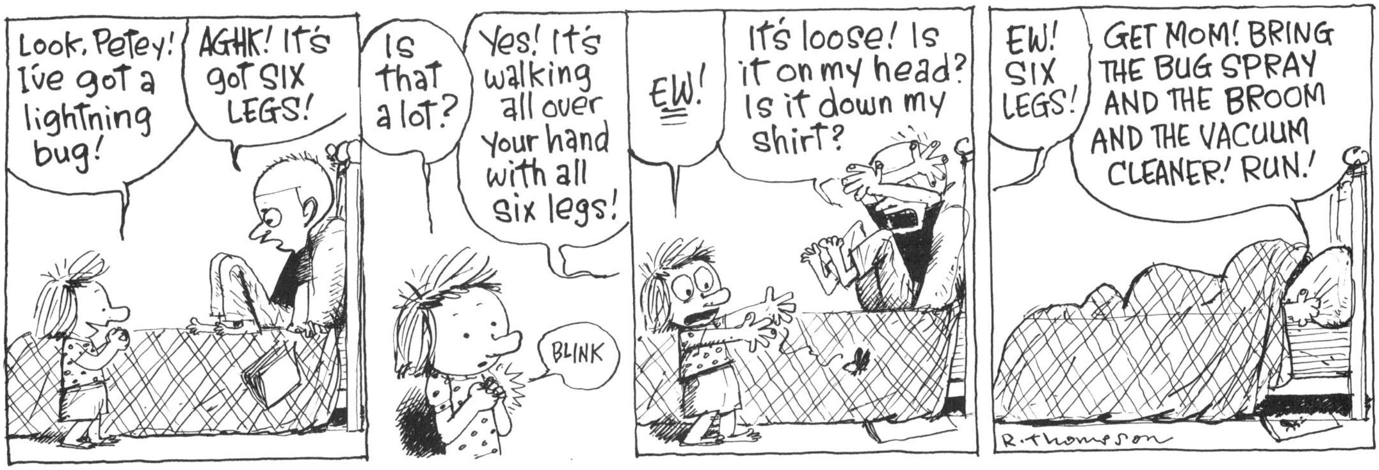
Look, Petey! I've got a lightning bug!
AGHK! It's got SIX LEGS!
Is that a lot?
Yes! It's walking all over your hand with all six legs!
BLINK
EW!
It's loose! Is it on my head? Is it down my shirt?
EW! SIX LEGS!
GET MOM! BRING THE BUG SPRAY AND THE BROOM AND THE VACUUM CLEANER! RUN!
R. Thompson

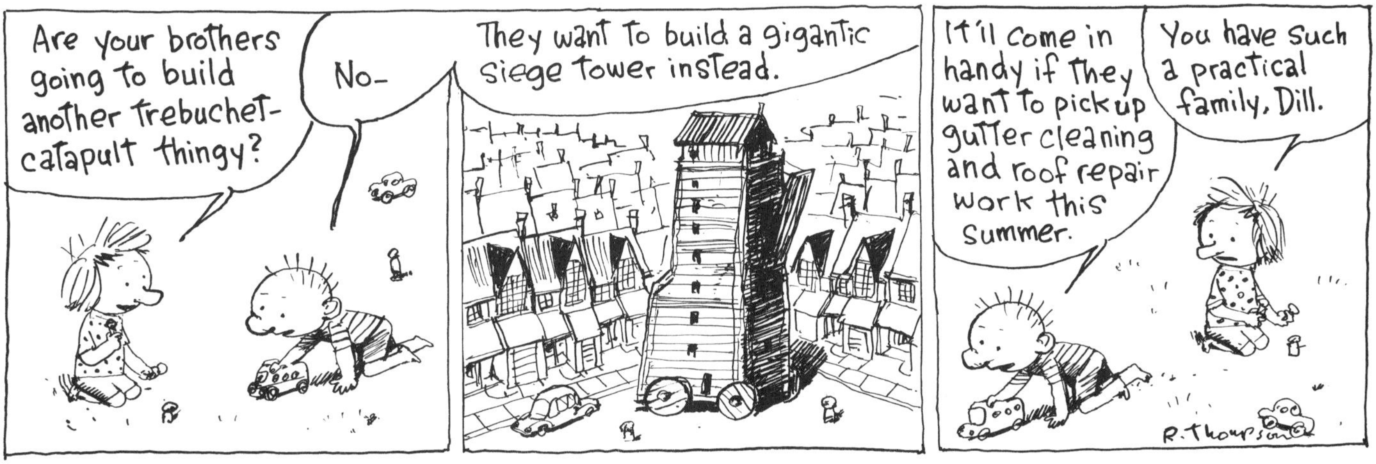
Are your brothers going to build another trebuchet-catapult thingy?
No–
They want to build a gigantic siege tower instead.
It'll come in handy if they want to pick up gutter cleaning and roof repair work this summer.
You have such a practical family, Dill.
R. Thompson

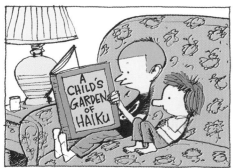

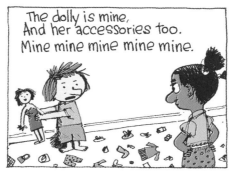

A CHILD'S GARDEN OF HAIKU
The dolly is mine,
And her accessories too.
Mine mine mine mine mine.
Bowl of cereal,
Its marshmallows now eaten.
May I be excused?
LUCKY STARS
Get up, go to work,
What does Daddy do all day?
Hamster in a wheel.
Have you not been told,
Eat pudding at the table?
Look at that sofa!
Spare and unrhymed verse,
Subtle, dense and allusive.
A CHILD'S GARDEN OF HAIKU
Give me Mother Goose.
R. Thompson

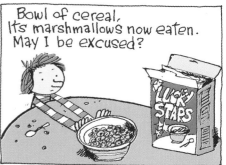

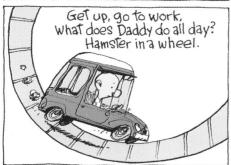

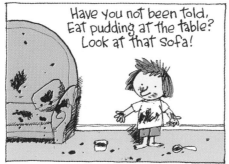

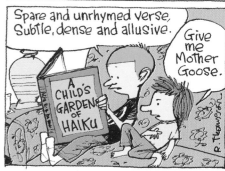

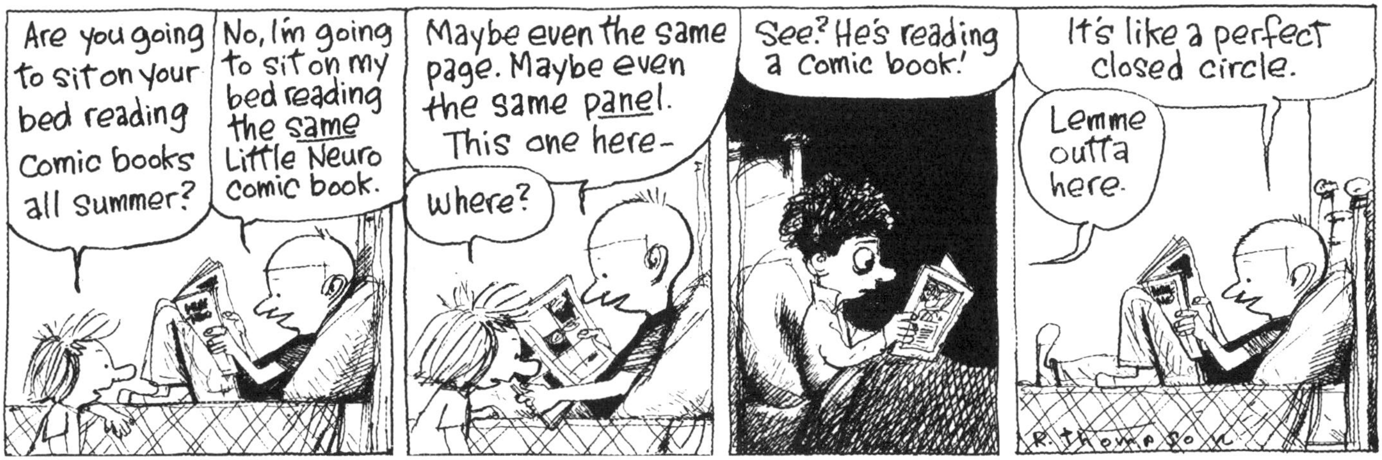
Are you going to sit on your bed reading comic books all summer?
No, I'm going to sit on my bed reading the same Little Neuro comic book.
Maybe even the same page. Maybe even the same panel. This one here–
Where?
See? He's reading a comic book!
It's like a perfect closed circle.
Lemme outta here.
R. Thompson

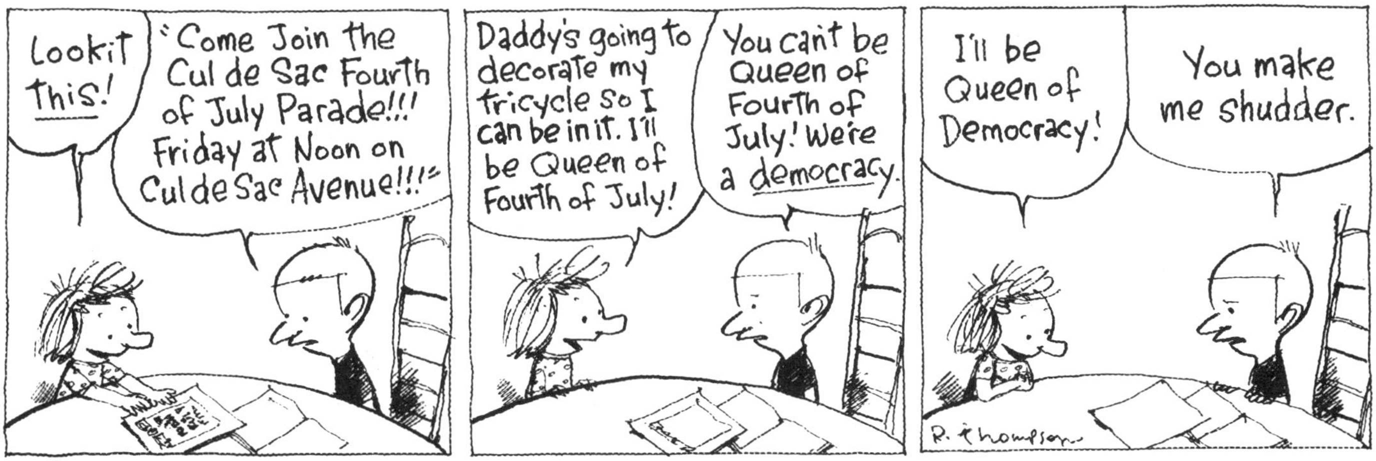
Lookit This!
"Come Join the Cul de Sac Fourth of July Parade!!! Friday at Noon on Cul de Sac Avenue!!!"
Daddy's going to decorate my tricycle so I can be in it. I'll be Queen of Fourth of July!
You can't be Queen of Fourth of July! We're a democracy.
I'll be Queen of Democracy!
You make me shudder.
R. Thompson

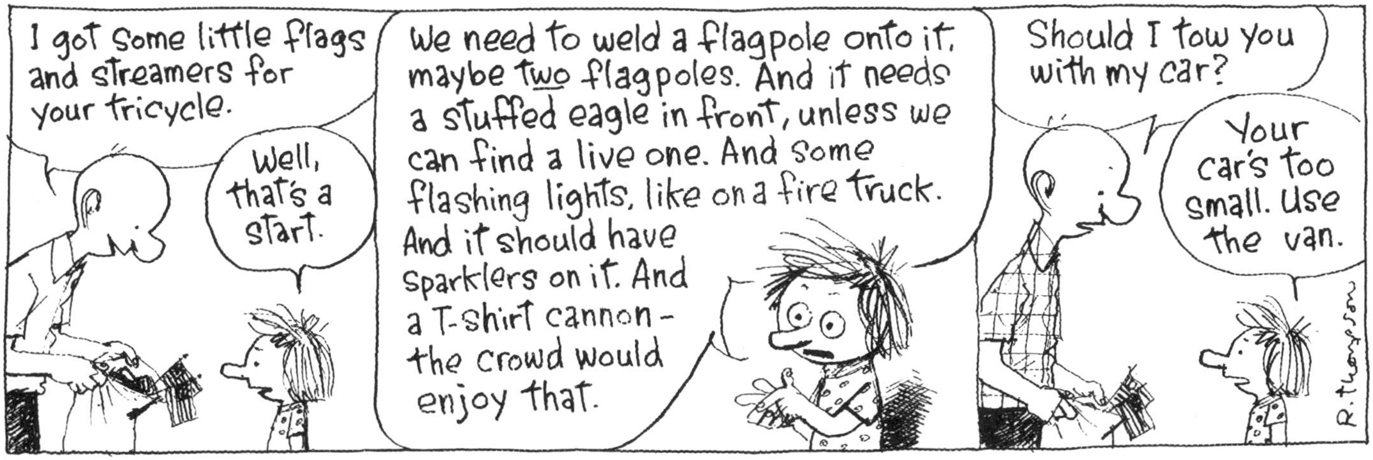
I got some little flags and streamers for your tricycle.
Well, that's a start.
We need to weld a flagpole onto it, maybe two flagpoles. And it needs a stuffed eagle in front, unless we can find a live one. And some flashing lights, like on a fire truck.
And it should have sparklers on it. And a T-shirt cannon – the crowd would enjoy that.
Should I tow you with my car?
Your car's too small. Use the van.
R. Thompson

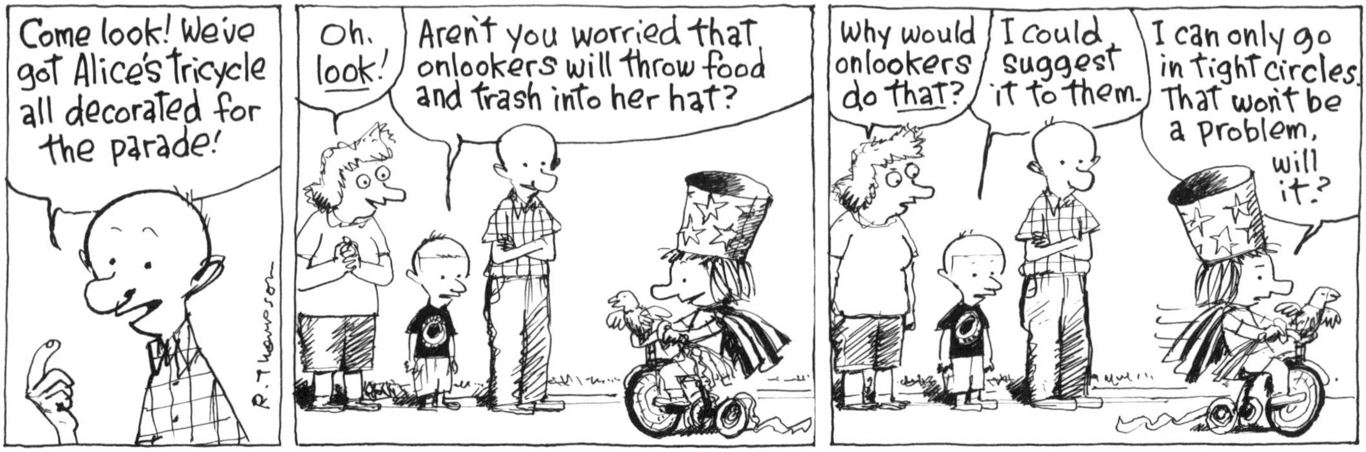
Come look! We've got Alice's tricycle all decorated for the parade!
Oh, look!
Aren't you worried that onlookers will throw food and trash into her hat?
Why would onlookers do that?
I could suggest it to them.
I can only go in tight circles. That won't be a problem, will it?

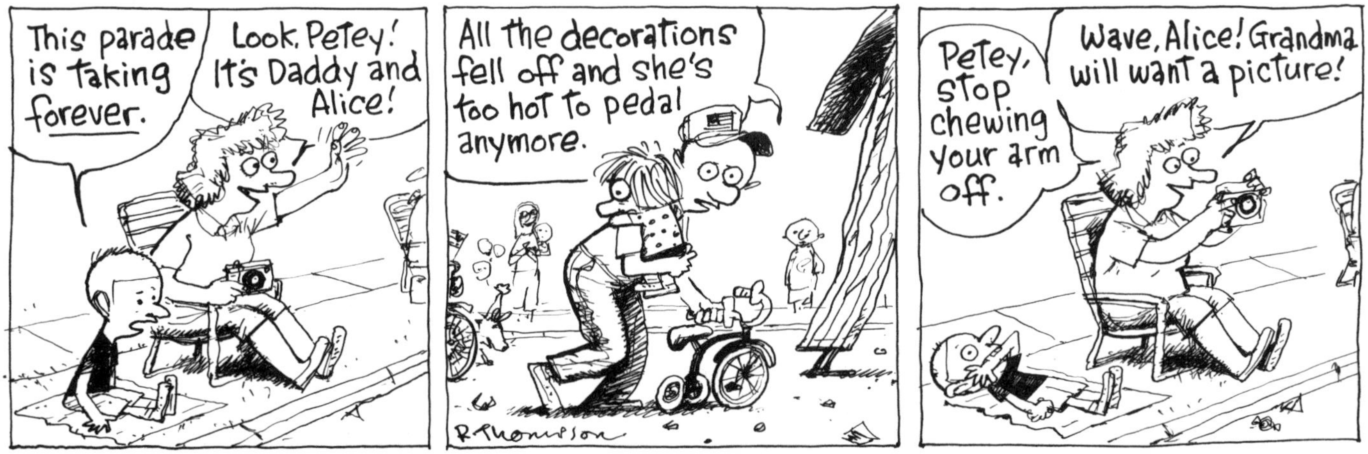
This parade is taking forever.
Look, Petey! It's Daddy and Alice!
All the decorations fell off and she's too hot to pedal anymore.
Petey, stop chewing your arm off.
Wave, Alice! Grandma will want a picture!

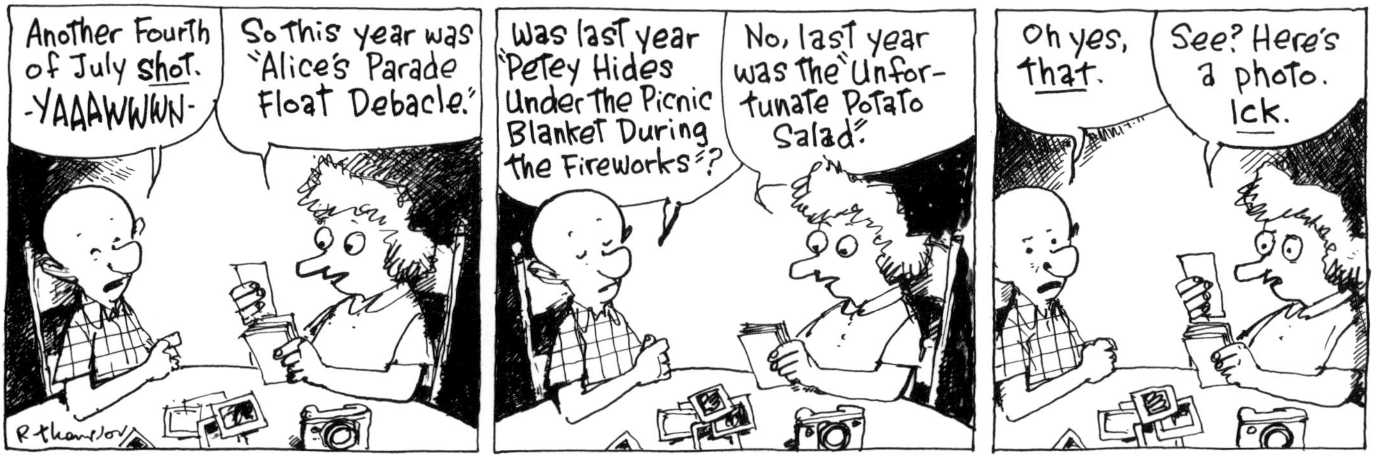
Another Fourth of July shot. -YAAAWWWN-
So this year was "Alice's Parade Float Debacle."
Was last year "Petey Hides Under the Picnic Blanket During the Fireworks"?
No, last year was the "Unfortunate Potato Salad."
Oh yes, that.
See? Here's a photo. Ick.

Butterflies are so pretty.
Ah, but appearances can be deceptive.
Have you heard of the Butterfly Effect?
No.
What are they teaching kids these days?
It's the theory that a thing as small as the beat of a butterfly's wings can influence vast global weather systems.
Thus, my slightest gesture, my merest lazy twitch, could summon tornadoes, hurricanes, droughts, freak rains of frogs!
Uh.
HA! Think of the POWER! WHAT ROUGH BEAST FLUTTERS IN YON FIELD? IT IS I, BRINGER OF CATASTRO-
SQUISH.
What-
IT WAS SELF-DEFENSE, I SWEAR.
R. thompson

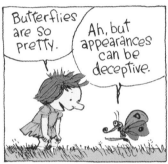

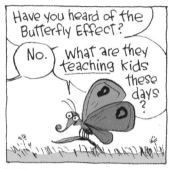

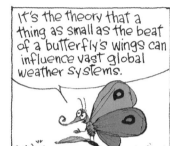

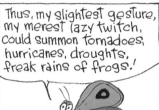

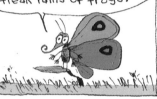

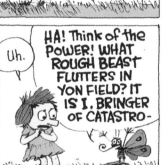

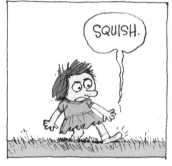

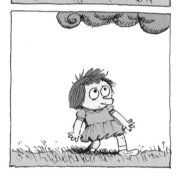

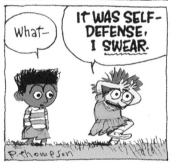

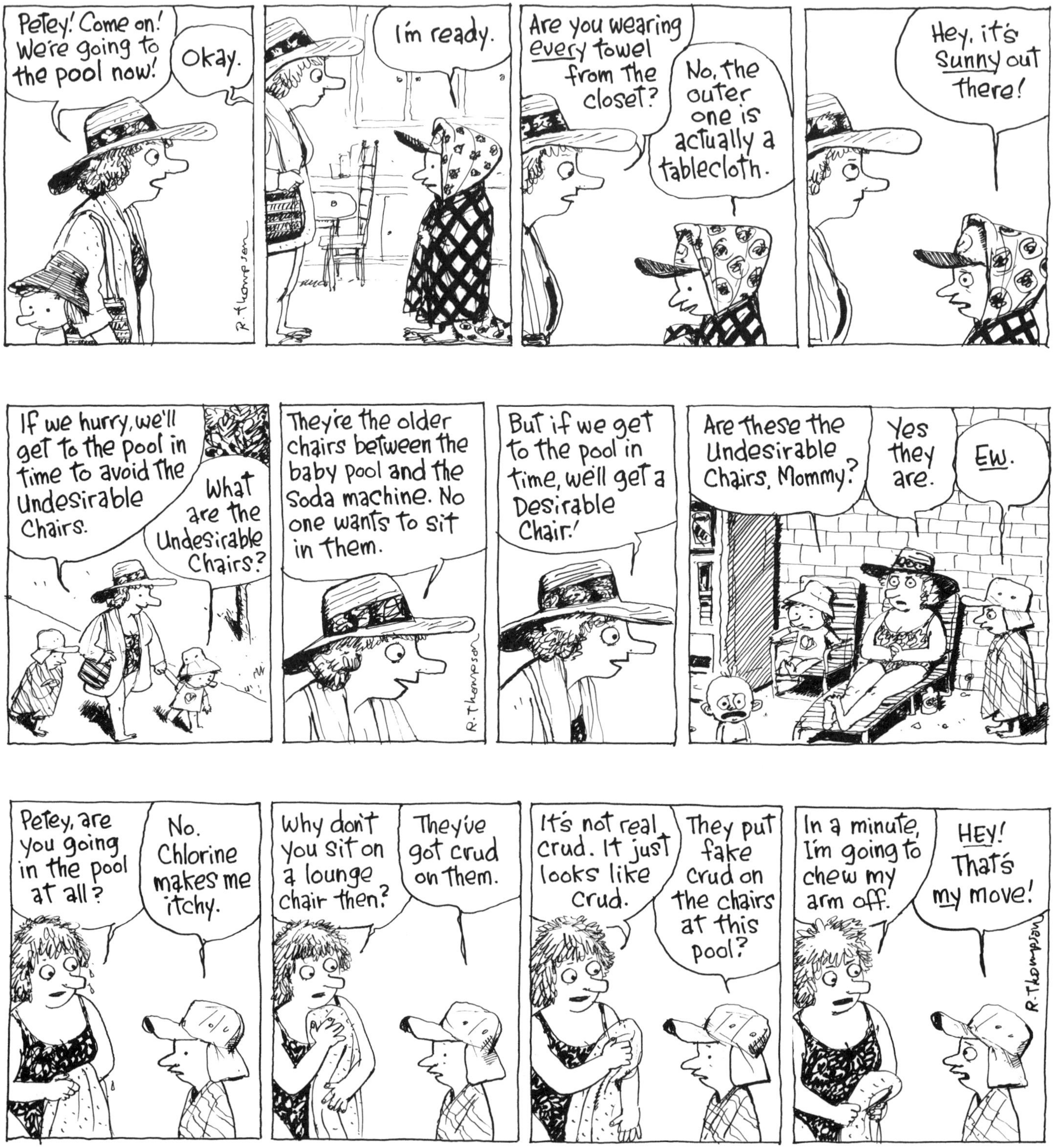
Petey! Come on! We're going to the pool now!
Okay.
I'm ready.
Are you wearing every towel from the closet?
No, the outer one is actually a tablecloth.
Hey, it's sunny out there!
If we hurry, we'll get to the pool in time to avoid the Undesirable Chairs.
What are the Undesirable Chairs?
They're the older chairs between the baby pool and the soda machine. No one wants to sit in them.
But if we get to the pool in time, we'll get a Desirable Chair!
Are these the Undesirable Chairs, Mommy?
Yes they are.
Ew.
Petey, are you going in the pool at all?
No. Chlorine makes me itchy.
Why don't you sit on a lounge chair then?
They've got crud on them.
It's not real crud. It just looks like crud.
They put fake crud on the chairs at this pool?
In a minute, I'm going to chew my arm off.
HEY! That's my move!
R. Thompson

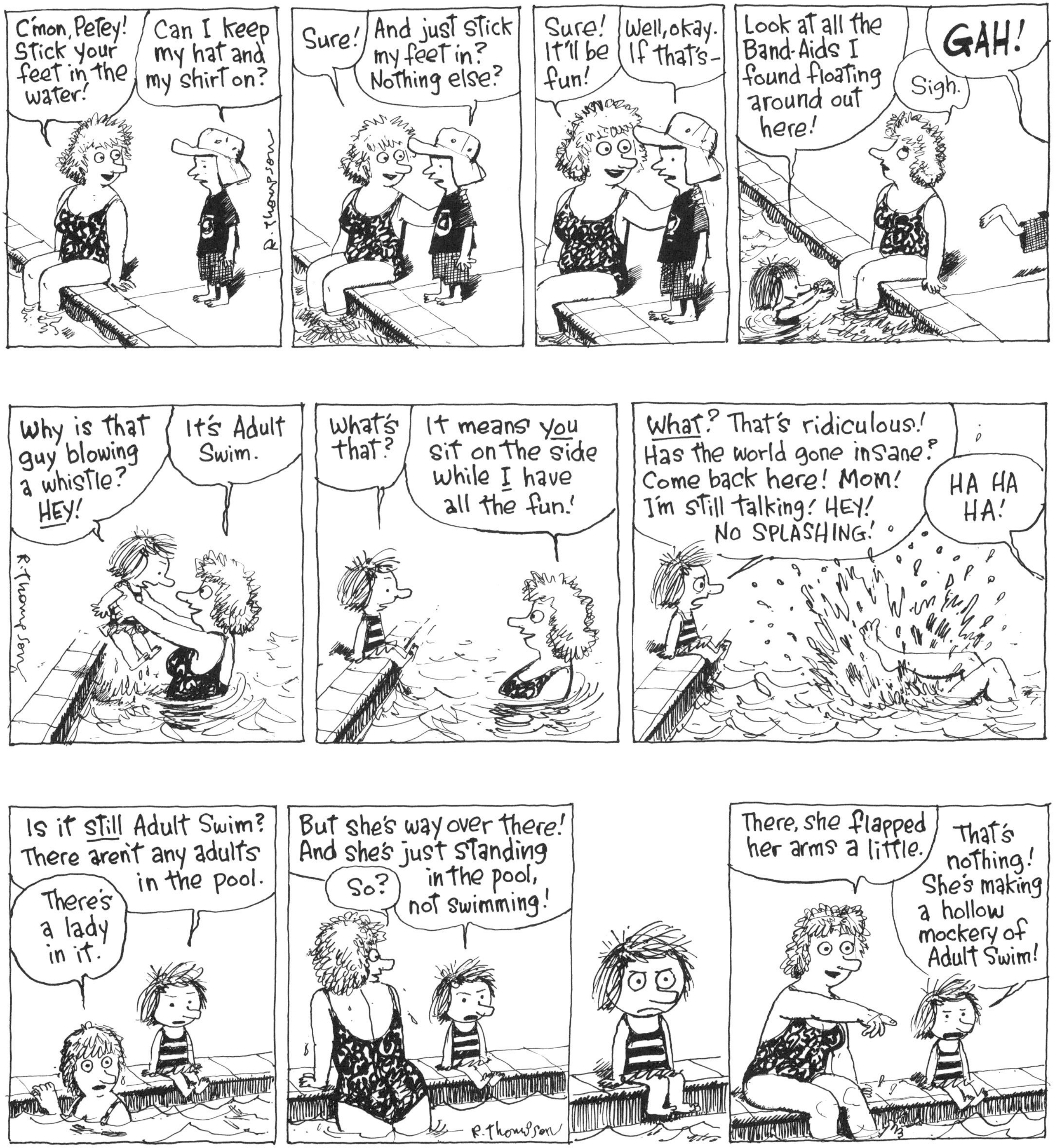
C'mon, Petey! Stick your feet in the water!
Can I keep my hat and my shirt on?
Sure!
And just stick my feet in? Nothing else?
Sure! It'll be fun!
Well, okay. If that's–
Look at all the Band-Aids I found floating around out here!
Sigh.
GAH!
Why is that guy blowing a whistle? HEY!
It's Adult Swim.
What's that?
It means you sit on the side while I have all the fun!
What? That's ridiculous! Has the world gone insane? Come back here! Mom! I'm still talking! HEY! NO SPLASHING!
HA HA HA!
Is it still Adult Swim? There aren't any adults in the pool.
There's a lady in it.
But she's way over there! And she's just standing in the pool, not swimming!
So?
There, she flapped her arms a little.
That's nothing! She's making a hollow mockery of Adult Swim!
R. Thompson

What is that?
Belgian llama cheese. I bought it at the Allfoods Market.
Oh, that place. They're always so serious there.
Yeah. It cost 12 bucks. Smell it.
YEEGHK!
I was hoping it'd be good. Phooey.
You've got cheese-buyer's remorse?
I do. It's sad.
MOLD
Oh boy! A Fuzzikin interactive pet like on TV! I'm going to name her Elspeth! Thanks, Dad!
It's going to smell up her room.
But it's not a total loss!
R. Thompson

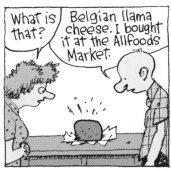

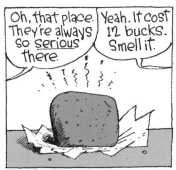

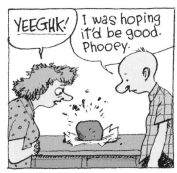

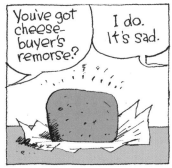

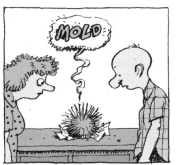

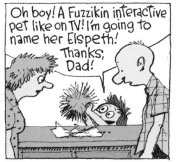

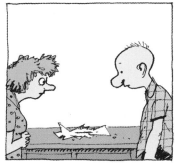

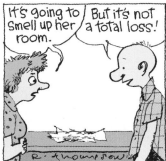

Look at this! Isn't it great? Help me pull it up!
Why?
R. Thompson
I'll give it to my Mom! GRUNT She'll love it!
Better slap the bugs off.
Years from now, when I've done something really awful, Mom'll look back on how I gave her this giant flower and think how I'm wonderful, deep down.
Wow! Planning ahead! I never do stuff like that!
Mom! Look what I picked for you!
Oh! Is that a flower?
I think so. Do you like it?
Yes! Let's get it in some water and put it on the table!
See? Mom is just crazy about big, flashy vegetation!
It better not have any bugs on it, 'cause it sounds like she's going to fix it for dinner.
R. Thompson
See what Alice picked for me?
Wow. Is it a flower?
I think so. It's got a thing on top that smells.
Huh! Where did you find it, Alice?
In our back-yard!
Really?
Hey, everyone knows our yard can't sustain life.
R. Thompson

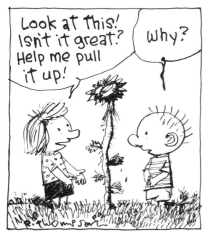

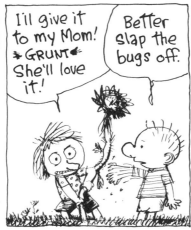

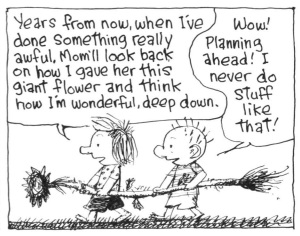

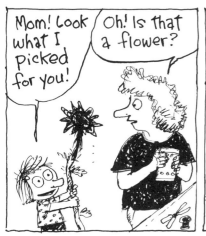

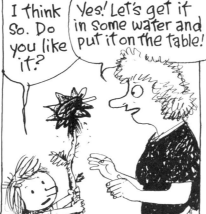

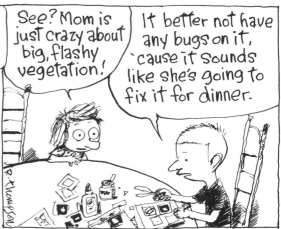

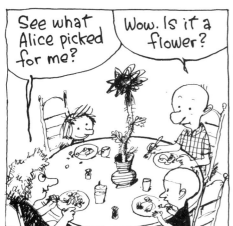

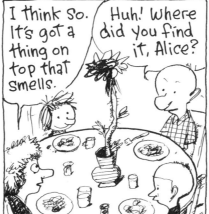

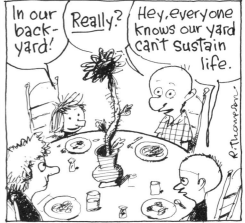

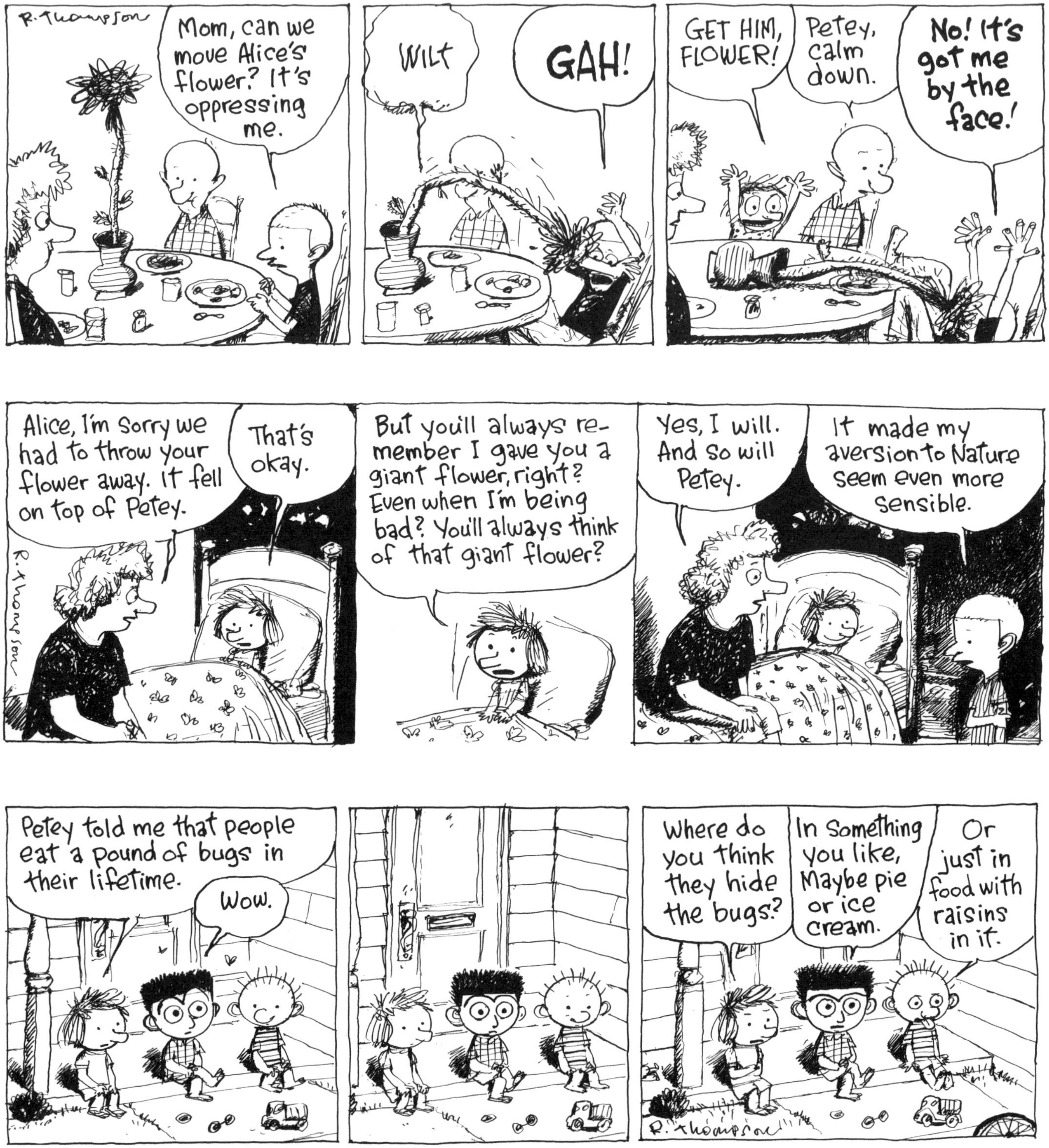
R. Thompson
Mom, can we move Alice's flower? It's oppressing me.
WILT
GAH!
GET HIM, FLOWER!
Petey, calm down.
No! It's got me by the face!
Alice, I'm sorry we had to throw your flower away. It fell on top of Petey.
That's okay.
R. Thompson
But you'll always remember I gave you a giant flower, right? Even when I'm being bad? You'll always think of that giant flower?
Yes, I will. And so will Petey.
It made my aversion to Nature seem even more sensible.
Petey told me that people eat a pound of bugs in their lifetime.
Wow.
Where do you think they hide the bugs?
In Something you like, Maybe pie or ice cream.
Or just in food with raisins in it.
R. Thompson

Dad, why are we stopping here?

Let's get some watermelons!

PULPY JOE'S PRODUCE

I hate produce.

PETEY.

Is he Pulpy Joe?

Me? Do you not know the story of Pulpy Joe?

They say he was a farmer with fancy ideas about growing the World's Largest Watermelon. They say he sold his soul to the Devil, at the Crossroads, at midnight...

Deal.

Deal.

But the watermelon Joe grew was puny. He mocked the Devil, who said that Joe's soul wasn't no bargain neither.

So the devil cursed him. Now Pulpy Joe wanders the land lookin' for his head, but in vain.

WOW! Produce is cool!

How about that?

Good day to you.

Did you just think that up?

Naw, it's a screenplay I'm writing. Do you think it'd work better with a grapefruit?

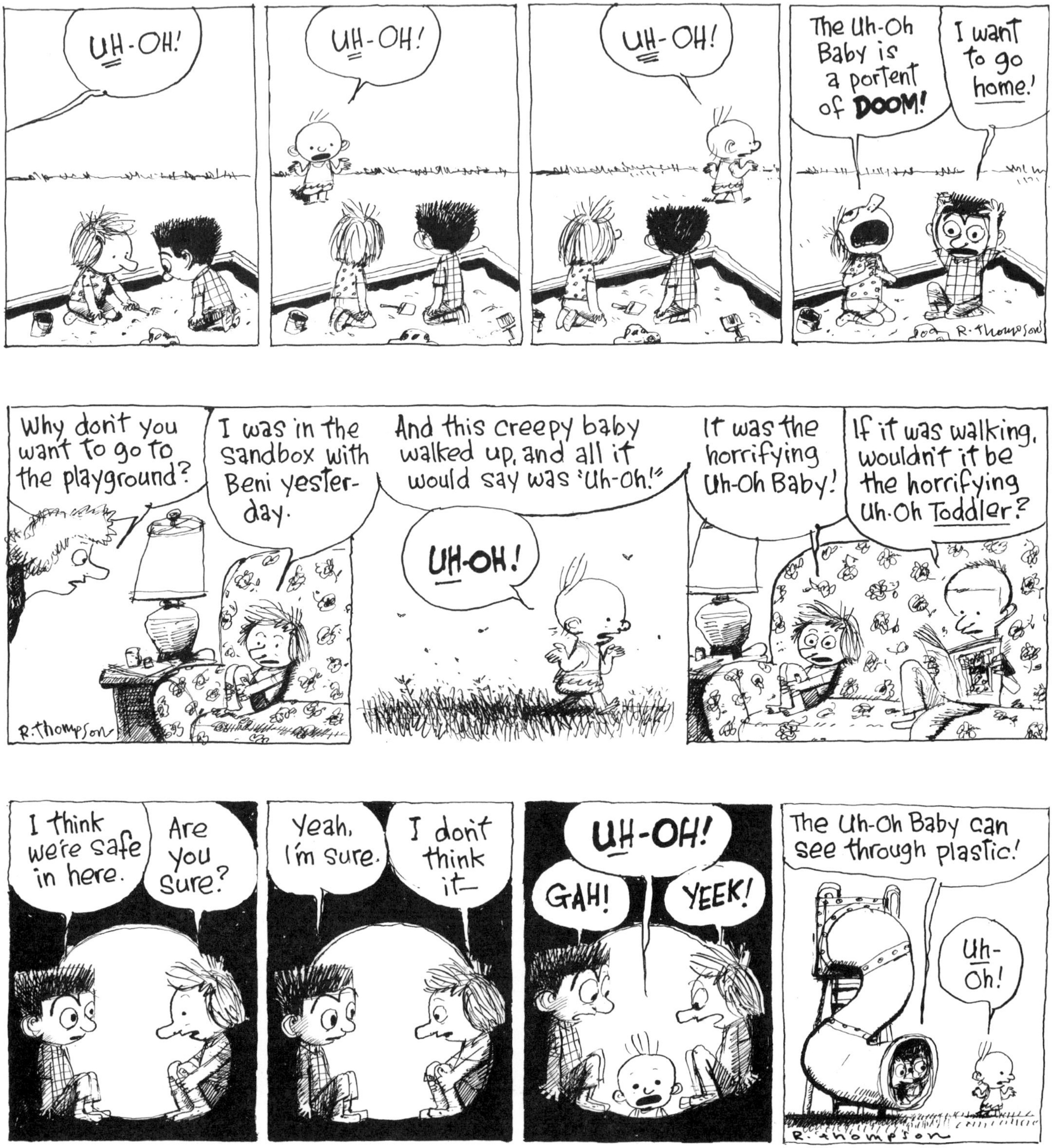
UH-OH!
UH-OH!
UH-OH!
The Uh-Oh Baby is a portent of DOOM!
I want to go home!
R. Thompson
Why don't you want to go to the playground?
R. Thompson
I was in the sandbox with Beni yesterday.
And this creepy baby walked up, and all it would say was "Uh-Oh!"
UH-OH!
It was the horrifying Uh-Oh Baby!
If it was walking, wouldn't it be the horrifying Uh-Oh Toddler?
I think we're safe in here.
Are you sure?
Yeah, I'm sure.
I don't think it—
UH-OH!
GAH!
YEEK!
The Uh-Oh Baby can see through plastic!
Uh-Oh!
R. Thompson

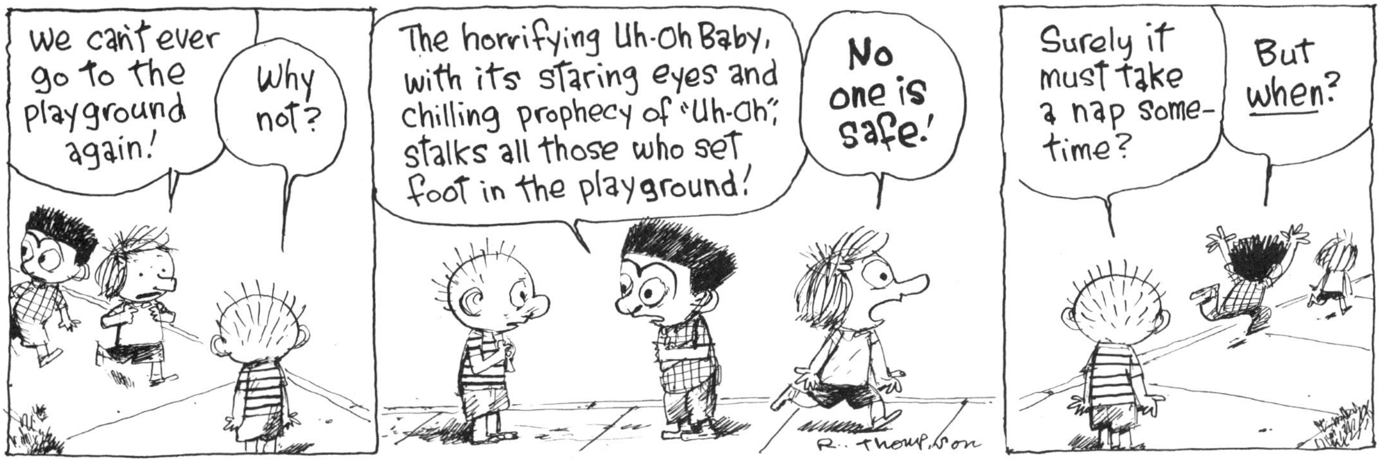
We can't ever go to the playground again!
Why not?
The horrifying Uh-Oh Baby, with its staring eyes and chilling prophecy of "Uh-Oh", stalks all those who set foot in the playground!
No one is safe!
Surely it must take a nap sometime?
But when?
R. Thompson

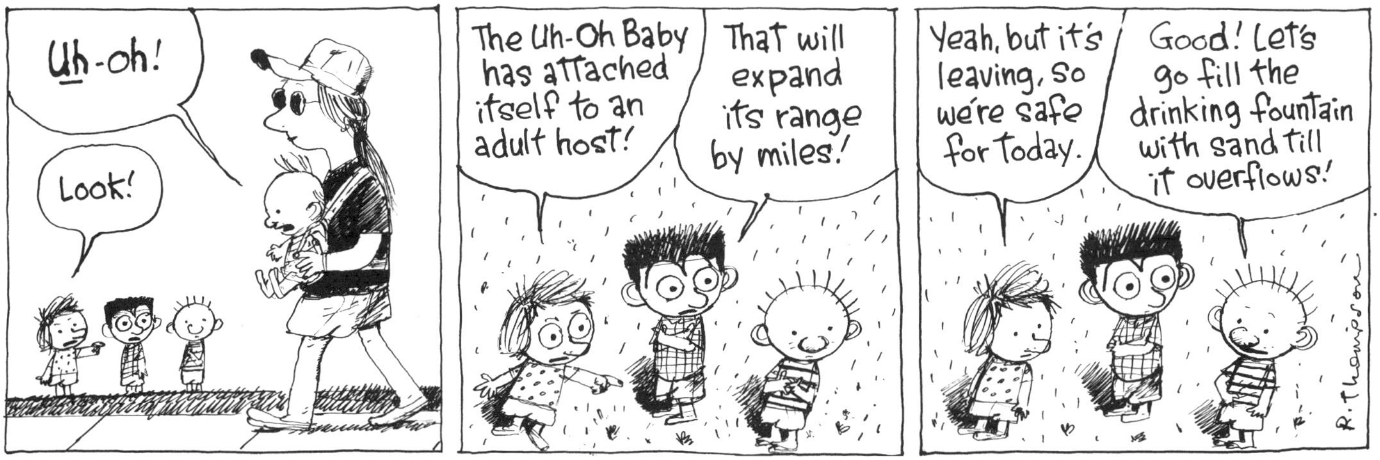
Uh-oh!
Look!
The Uh-Oh Baby has attached itself to an adult host!
That will expand its range by miles!
Yeah, but it's leaving, so we're safe for today.
Good! Let's go fill the drinking fountain with sand till it overflows!
R. Thompson

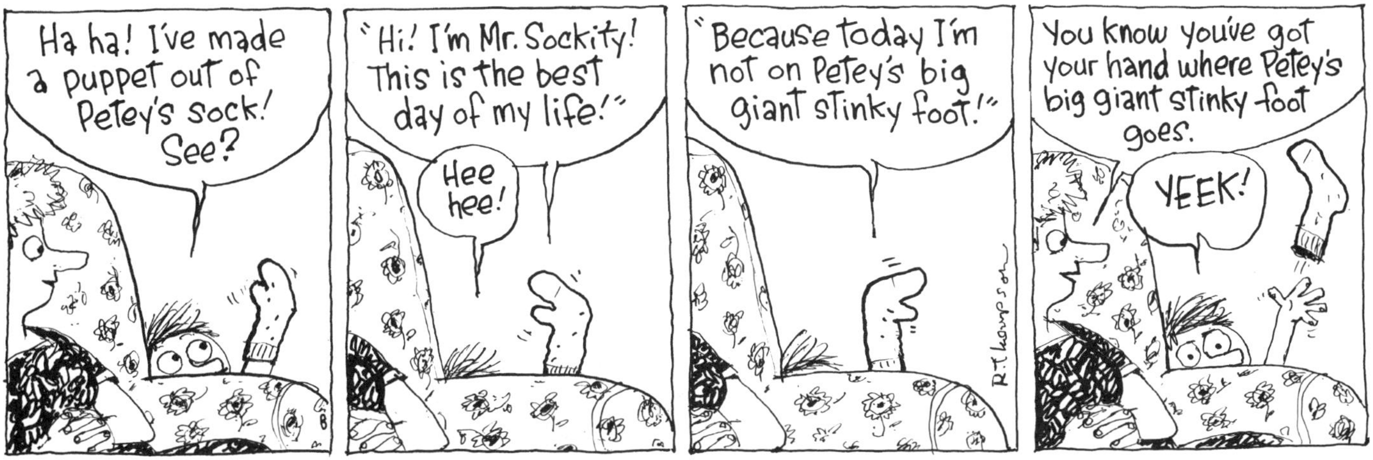
Ha ha! I've made a puppet out of Petey's sock! See?
"Hi! I'm Mr. Sockity! This is the best day of my life!"
Hee hee!
"Because today I'm not on Petey's big giant stinky foot!"
R. Thompson
You know you've got your hand where Petey's big giant stinky foot goes.
YEEK!

Ah, Peter! Checking out some Summer reading?

Hi, um, Ernesto. Yeah, I've got this book-

Let's see: "Dirk Dragonslapper Volume 1: The Trolls Revolt."

It's about a boy who rides around on a dragon-

Yes, I reviewed it on my blog...

You have a blog?

Yes. I found the book derivative and thin, like watered-down Tolkien. You do like Tolkien?

I've never been tolking.

LOL! The always quotable Peter! May I use that?

Yeah, okay.

Goodbye! Enjoy your little book!

Let's check out, Petey, where's your book?

I put it back. It's derivative, watered-down tolking.

Okay, Petey.

I'm getting the BIG POP-UP BOOK OF GIANT SQUIDS! See?

GAAAH!

LOOK! HE'S HERE!
What? Who's here?
It's our turn to take care of the class guinea pig.
Hi, Guinea Pig!
It's **Danders**. Mr. Danders. Why does no one ever remember my name?
He's all yours. My mom says no more pets in the house, especially yappy rodents who shed.
Zippy
R. Thompson
Welcome to my house, Guinea Pig.
Ah, very nice!
R. Thompson
This is my Mom!
The woman at the last house would not stop sneezing.
Zippy
And she vacuumed so relentlessly that I'm sure I suffered oxygen depletion.
You'll love it here! We never vacuum!
Guinea Pig, this is my Daddy.
Danders. Mr. Danders. Pleased to meet you.
I've got a spot ready for him in the utility room.
The WHAT?
It's where the washer-dryer and the mop are!
A janitor's closet and laundromat combined! I can't wait, he said with withering sarcasm.
R. Thompson

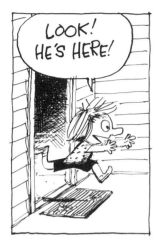

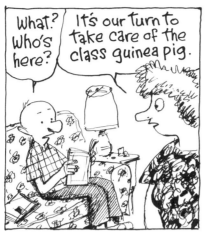

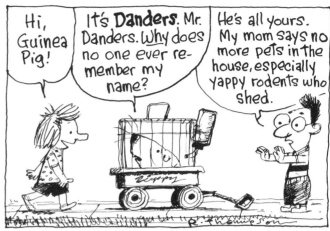

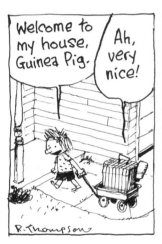

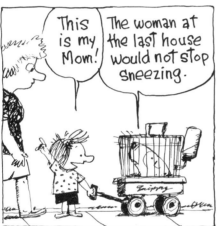

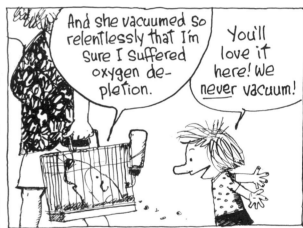

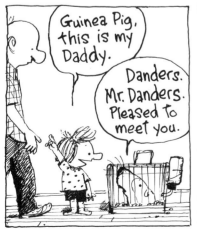

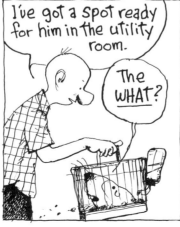

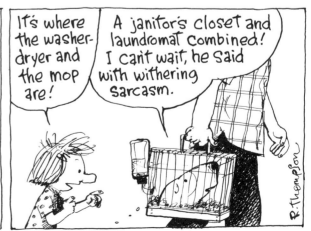

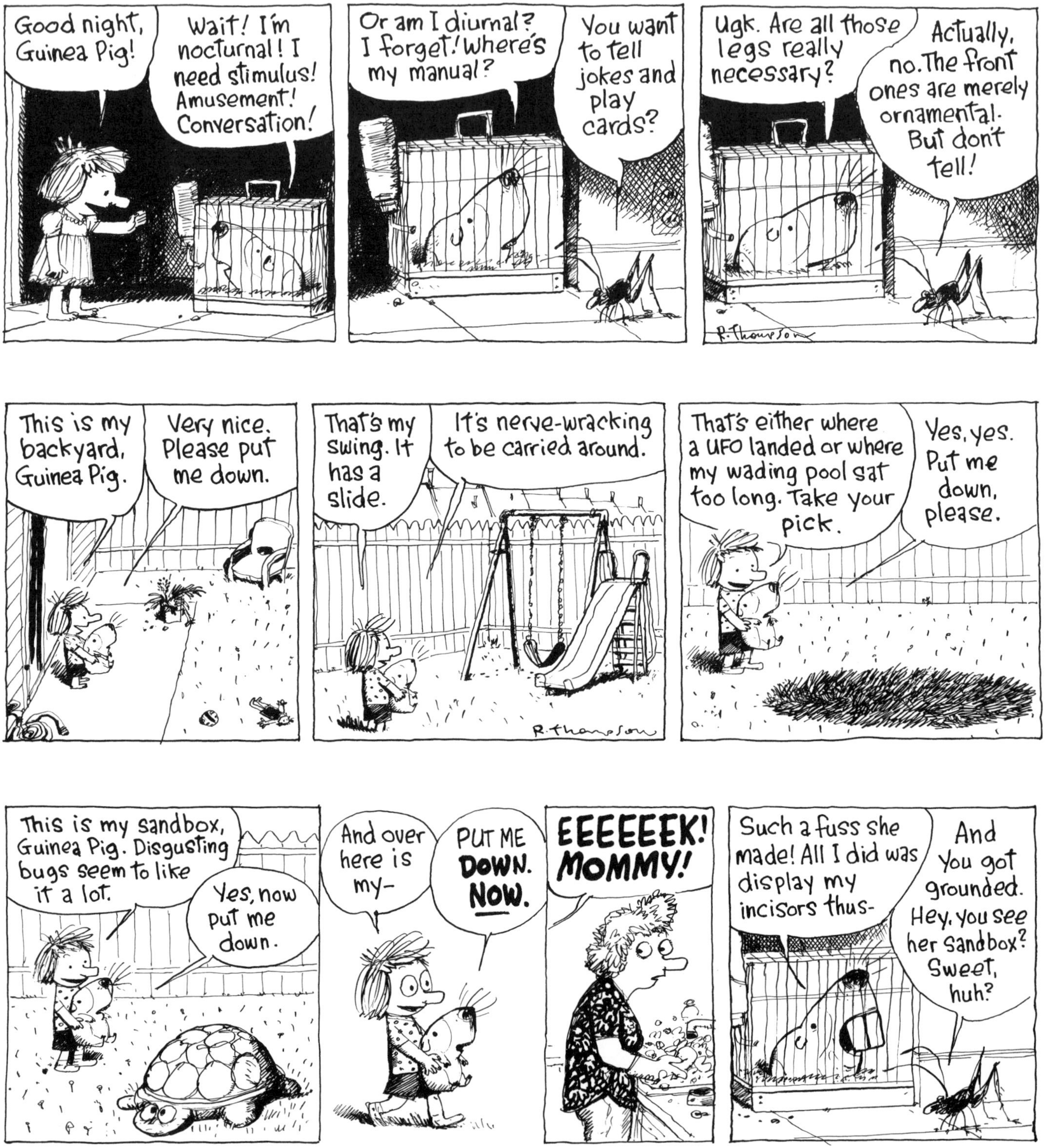
Good night, Guinea Pig!
Wait! I'm nocturnal! I need stimulus! Amusement! Conversation!
Or am I diurnal? I forget! Where's my manual?
You want to tell jokes and play cards?
Ugk. Are all those legs really necessary?
Actually, no. The front ones are merely ornamental. But don't tell!
R. Thompson
This is my backyard, Guinea Pig.
Very nice. Please put me down.
That's my swing. It has a slide.
It's nerve-wracking to be carried around.
That's either where a UFO landed or where my wading pool sat too long. Take your pick.
Yes, yes. Put me down, please.
R. Thompson
This is my sandbox, Guinea Pig. Disgusting bugs seem to like it a lot.
Yes, now put me down.
And over here is my–
PUT ME DOWN. NOW.
EEEEEEK! MOMMY!
Such a fuss she made! All I did was display my incisors thus–
And you got grounded. Hey, you see her sandbox? Sweet, huh?

All the pool chairs had crud on them this time.
Then why didn't you get in the pool, Petey?
Chlorine makes my skin shrink.
Oh, jeez, Petey. Alice, don't drag your towel.
Hello, Peter.
Mom! It's the kid who's even weirder than me!
Why don't you introduce your little friend?
He's, um-
Ernesto Lacuna, Mrs. Otterloop. Delighted to meet you!
Would you like to join us for dinner, Ernesto? Five bean salad and hot dogs?
Alas. I have a food allergy that manifests itself as a mild form of lycanthropy, so I must decline.
Another time perhaps?
R. Thompson
You could see him too? I thought he might be imaginary.
He's much too polite to be imaginary.
ALICE! Stop dragging your towel!
Boy, none of my imaginary friends wear two sweaters at the same time.

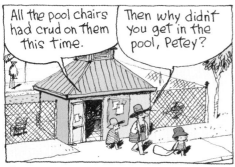

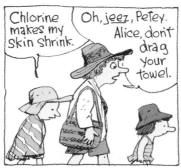

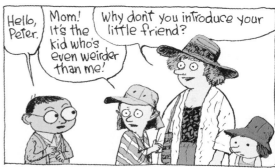

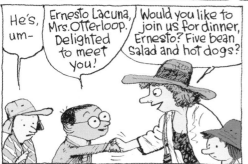

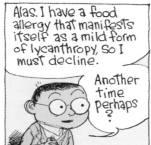

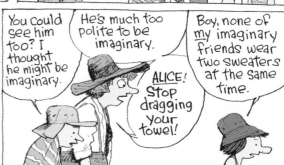

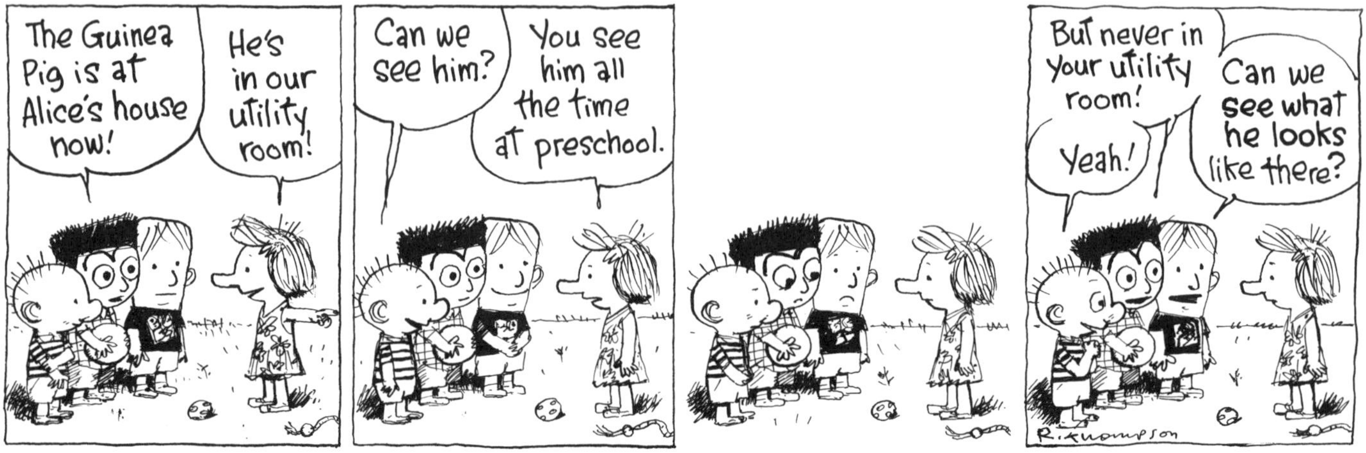
The Guinea Pig is at Alice's house now!
He's in our utility room!
Can we see him?
You see him all the time at preschool.
But never in your utility room!
Yeah!
Can we see what he looks like there?

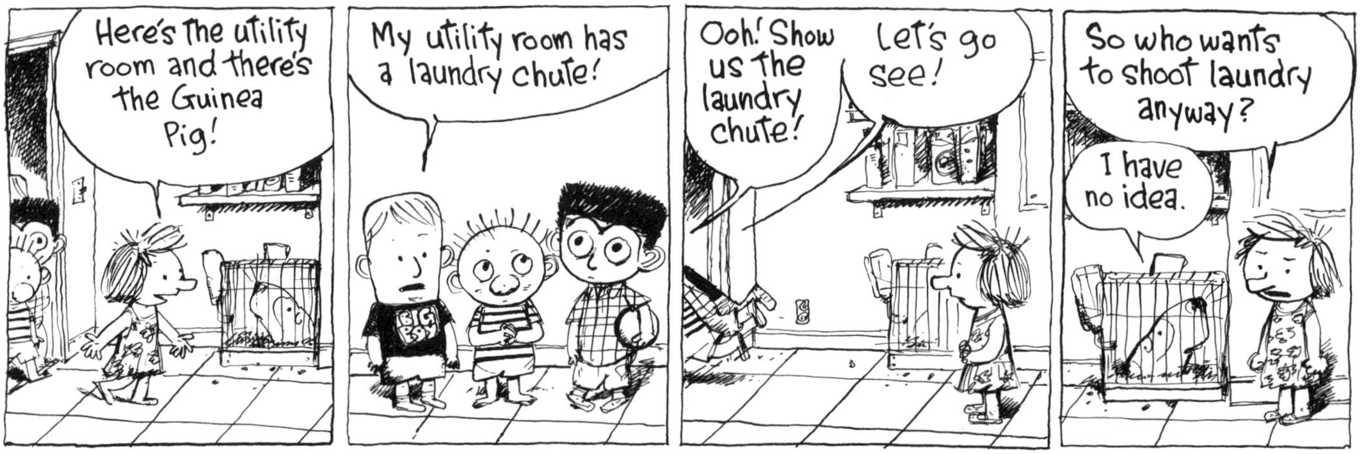
Here's the utility room and there's the Guinea Pig!
My utility room has a laundry chute!
Ooh! Show us the laundry chute!
Let's go see!
So who wants to shoot laundry anyway?
I have no idea.

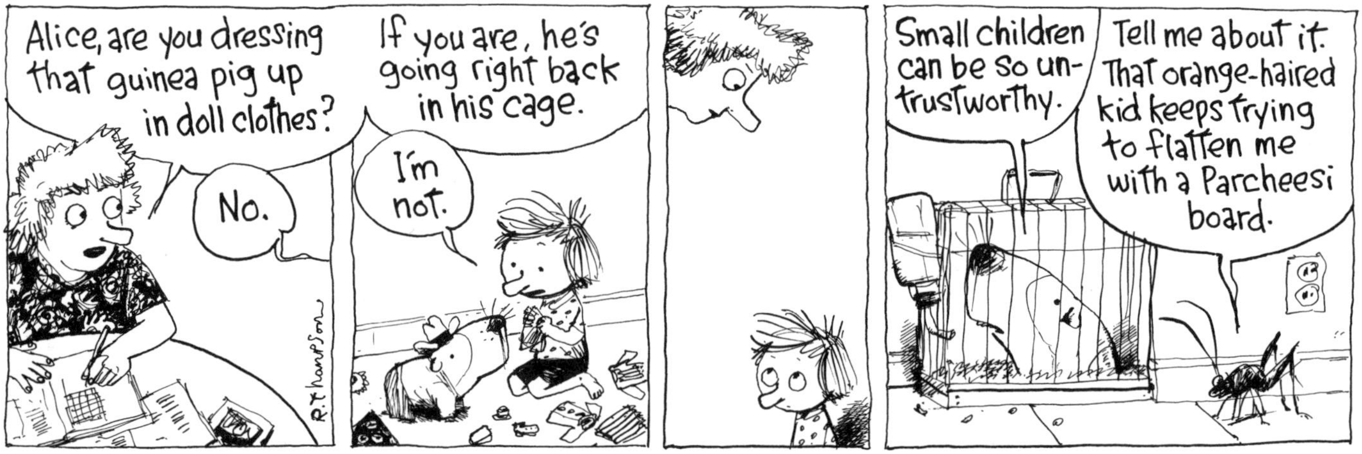
Alice, are you dressing that guinea pig up in doll clothes?
No.
If you are, he's going right back in his cage.
I'm not.
Small children can be so untrustworthy.
Tell me about it. That orange-haired kid keeps trying to flatten me with a Parcheesi board.

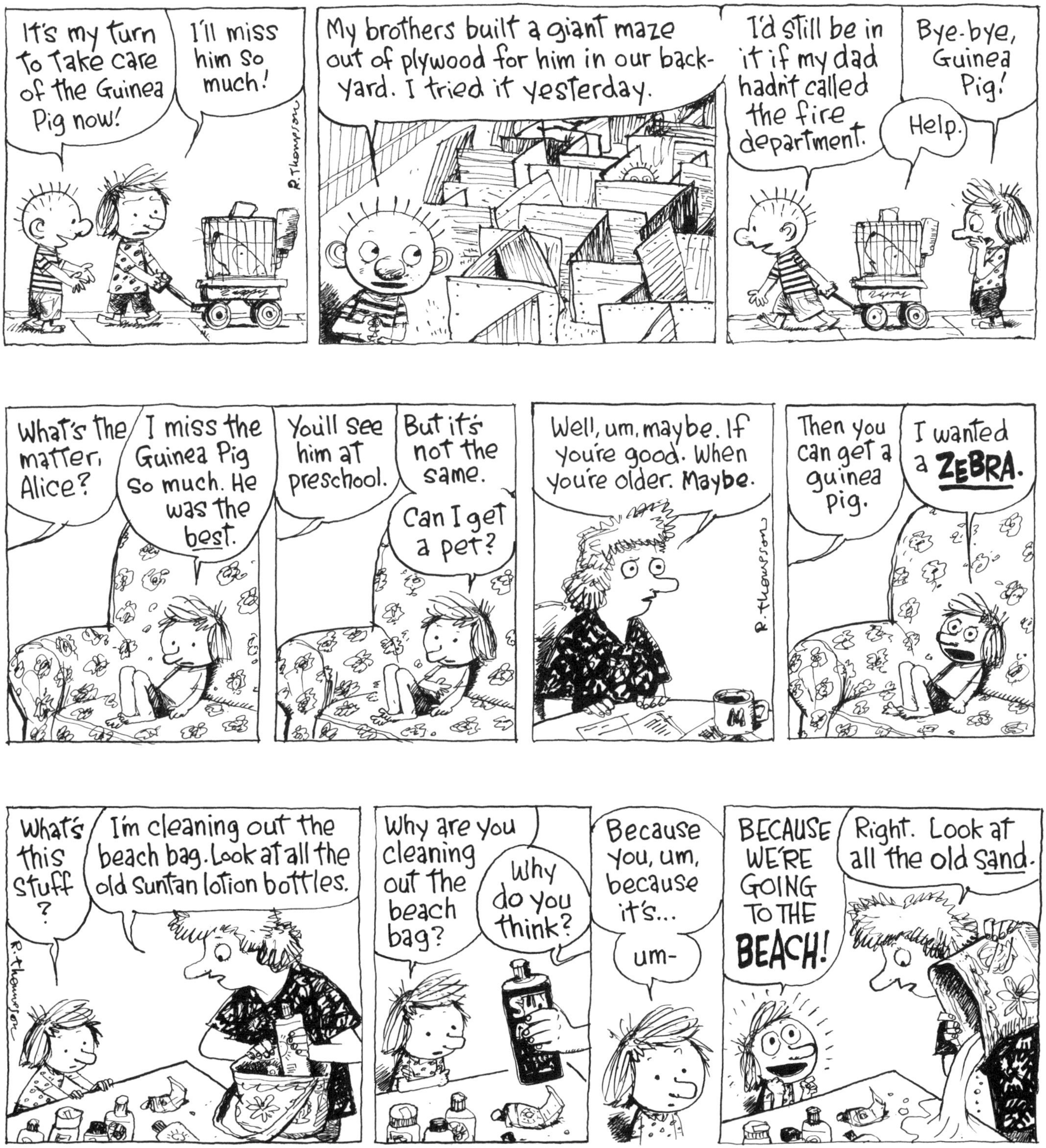
It's my turn to take care of the Guinea Pig now!
I'll miss him so much!
R. Thompson
My brothers built a giant maze out of plywood for him in our backyard. I tried it yesterday.
I'd still be in it if my dad hadn't called the fire department.
Bye-bye, Guinea Pig!
Help.
What's the matter, Alice?
I miss the Guinea Pig so much. He was the best.
You'll see him at preschool.
But it's not the same.
Can I get a pet?
Well, um, maybe. If you're good. When you're older. **Maybe**.
R. Thompson
Then you can get a guinea pig.
I wanted a **ZEBRA**.
What's this stuff?
I'm cleaning out the beach bag. Look at all the old suntan lotion bottles.
R. Thompson
Why are you cleaning out the beach bag?
Why do you think?
Because you, um, because it's...
um-
BECAUSE WE'RE GOING TO THE **BEACH**!
Right. Look at all the old sand.

What a great game!
How do you play?
You spin around for five minutes.
Then you try to pick out your house and run to it as fast as you can!
The winner makes it home safe.
The loser staggers into the wrong house and probably barfs!
What a great game!
R. Thompson

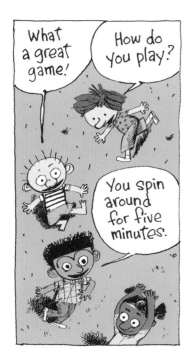

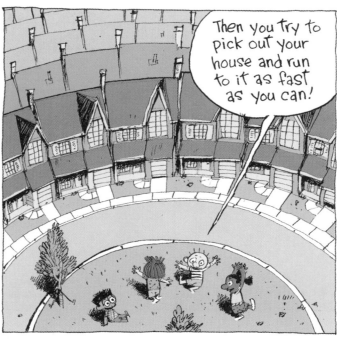

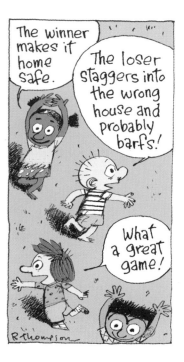

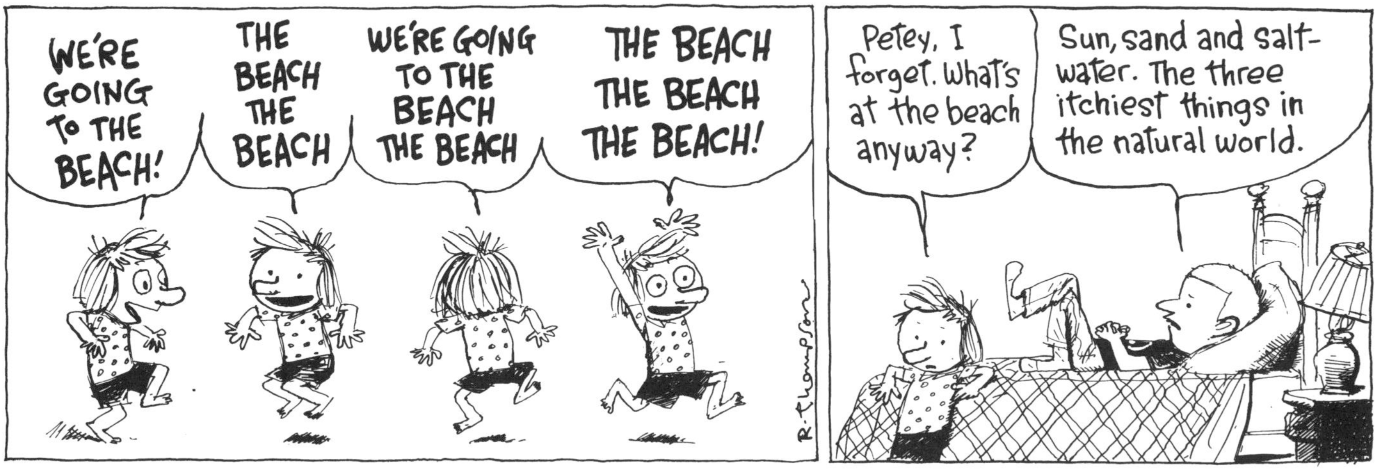
WE'RE GOING TO THE BEACH!
THE BEACH THE BEACH THE BEACH
WE'RE GOING TO THE BEACH THE BEACH
THE BEACH THE BEACH THE BEACH!
Petey, I forget. What's at the beach anyway?
Sun, sand and salt-water. The three itchiest things in the natural world.

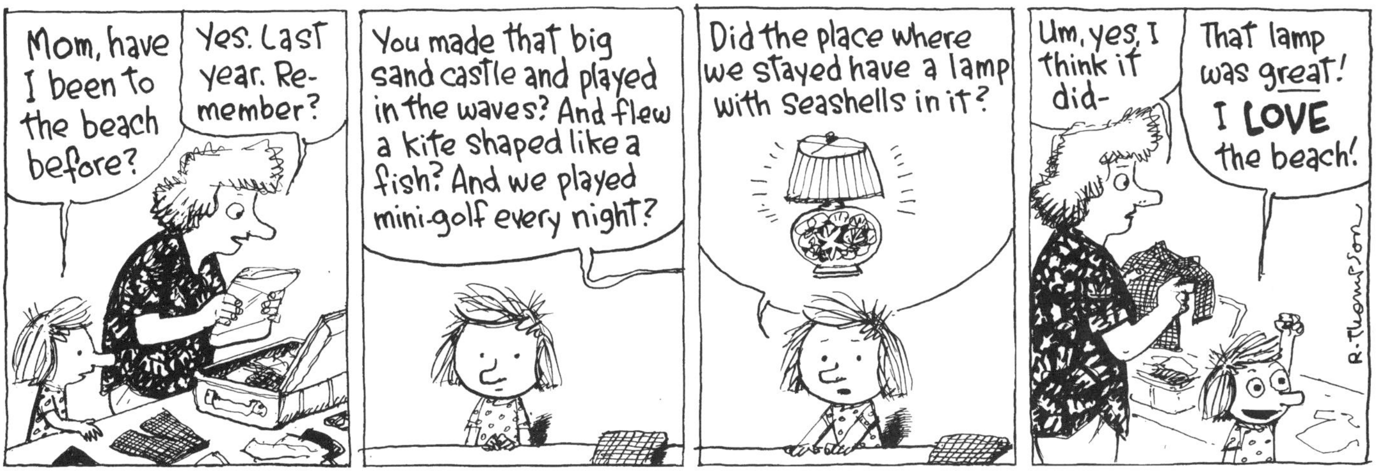
Mom, have I been to the beach before?
Yes. Last year. Re-member?
You made that big sand castle and played in the waves? And flew a kite shaped like a fish? And we played mini-golf every night?
Did the place where we stayed have a lamp with seashells in it?
Um, yes, I think it did-
That lamp was great! I LOVE the beach!

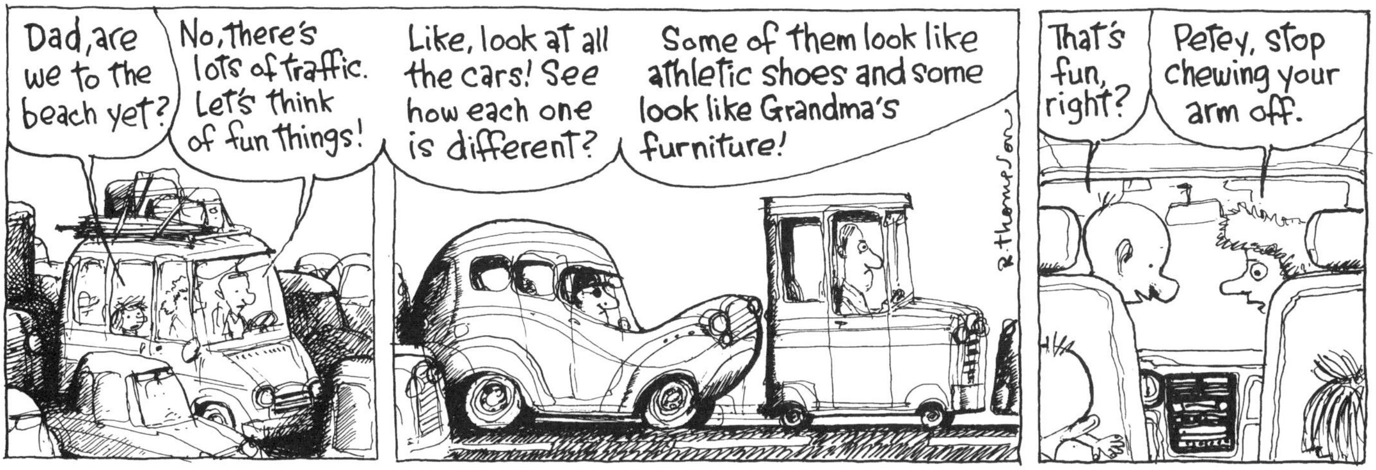
Dad, are we to the beach yet?
No, there's lots of traffic. Let's think of fun things!
Like, look at all the cars! See how each one is different?
Some of them look like athletic shoes and some look like Grandma's furniture!
That's fun, right?
Petey, stop chewing your arm off.

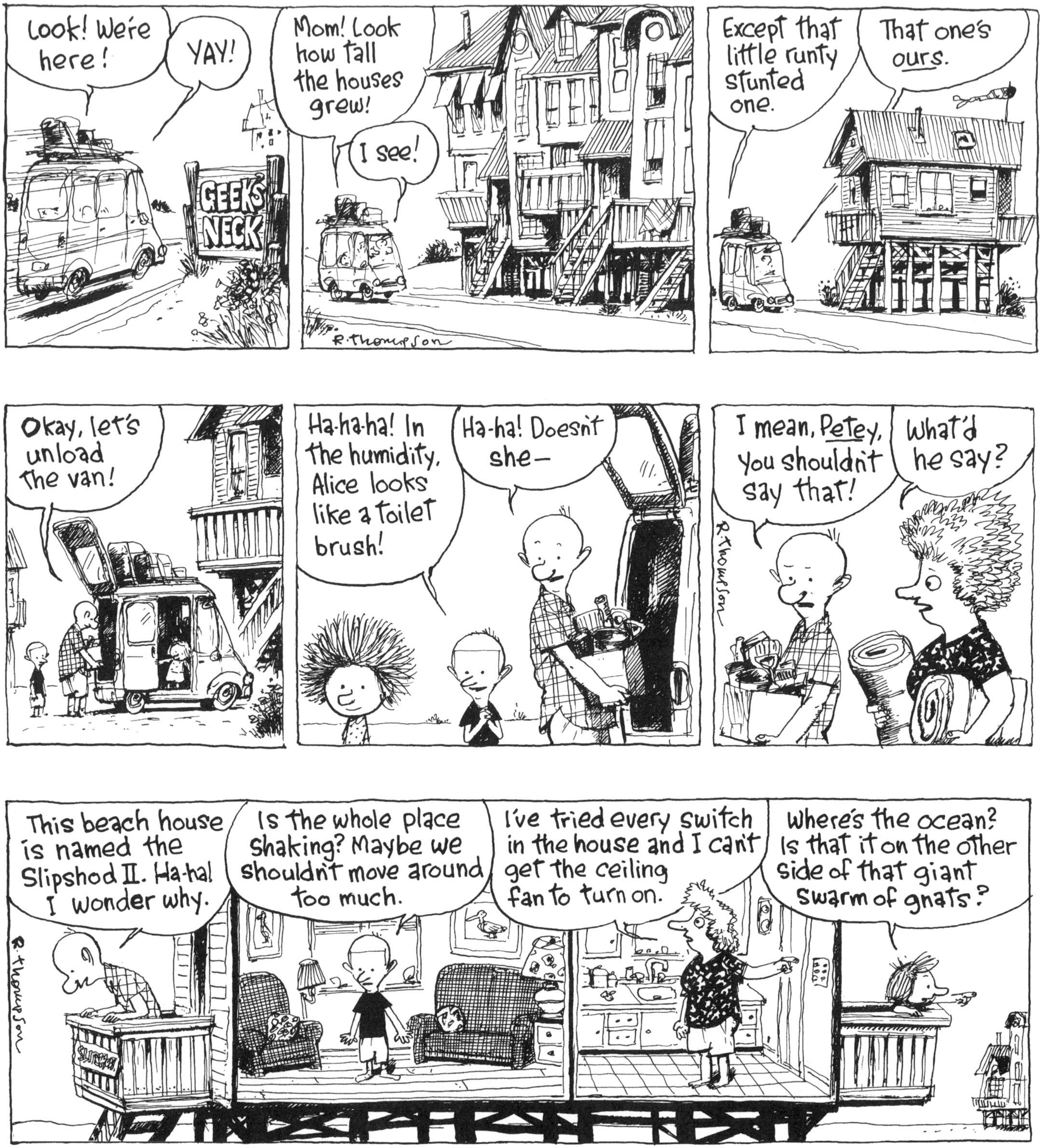
Look! We're here!
YAY!
GEEKS NECK
Mom! Look how tall the houses grew!
I see!
R. Thompson
Except that little runty stunted one.
That one's ours.
Okay, let's unload the van!
Ha-ha-ha! In the humidity, Alice looks like a toilet brush!
Ha-ha! Doesn't she—
I mean, Petey, you shouldn't say that!
What'd he say?
R. Thompson
This beach house is named the Slipshod II. Ha-ha! I wonder why.
R. Thompson
Is the whole place shaking? Maybe we shouldn't move around too much.
I've tried every switch in the house and I can't get the ceiling fan to turn on.
Where's the ocean? Is that it on the other side of that giant swarm of gnats?

You know what? If I say your names together real fast, it sounds like some kind of bad-tasting medicine. Alice-Beni-Dill. See?
ALICE-BENI-DILL, ALICE-BENI-DILL,
IT'S THE MEDICINE THAT MAKES YOU ILL!
ALICE-BENI-DILL, ALICE-BENI-DILL,
IF YOU NEED A PILL TO MAKE YOU ILL,
TRY SOME ALICE-BENI-DILL!
When I'm older, I hope to understand sophisticated humor.
I look forward to an enhanced appreciation of the dance.

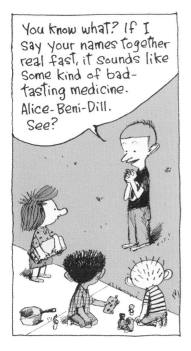

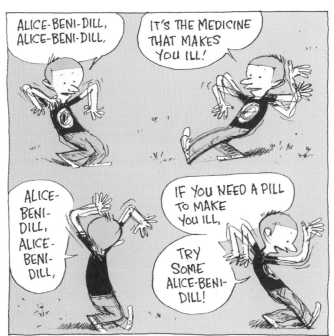

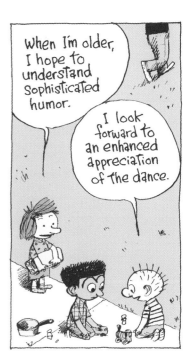

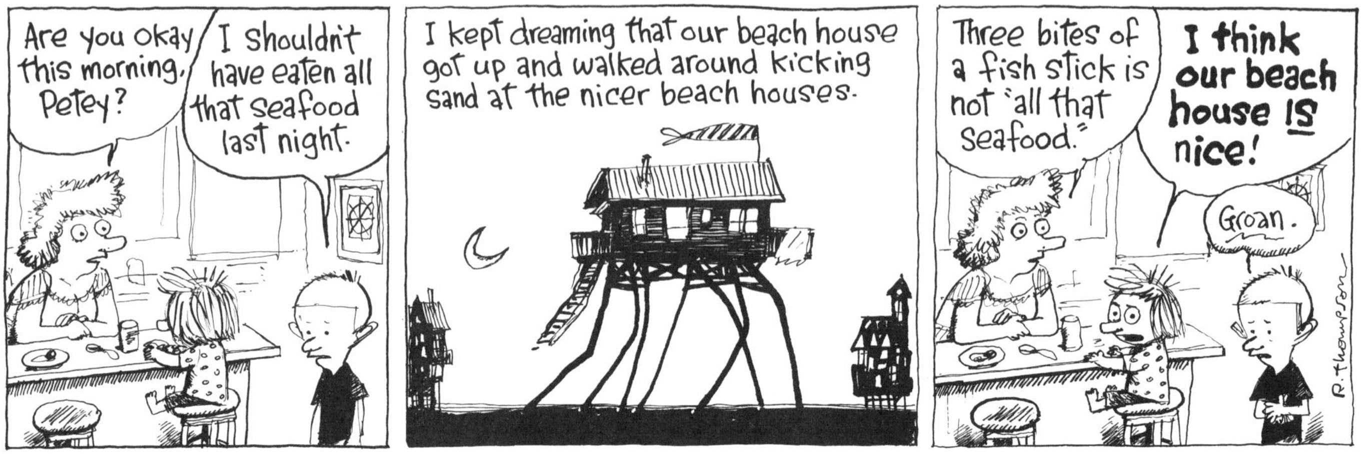
Are you okay this morning, Petey?
I shouldn't have eaten all that seafood last night.
I kept dreaming that our beach house got up and walked around kicking sand at the nicer beach houses.
Three bites of a fish stick is not "all that seafood."
I think our beach house IS nice!
Groan.

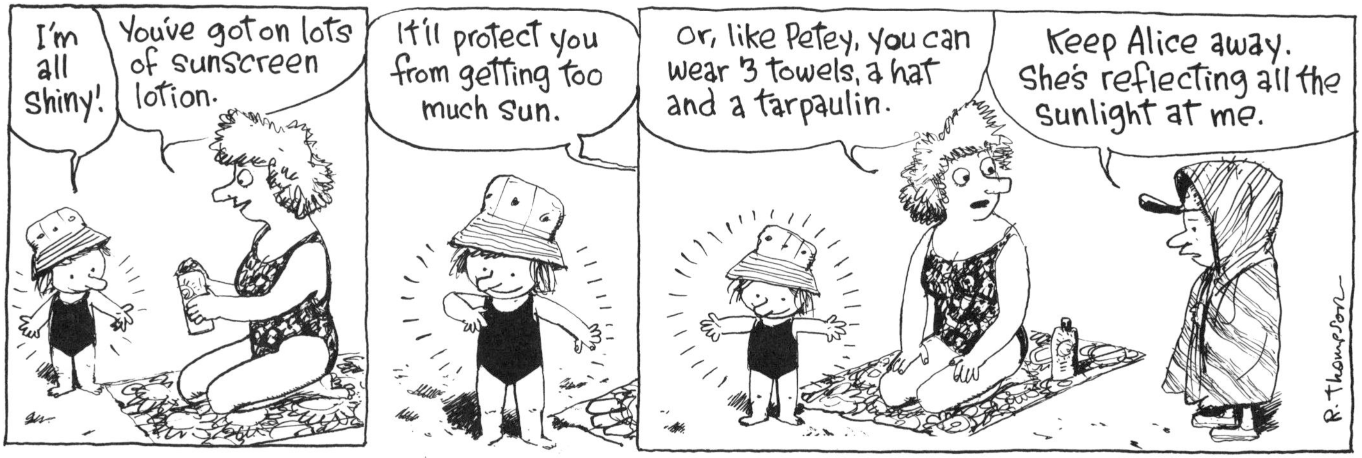
I'm all shiny!
You've got on lots of sunscreen lotion.
It'll protect you from getting too much sun.
Or, like Petey, you can wear 3 towels, a hat and a tarpaulin.
Keep Alice away. She's reflecting all the sunlight at me.

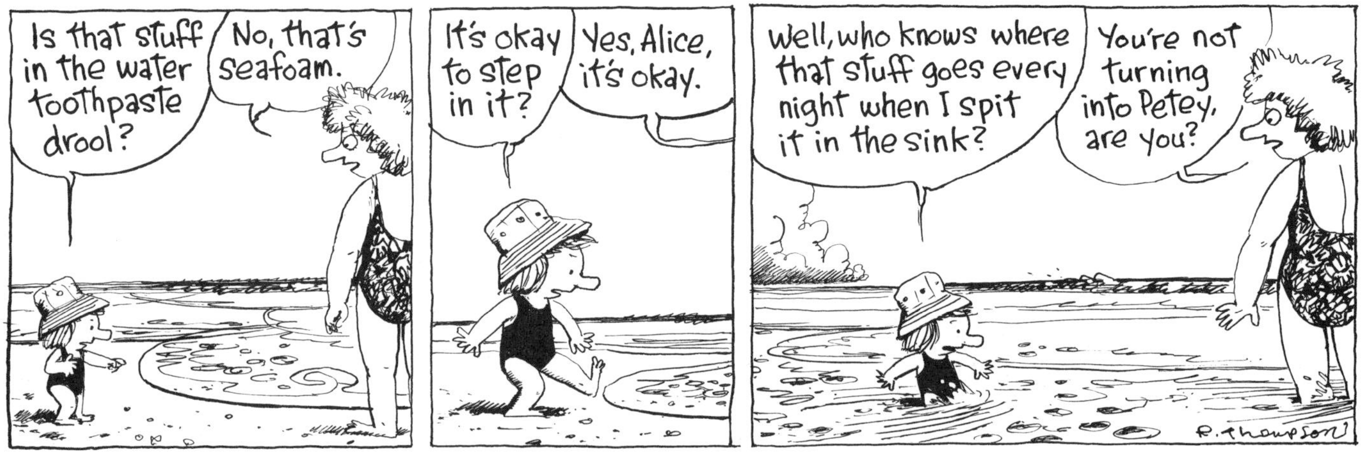
Is that stuff in the water toothpaste drool?
No, that's seafoam.
It's okay to step in it?
Yes, Alice, it's okay.
Well, who knows where that stuff goes every night when I spit it in the sink?
You're not turning into Petey, are you?

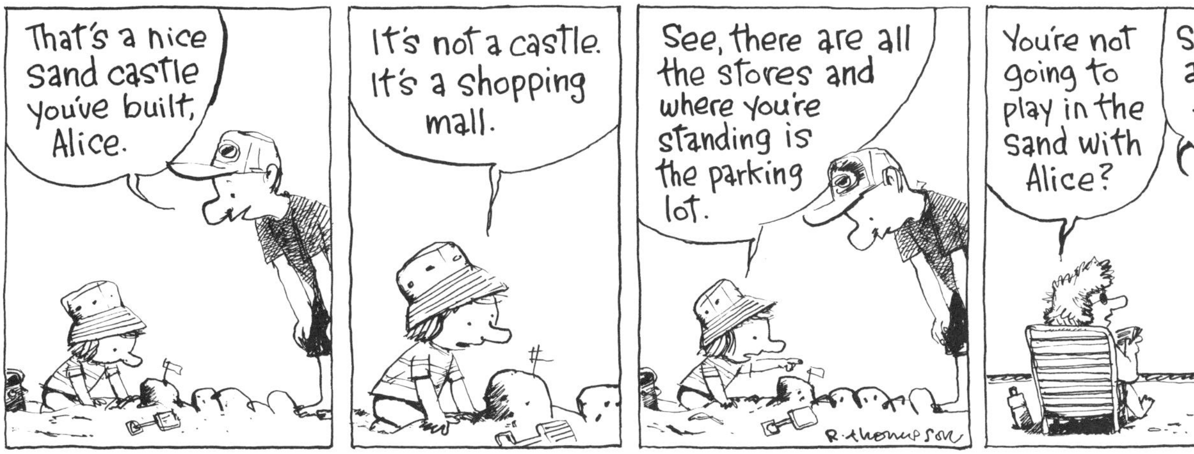
That's a nice sand castle you've built, Alice.
It's not a castle. It's a shopping mall.
See, there are all the stores and where you're standing is the parking lot.
You're not going to play in the sand with Alice?
She's too advanced for me.
R. thompson

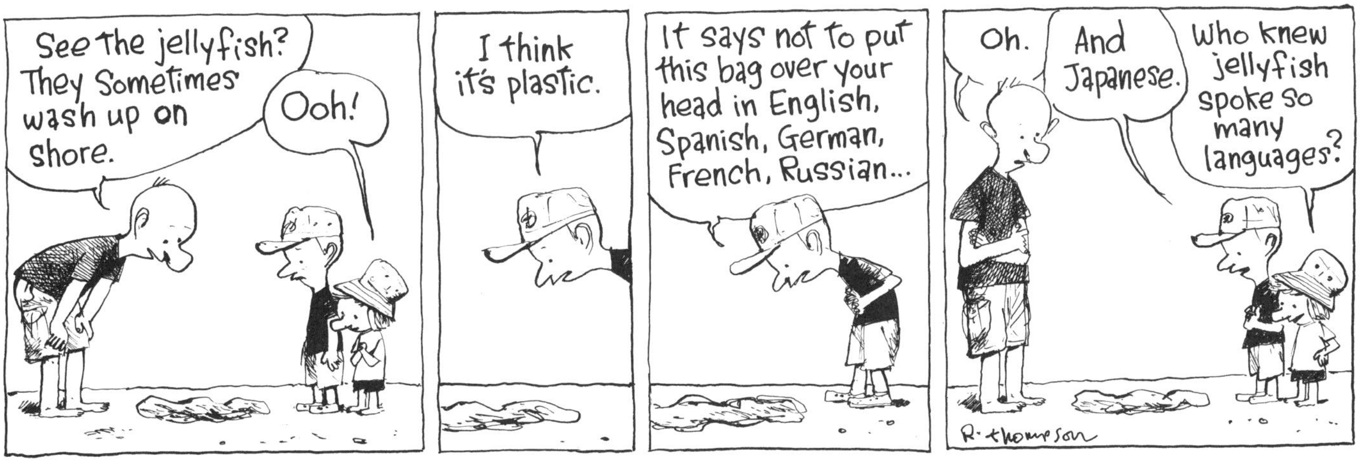
See the jellyfish? They sometimes wash up on shore.
Ooh!
I think it's plastic.
It says not to put this bag over your head in English, Spanish, German, French, Russian...
Oh.
And Japanese.
Who knew jellyfish spoke so many languages?
R. thompson

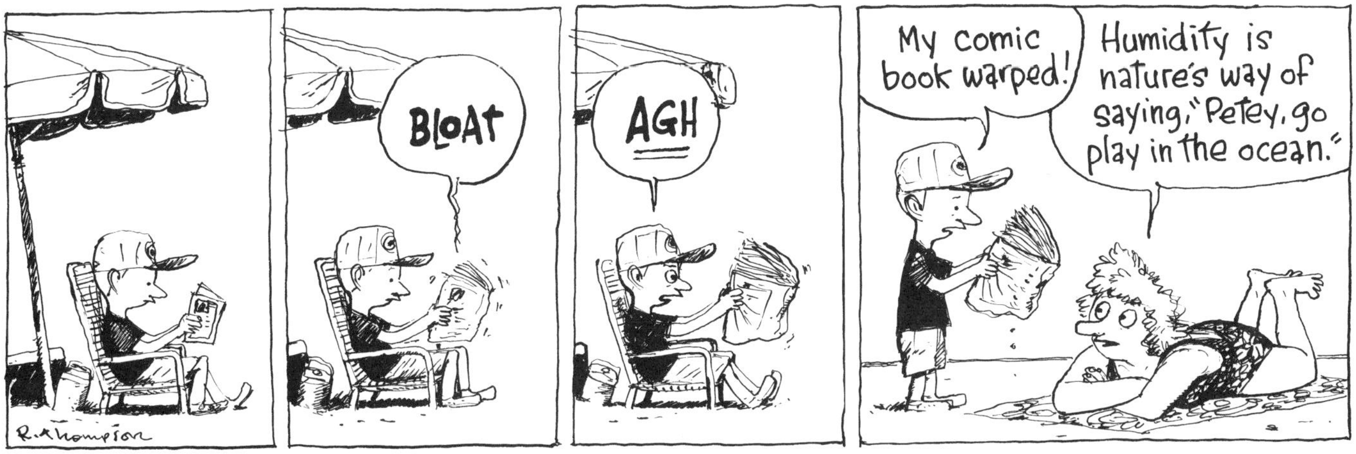
R. thompson
BLOAT
AGH
My comic book warped!
Humidity is nature's way of saying, "Petey, go play in the ocean."

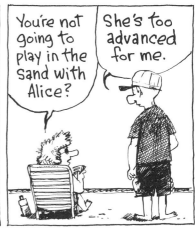

ALICE! That's enough TV!
Huh?
CLICK
You spend too much time in front of the TV with your eyes all bugged out.
So?
It's a waste of time and it's bad for your eyes! I'll bet it's stretching your optic nerve like a rubber band!
Huh?
I'll bet your optic nerve is six feet long! I'll bet your eyeballs will pop out like yo-yos if you keep watching so much TV.
Really?
R. thompson
Now go outside and play!
Okay!
Guess what! I've almost learned how to extend my eyeballs on stalks!
I'm glad somebody is using their time wisely.

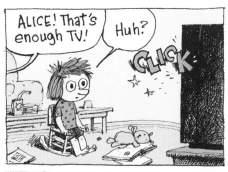

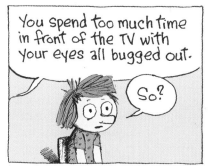

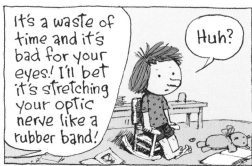

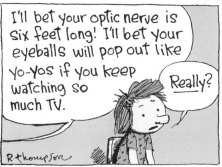

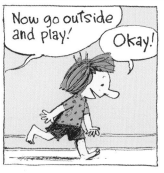

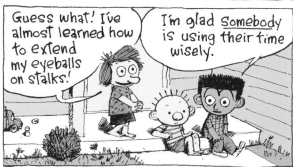

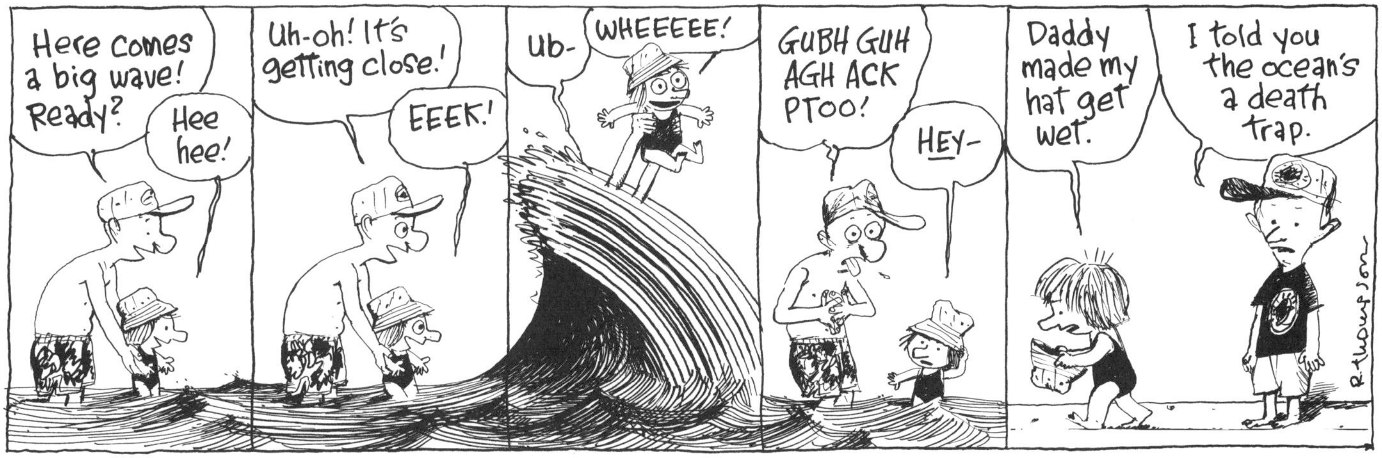
Here comes a big wave! Ready?
Hee hee!
Uh-oh! It's getting close!
EEEK!
Ub-
WHEEEEE!
GUBH GUH AGH ACK PTOO!
HEY-
Daddy made my hat get wet.
I told you the ocean's a death trap.
R. Thompson

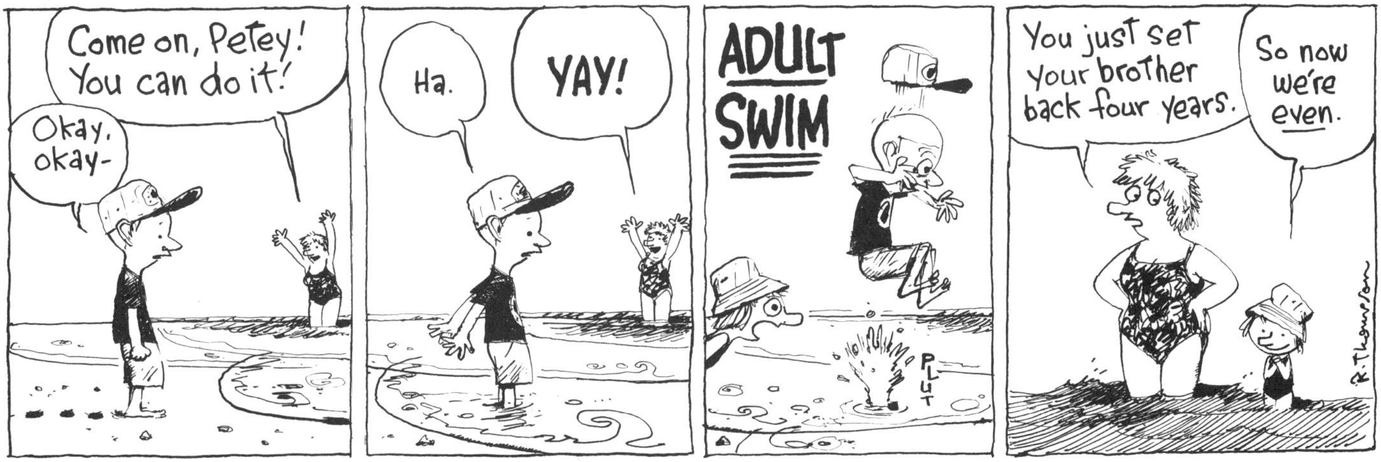
Come on, Petey! You can do it!
Okay, okay-
Ha.
YAY!
ADULT SWIM
PLUT
You just set your brother back four years.
So now we're even.
R. Thompson

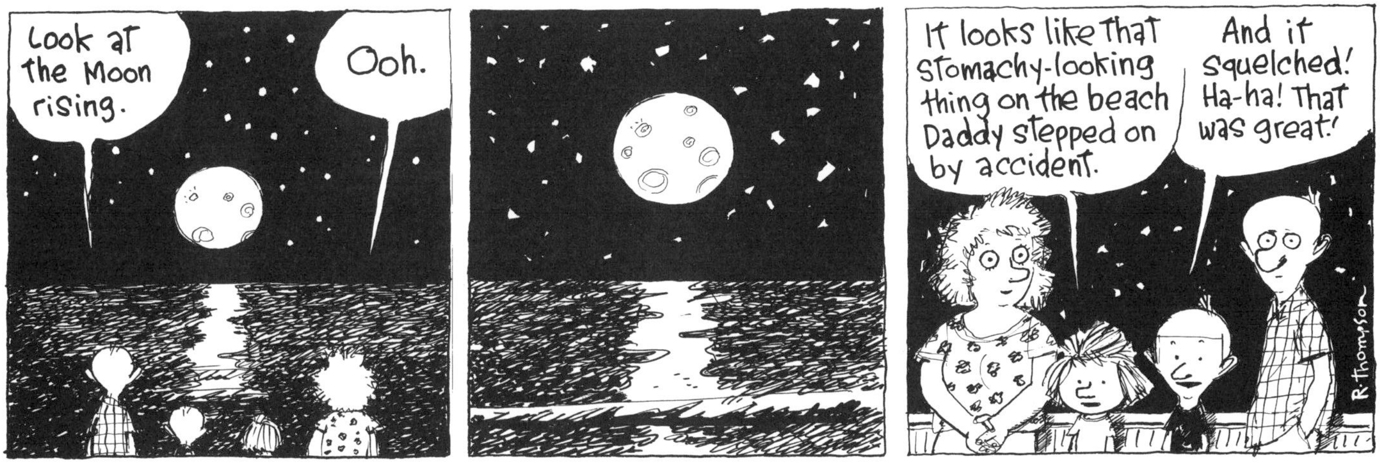
Look at the Moon rising.
Ooh.
It looks like that stomachy-looking thing on the beach Daddy stepped on by accident.
And it squelched! Ha-ha! That was great!
R. Thompson

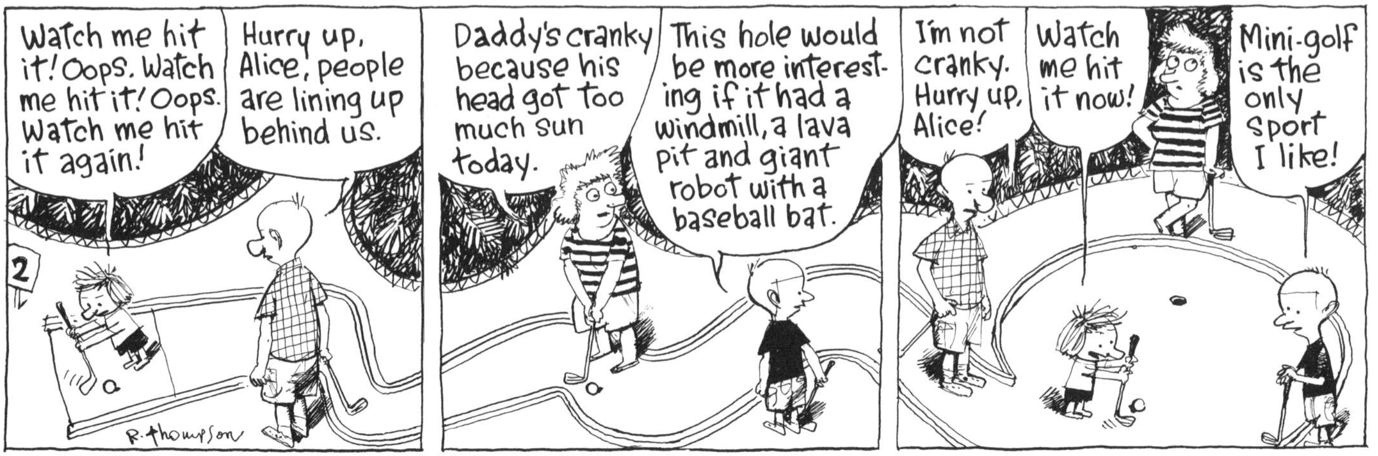
Watch me hit it! Oops. Watch me hit it! Oops. Watch me hit it again!
Hurry up, Alice, people are lining up behind us.
2
R. Thompson
Daddy's cranky because his head got too much sun today.
This hole would be more interesting if it had a windmill, a lava pit and giant robot with a baseball bat.
I'm not cranky. Hurry up, Alice!
Watch me hit it now!
Mini-golf is the only sport I like!

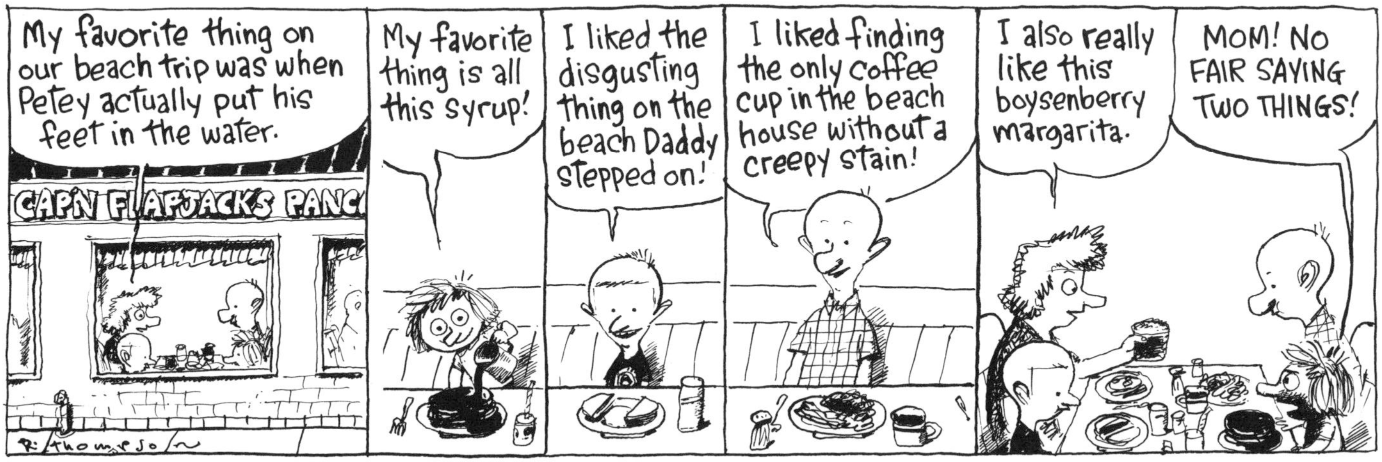
My favorite thing on our beach trip was when Petey actually put his feet in the water.
CAP'N FLAPJACK'S PANC
R. Thompson
My favorite thing is all this syrup!
I liked the disgusting thing on the beach Daddy stepped on!
I liked finding the only coffee cup in the beach house without a creepy stain!
I also really like this boysenberry margarita.
MOM! NO FAIR SAYING TWO THINGS!

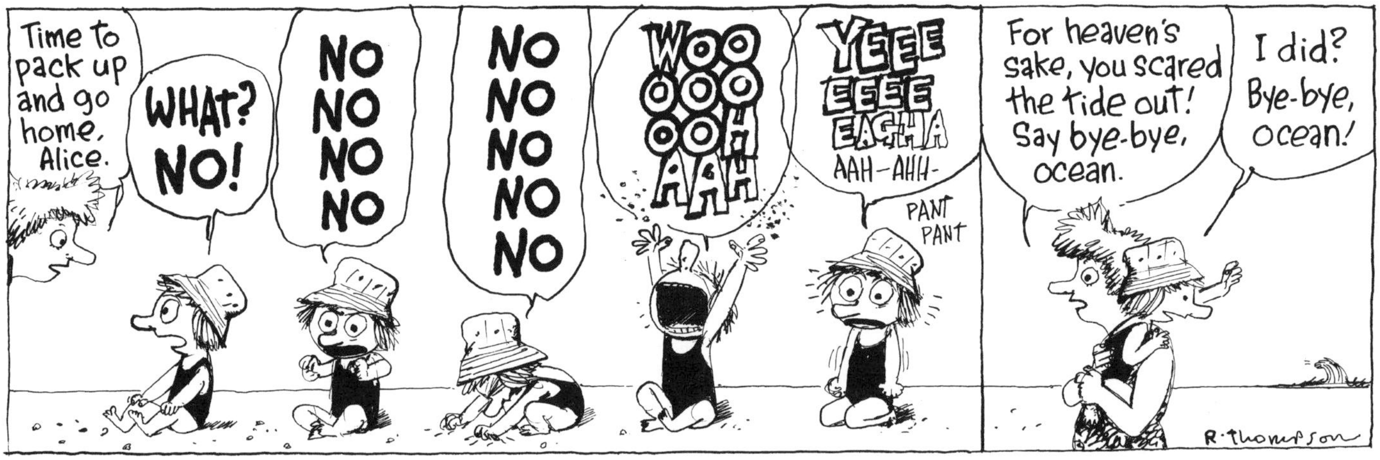
Time to pack up and go home, Alice.
WHAT? NO!
NO NO NO NO
NO NO NO NO NO
WOOOOOOOOHAAH
YEEEEEEEAGHA AAH-AHH-
PANT PANT
For heaven's sake, you scared the tide out! Say bye-bye, ocean.
I did? Bye-bye, ocean!
R. Thompson

How about this bookbag, Petey?
I like my old one.
BACK TO SCHOOL SAVINGS
Your old one is falling apart.
This bag is made of ultra-light waterproof 1,000 denier polyester. It was tested in the Himalayas!
I don't like it.
R. Thompson
It says they successfully hauled the complete works of Charles Dickens up Mount Everest in one of these bags!
And it's got a built-in parachute!
I don't- wait- what?
This ring opens the chute.
This?
BANG
GAH!
MOM
This bag is fine.
8/31
Mom is a dangerous lunatic.
No she's not. She's getting me this lunchbox that makes its own cheese sandwiches by magic!

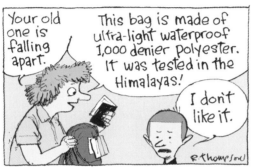

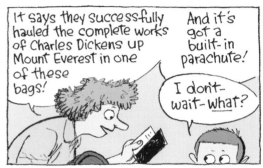

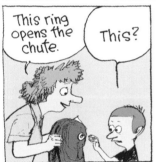

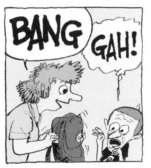

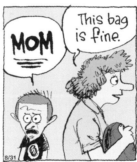

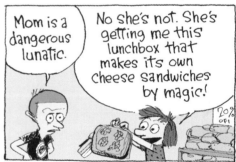

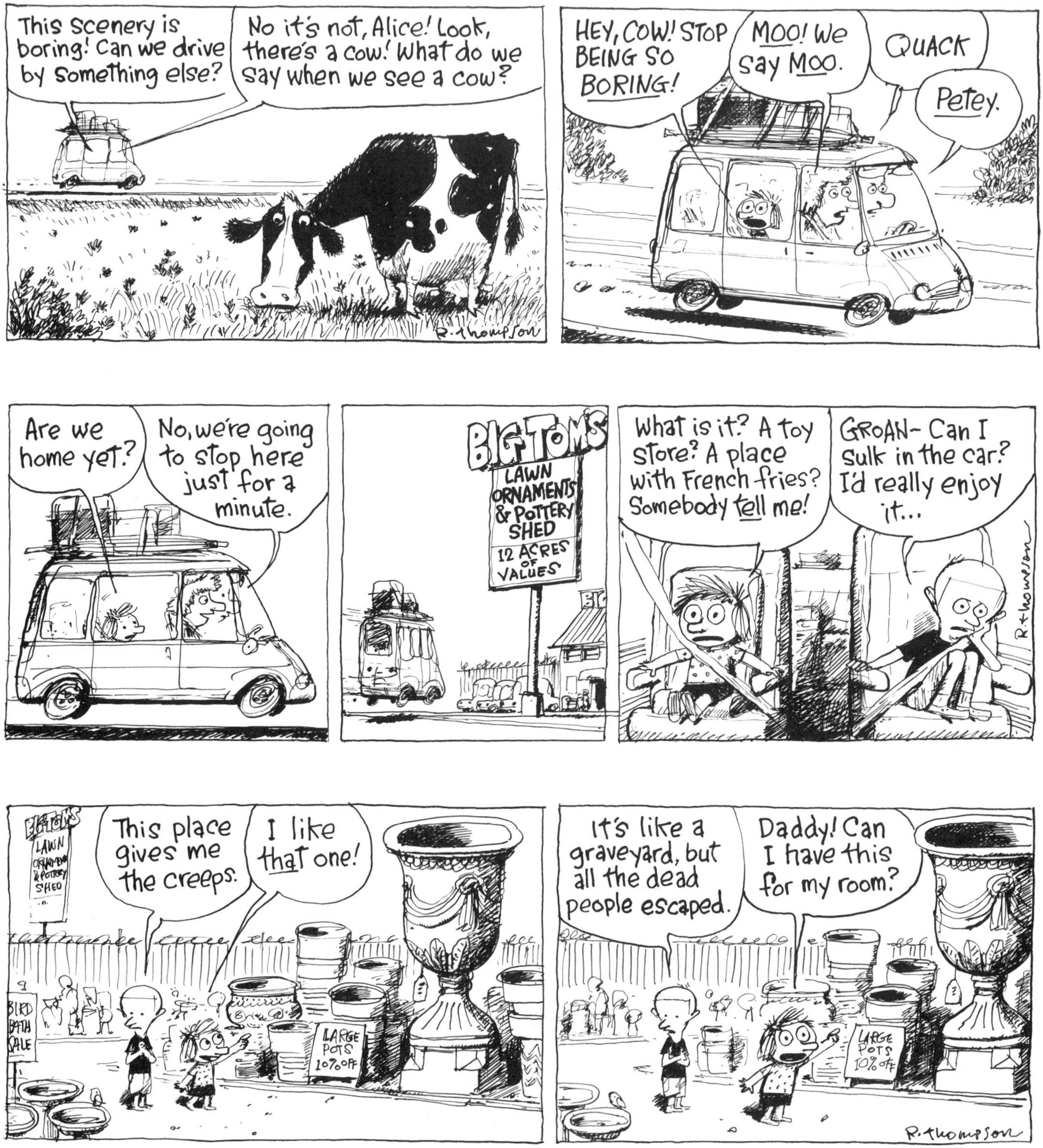
This scenery is boring! Can we drive by something else?
No it's not, Alice! Look, there's a cow! What do we say when we see a cow?
R. thompson
HEY, COW! STOP BEING SO BORING!
MOO! We say MOO.
QUACK
Petey.
Are we home yet?
No, we're going to stop here just for a minute.
BIG TOM'S
LAWN ORNAMENTS & POTTERY SHED
12 ACRES OF VALUES
What is it? A toy store? A place with French fries? Somebody tell me!
GROAN- Can I sulk in the car? I'd really enjoy it...
R. thompson
This place gives me the creeps.
I like that one!
LARGE POTS 10% OFF
It's like a graveyard, but all the dead people escaped.
Daddy! Can I have this for my room?
LARGE POTS 10% OFF
R. thompson

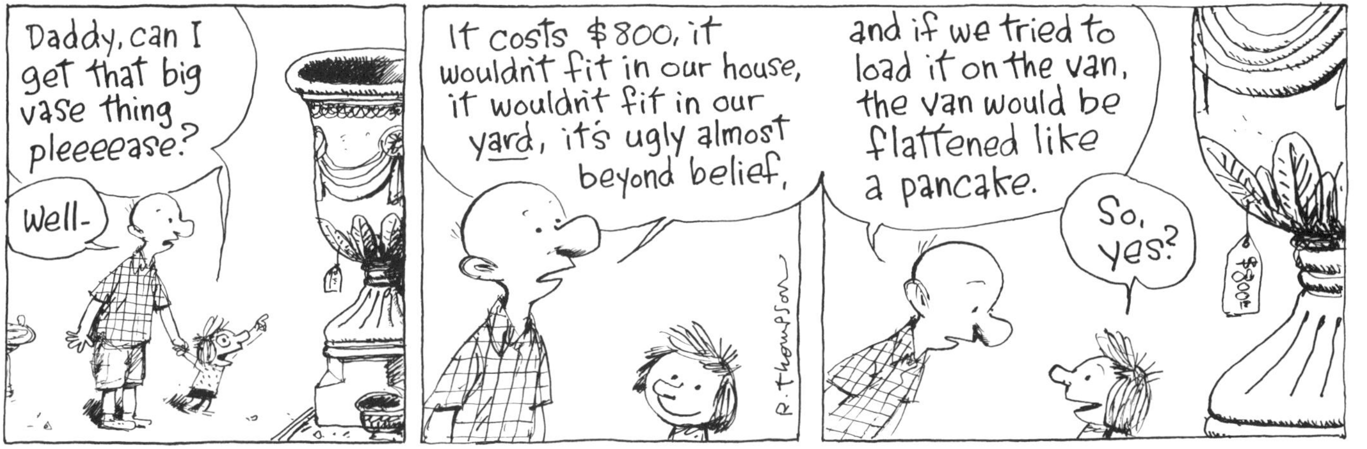
Daddy, can I get that big vase thing pleeeeease?
Well-
It costs $800, it wouldn't fit in our house, it wouldn't fit in our yard, it's ugly almost beyond belief,
and if we tried to load it on the van, the van would be flattened like a pancake.
So, yes?
$800
R. Thompson

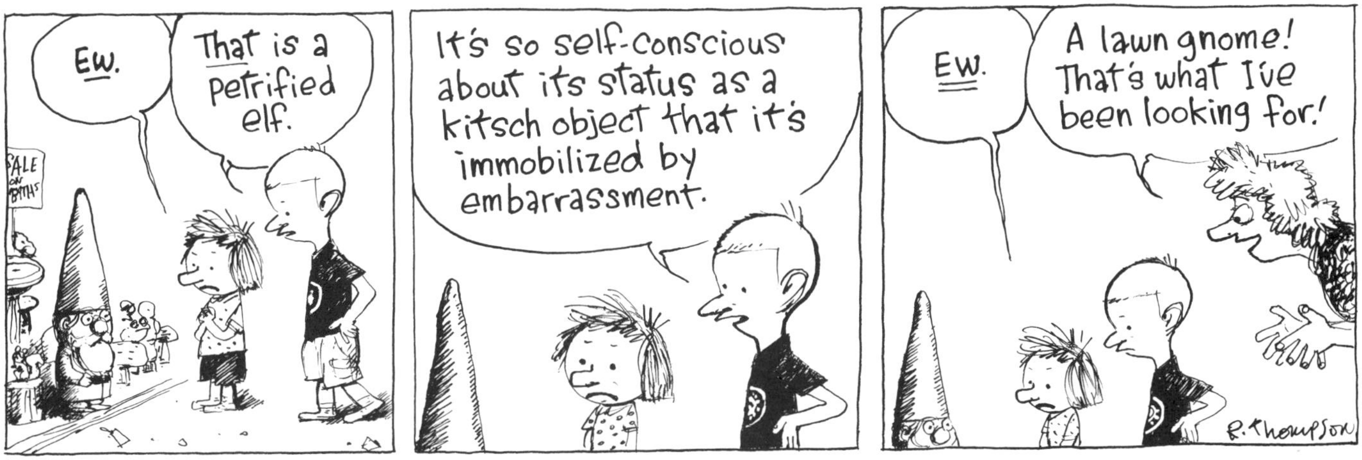
Ew.
That is a petrified elf.
SALE
It's so self-conscious about its status as a kitsch object that it's immobilized by embarrassment.
Ew.
A lawn gnome! That's what I've been looking for!
R. Thompson

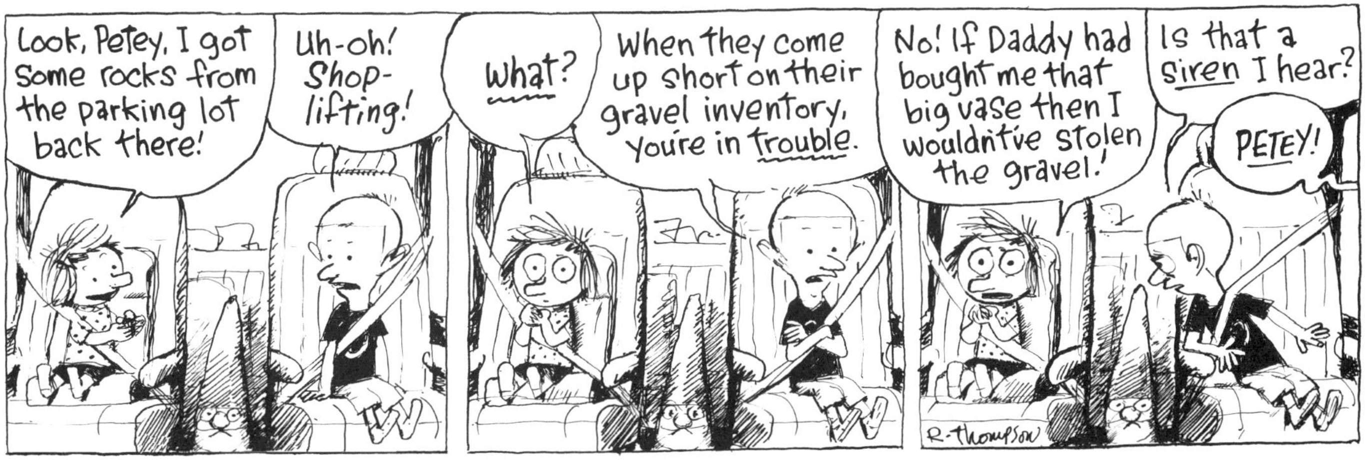
Look, Petey, I got some rocks from the parking lot back there!
Uh-oh! Shoplifting!
What?
When they come up short on their gravel inventory, you're in trouble.
No! If Daddy had bought me that big vase then I wouldn't've stolen the gravel!
Is that a siren I hear?
PETEY!
R. Thompson

Tell us about your first week back at school, Petey.

Well—

The halls are all painted a different beige than last year. I hate it.

My teacher arranged all the desks like the continents of the world as a learning experience. I'm in Antarctica.

And the worst is, our class nickname is the Sea Cucumbers.

THE SEA CUCUMBERS

SWIMMING IN A SEA OF LEARNING!

Why do things have to change every year?

When distressed, a sea cucumber can extrude its own stomach as a defense mechanism.

AGH

I thought that would cheer you up.

Maybe you need glasses.

I'd like to try that stomach thing.

84

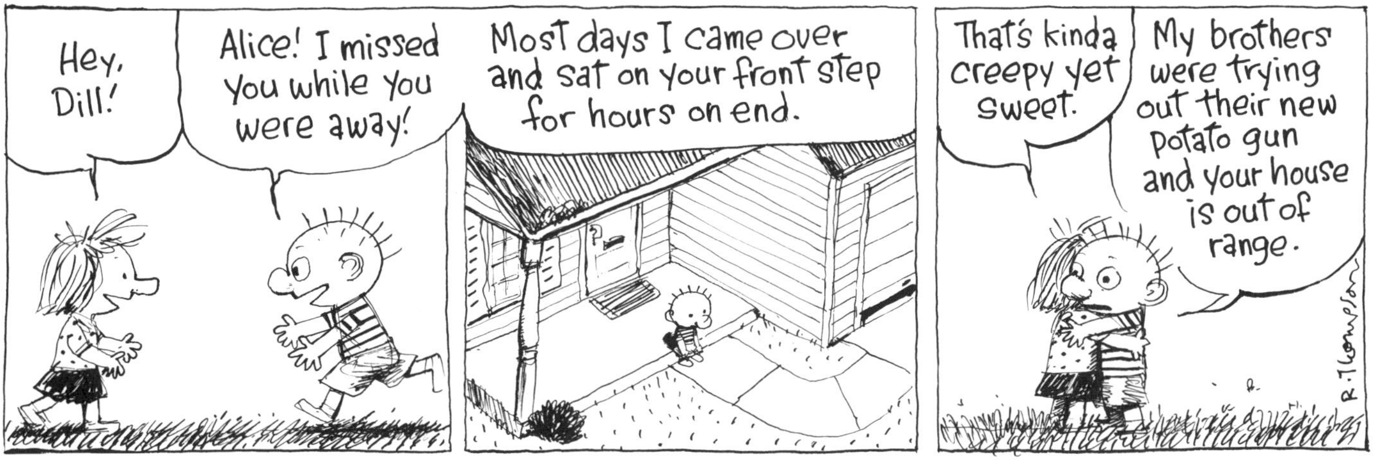
Hey, Dill!
Alice! I missed you while you were away!
Most days I came over and sat on your front step for hours on end.
That's kinda creepy yet sweet.
My brothers were trying out their new potato gun and your house is out of range.
R. Thompson

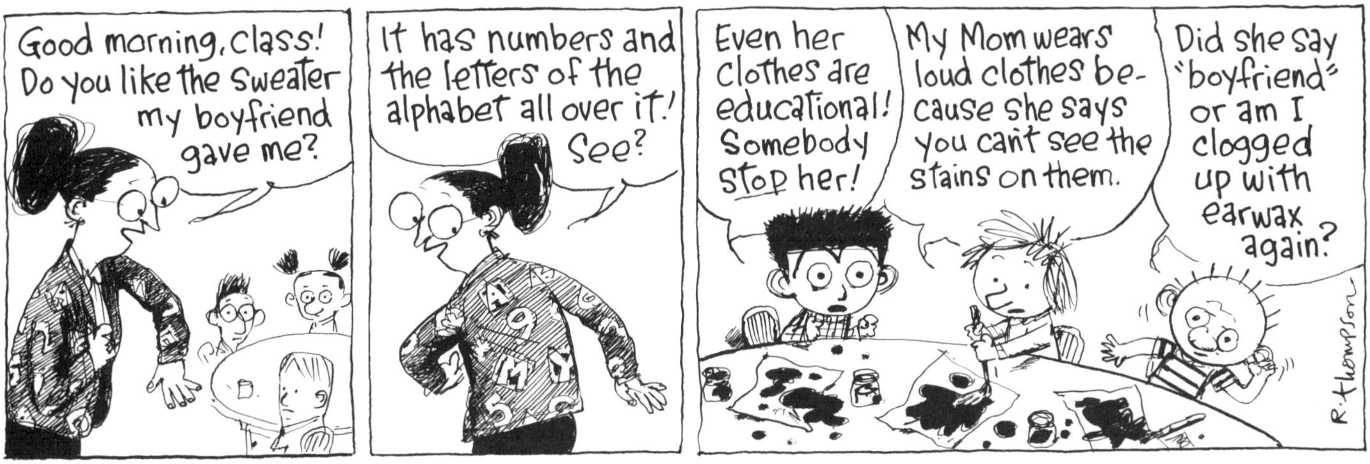
Good morning, class! Do you like the sweater my boyfriend gave me?
It has numbers and the letters of the alphabet all over it! See?
Even her clothes are educational! Somebody stop her!
My Mom wears loud clothes because she says you can't see the stains on them.
Did she say "boyfriend" or am I clogged up with earwax again?
R. Thompson

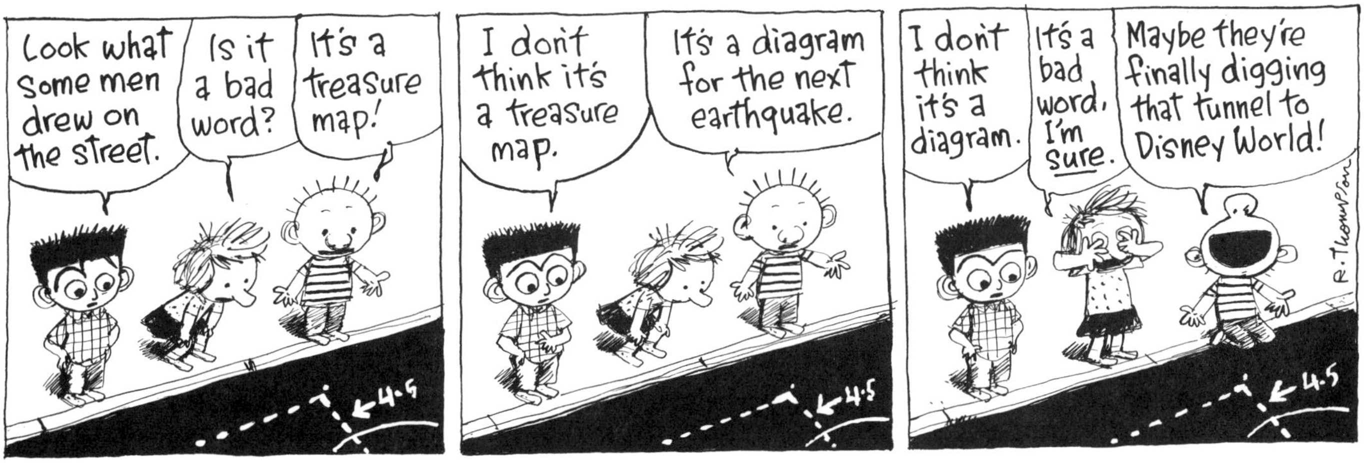
Look what some men drew on the street.
Is it a bad word?
It's a treasure map!
I don't think it's a treasure map.
It's a diagram for the next earthquake.
I don't think it's a diagram.
It's a bad word, I'm sure.
Maybe they're finally digging that tunnel to Disney World!
R. Thompson

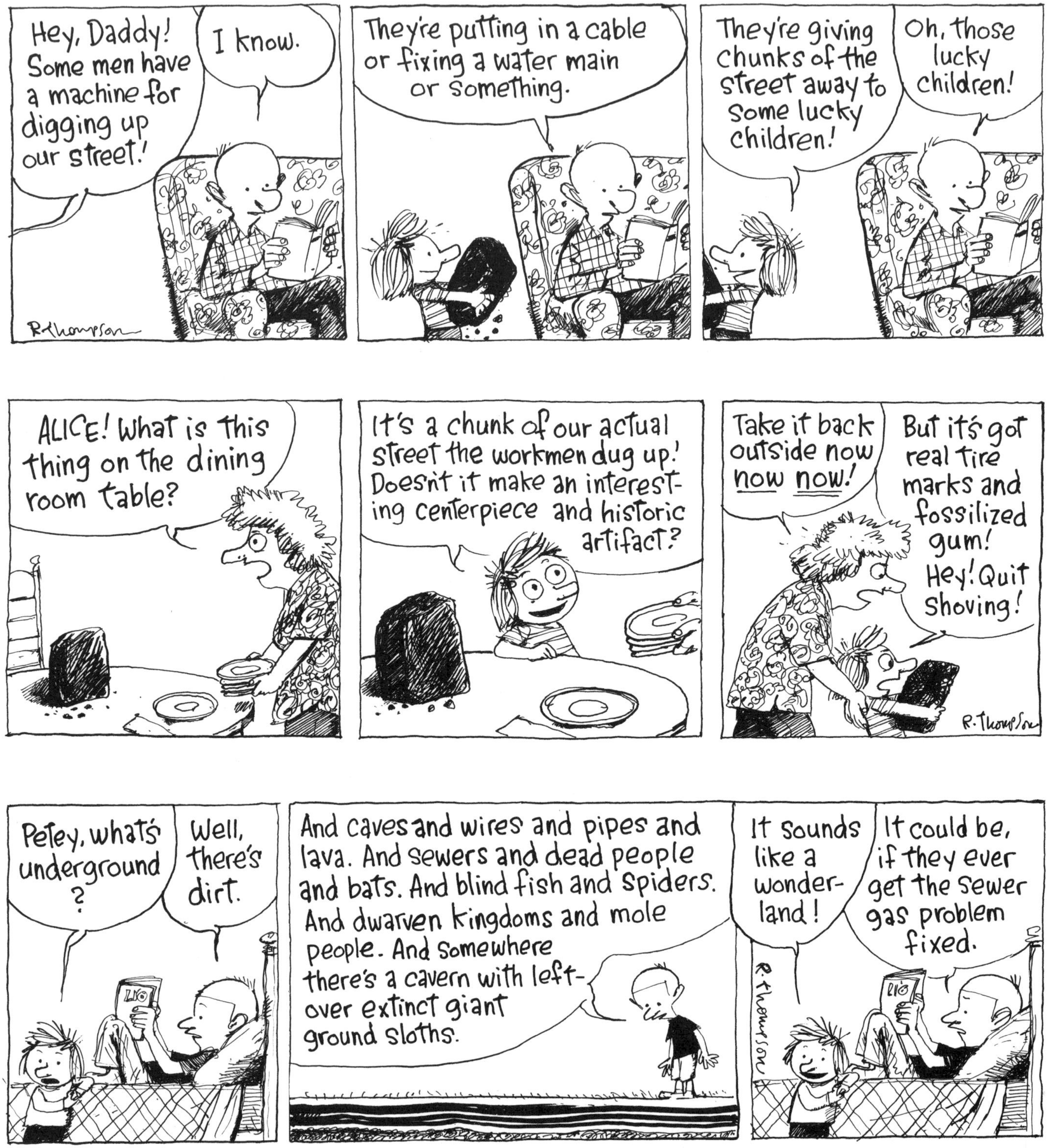
Hey, Daddy! Some men have a machine for digging up our street!
I know.
They're putting in a cable or fixing a water main or something.
They're giving chunks of the street away to some lucky children!
Oh, those lucky children!
R. Thompson
ALICE! What is this thing on the dining room table?
It's a chunk of our actual street the workmen dug up! Doesn't it make an interesting centerpiece and historic artifact?
Take it back outside now now now!
But it's got real tire marks and fossilized gum! Hey! Quit shoving!
R. Thompson
Petey, what's underground?
Well, there's dirt.
And caves and wires and pipes and lava. And sewers and dead people and bats. And blind fish and spiders. And dwarven kingdoms and mole people. And somewhere there's a cavern with left-over extinct giant ground sloths.
R. Thompson
It sounds like a wonder-land!
It could be, if they ever get the sewer gas problem fixed.

We've got a lawn gnome!
Is that allowed?
The neighborhood rules say you can have up to two man-made lawn objects.
We've got a burro with a cart. They count as two.
We've got a whirligig and a frog under a mushroom.
And a daisy doormat that's awaiting adjudication.
We've got a "Squirrel Crossing" sign and a cherub fountain birdbath that scares away all the squirrels.
We've got a pet cemetery, various dirtbike parts, a clothes dryer, a carpet sample display and my brother's newest trebuchet.
Didn't the neighborhood rules guy with the clipboard complain?
He tried to. He came down in the next county, but his clipboard has never been found.
R. Thompson

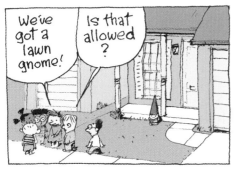

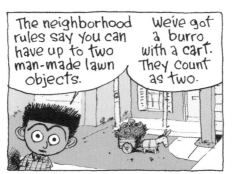

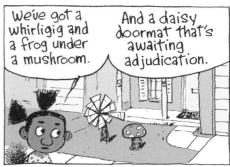

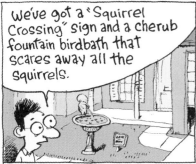

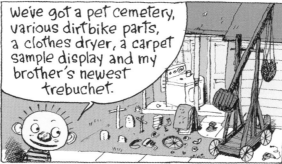

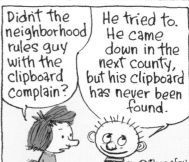

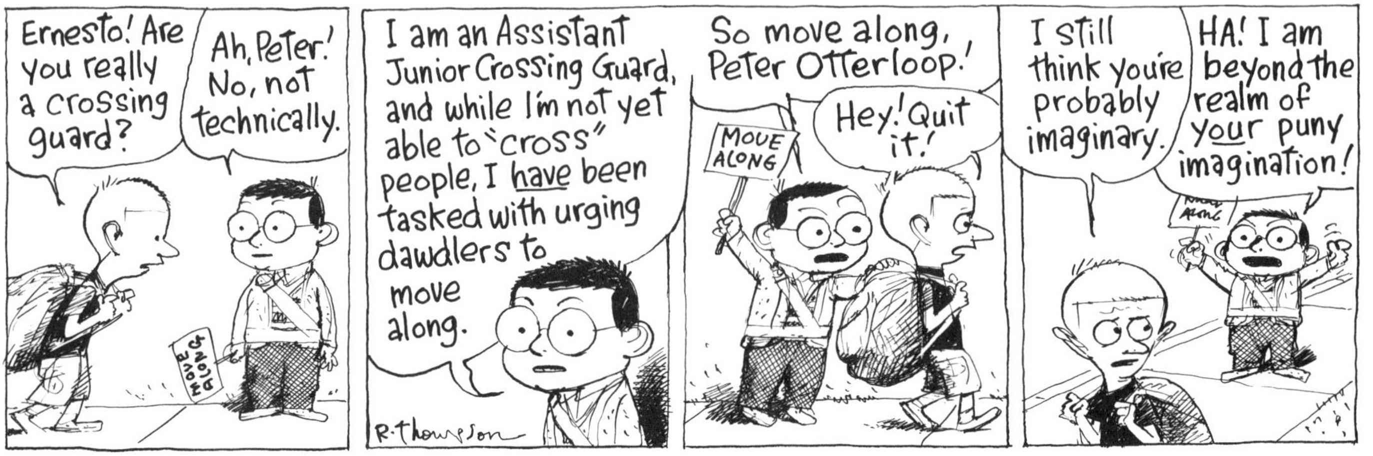
Ernesto! Are you really a crossing guard?
Ah, Peter! No, not technically.
MOVE ALONG
I am an Assistant Junior Crossing Guard, and while I'm not yet able to "cross" people, I have been tasked with urging dawdlers to move along.
R. Thompson
So move along, Peter Otterloop!
MOVE ALONG
Hey! Quit it!
I still think you're probably imaginary.
HA! I am beyond the realm of your puny imagination!

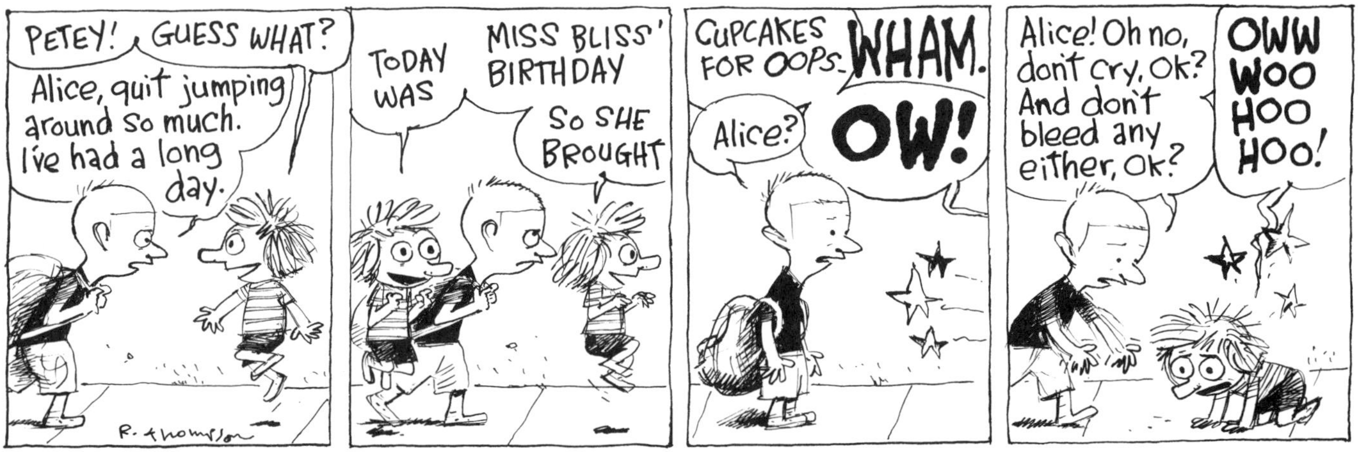
PETEY!
GUESS WHAT?
Alice, quit jumping around so much. I've had a long day.
R. Thompson
TODAY WAS
MISS BLISS' BIRTHDAY
SO SHE BROUGHT
CUPCAKES FOR OOPS–
WHAM.
Alice?
OW!
Alice! Oh no, don't cry, Ok? And don't bleed any either, Ok?
OWW WOO HOO HOO!

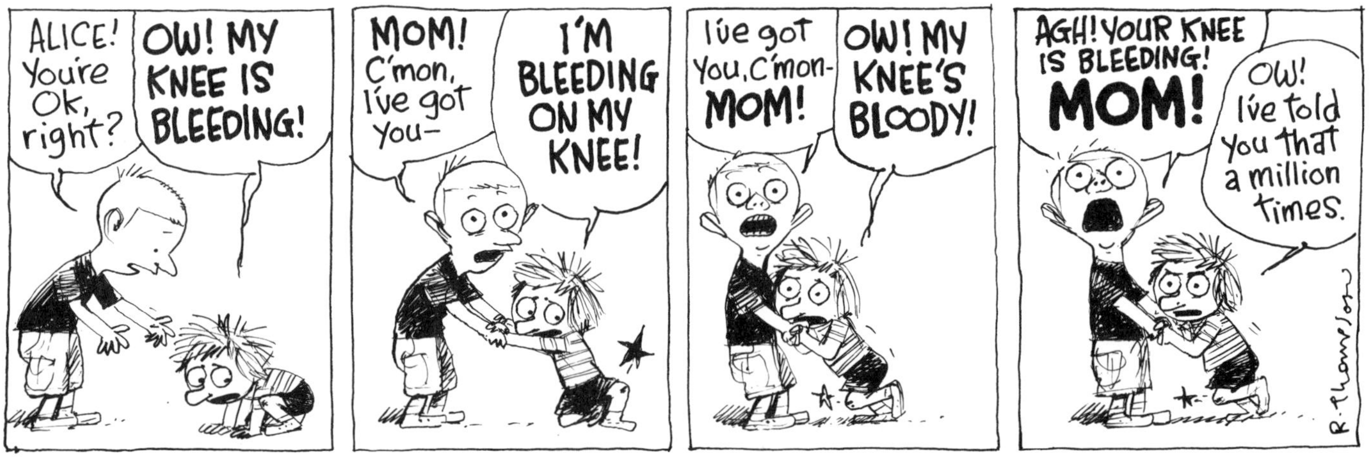
ALICE! You're Ok, right?
OW! MY KNEE IS BLEEDING!
MOM! C'mon, I've got you–
I'M BLEEDING ON MY KNEE!
I've got you, C'mon– MOM!
OW! MY KNEE'S BLOODY!
AGH! YOUR KNEE IS BLEEDING! MOM!
OW! I've told you that a million times.
R. Thompson

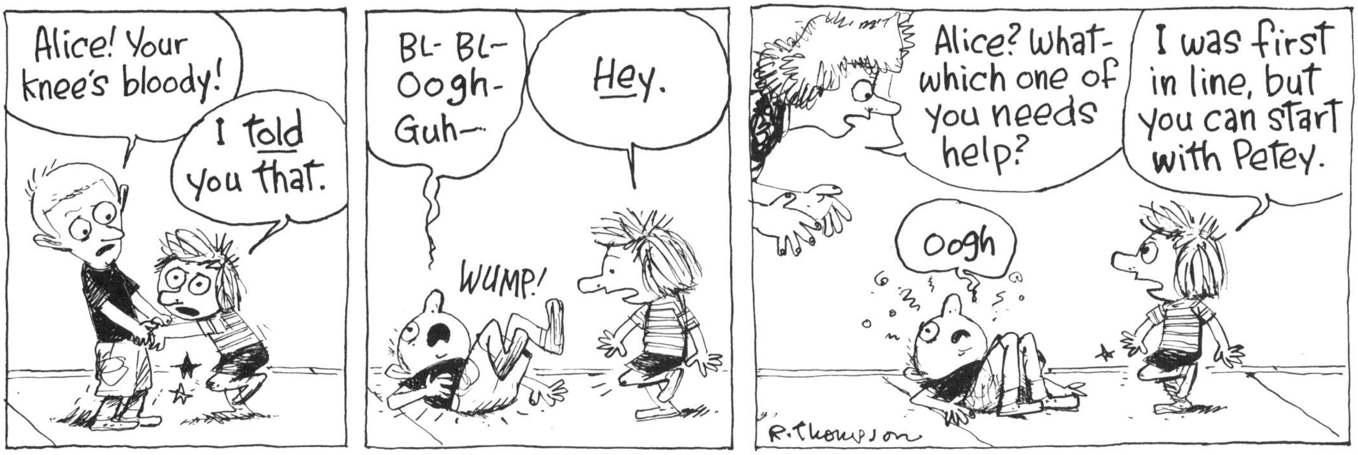
Alice! Your knee's bloody!
I told you that.
BL- BL- Oogh- Guh—
WUMP!
Hey.
Alice? What- which one of you needs help?
I was first in line, but you can start with Petey.
Oogh

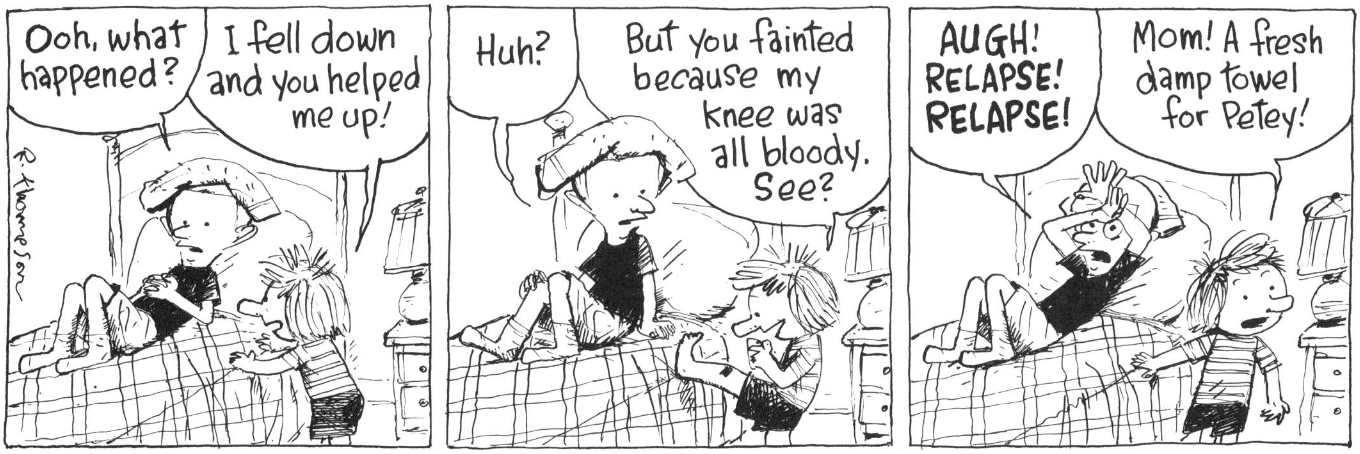
Ooh, what happened?
I fell down and you helped me up!
Huh?
But you fainted because my knee was all bloody. See?
AUGH! RELAPSE! RELAPSE!
Mom! A fresh damp towel for Petey!

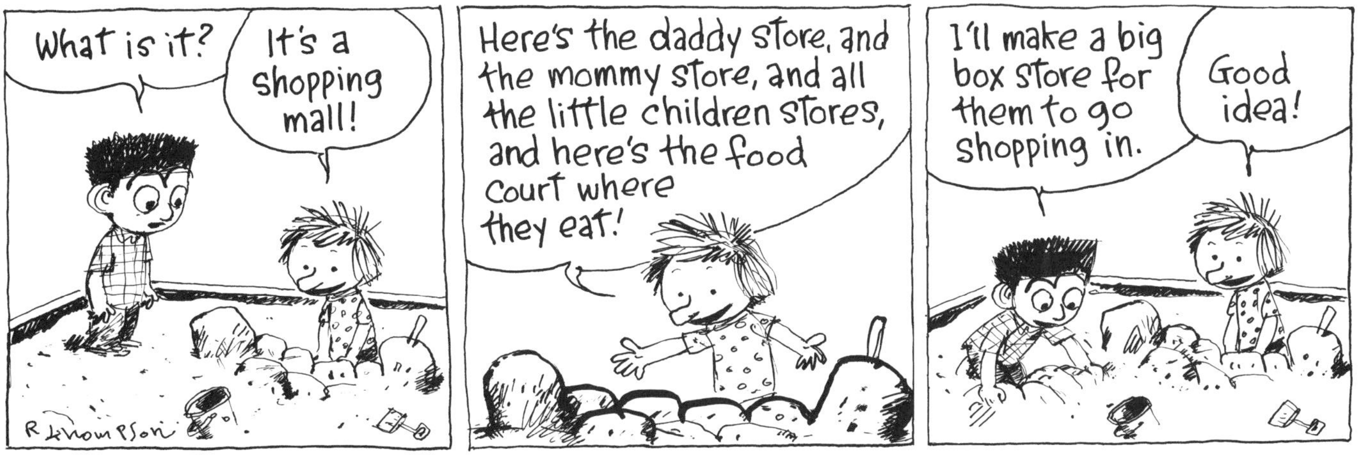
What is it?
It's a shopping mall!
Here's the daddy store, and the mommy store, and all the little children stores, and here's the food court where they eat!
I'll make a big box store for them to go shopping in.
Good idea!

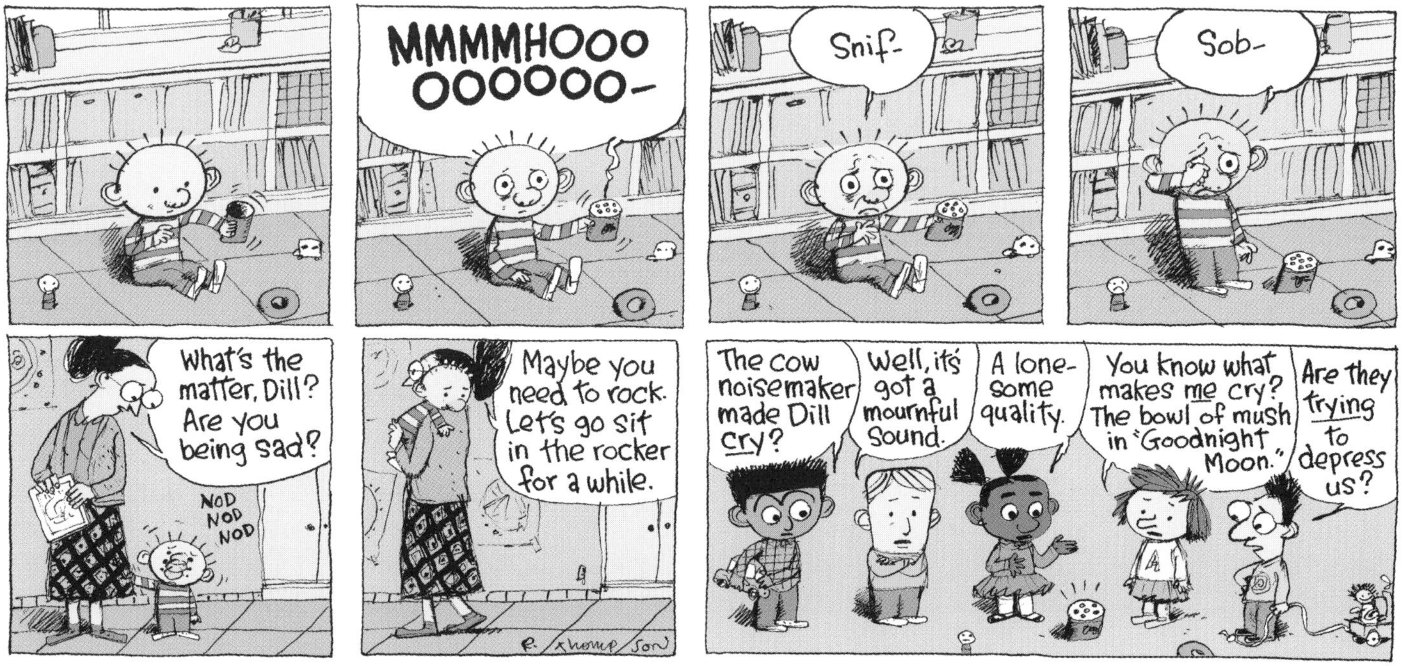
MMMMHOOO OOOOOO-
Snif-
Sob-
What's the matter, Dill? Are you being sad?
NOD NOD NOD
Maybe you need to rock. Let's go sit in the rocker for a while.
R. Thompson
The cow noisemaker made Dill cry?
Well, it's got a mournful sound.
A lonesome quality.
You know what makes me cry? The bowl of mush in "Goodnight Moon."
Are they trying to depress us?

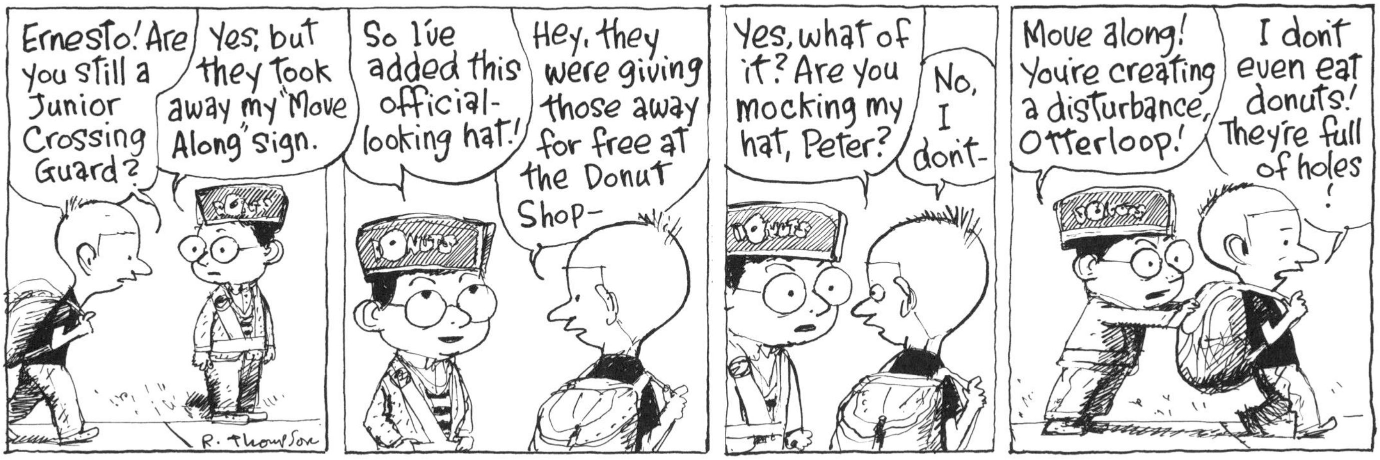
Ernesto! Are you still a Junior Crossing Guard?
Yes, but they took away my "Move Along" sign.
So I've added this official-looking hat!
Hey, they were giving those away for free at the Donut Shop-
DONUTS
Yes, what of it? Are you mocking my hat, Peter?
No, I don't-
Move along! You're creating a disturbance, Otterloop!
I don't even eat donuts! They're full of holes!

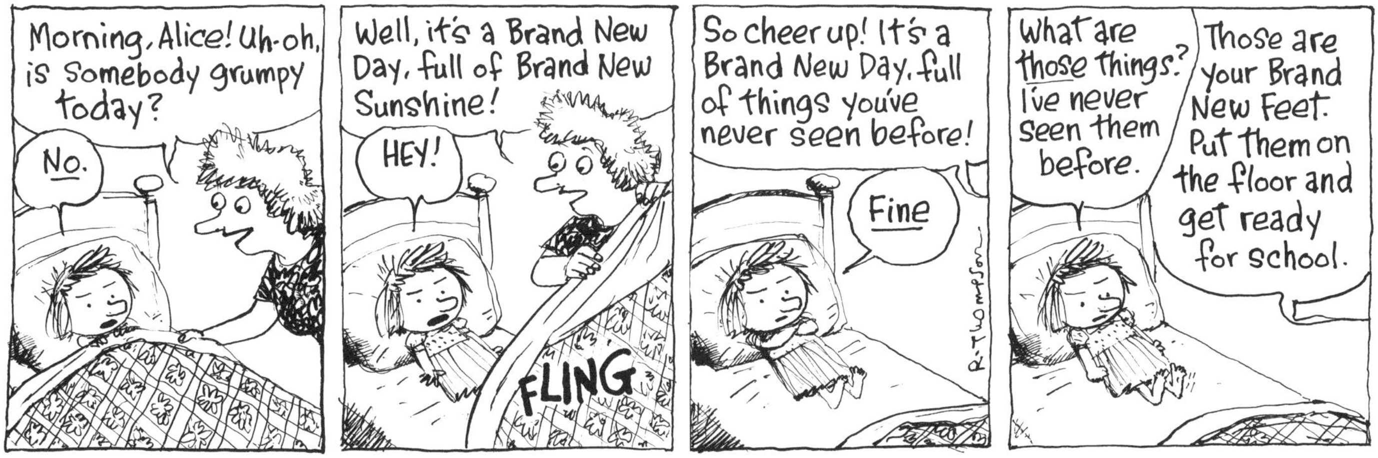
Morning, Alice! Uh-oh, is somebody grumpy today?
No.
Well, it's a Brand New Day, full of Brand New Sunshine!
HEY!
FLING
So cheer up! It's a Brand New Day, full of things you've never seen before!
Fine
What are those things? I've never seen them before.
Those are your Brand New Feet. Put them on the floor and get ready for school.

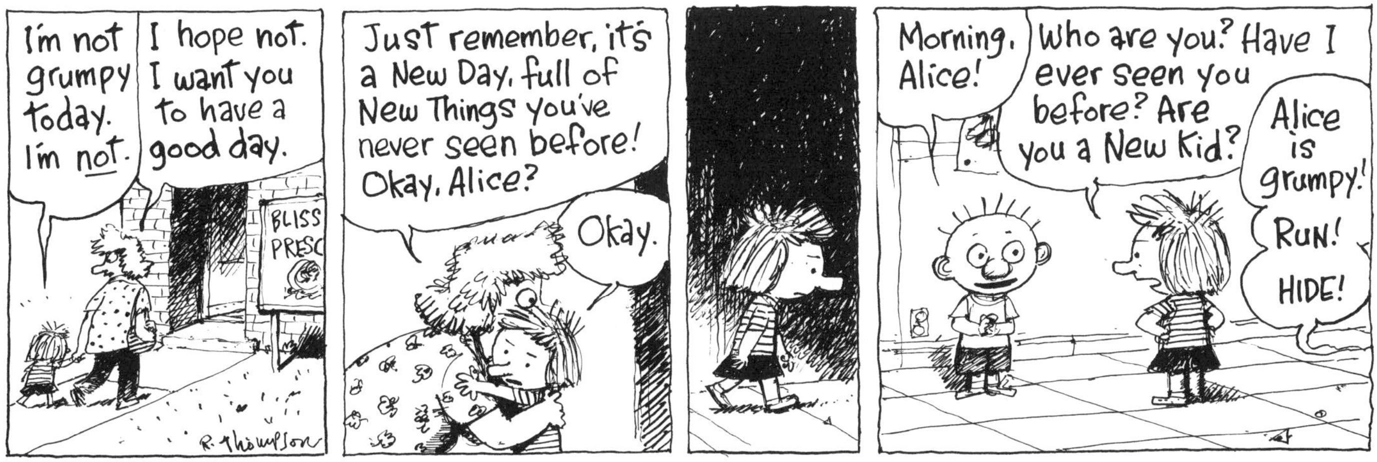
I'm not grumpy today. I'm not.
I hope not. I want you to have a good day.
BLISS
PRESC
Just remember, it's a New Day, full of New Things you've never seen before! Okay, Alice?
Okay.
Morning, Alice!
Who are you? Have I ever seen you before? Are you a New Kid?
Alice is grumpy!
RUN!
HIDE!

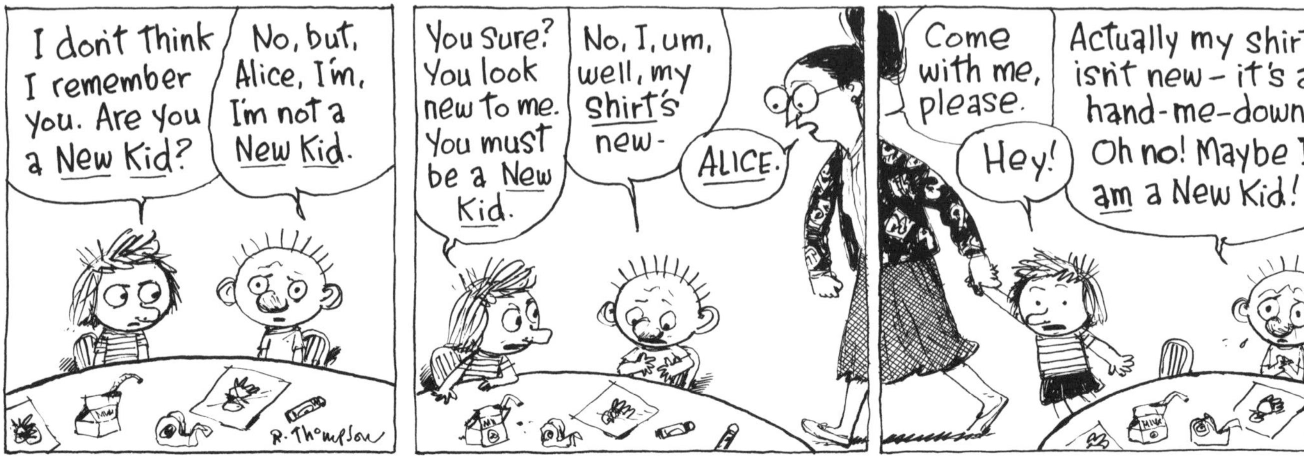
I don't Think I remember you. Are you a New Kid?
No, but, Alice, I'm, I'm not a New Kid.
You sure? You look new to me. You must be a New Kid.
No, I, um, well, my shirt's new-
ALICE.
Come with me, please.
Hey!
Actually my shirt isn't new - it's a hand-me-down. Oh no! Maybe I am a New Kid!
R. Thompson

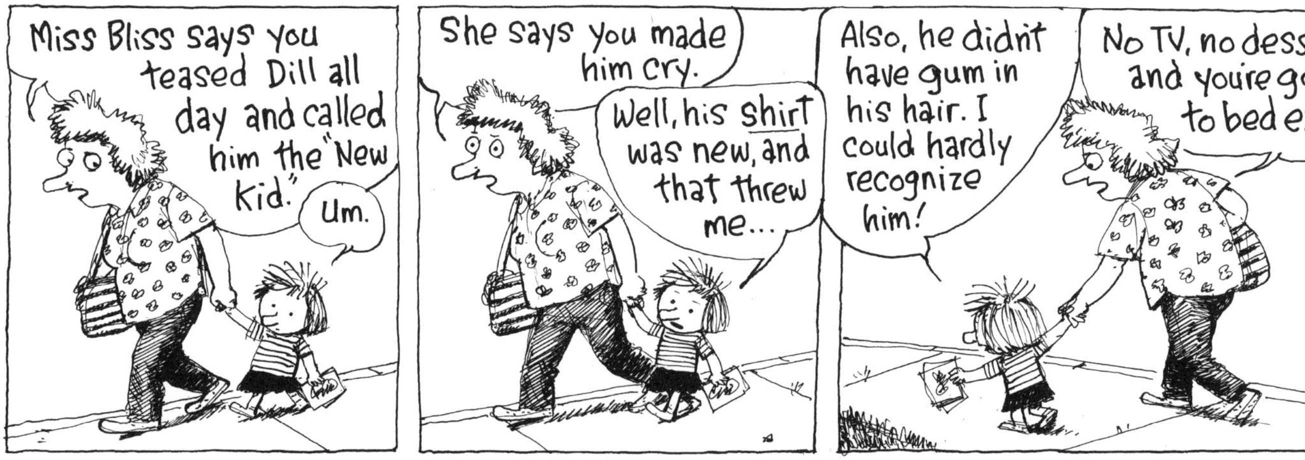
Miss Bliss says you teased Dill all day and called him the "New Kid."
Um.
She says you made him cry.
Well, his shirt was new, and that threw me...
Also, he didn't have gum in his hair. I could hardly recognize him!
No TV, no dessert, and you're going to bed early.
R. Thompson

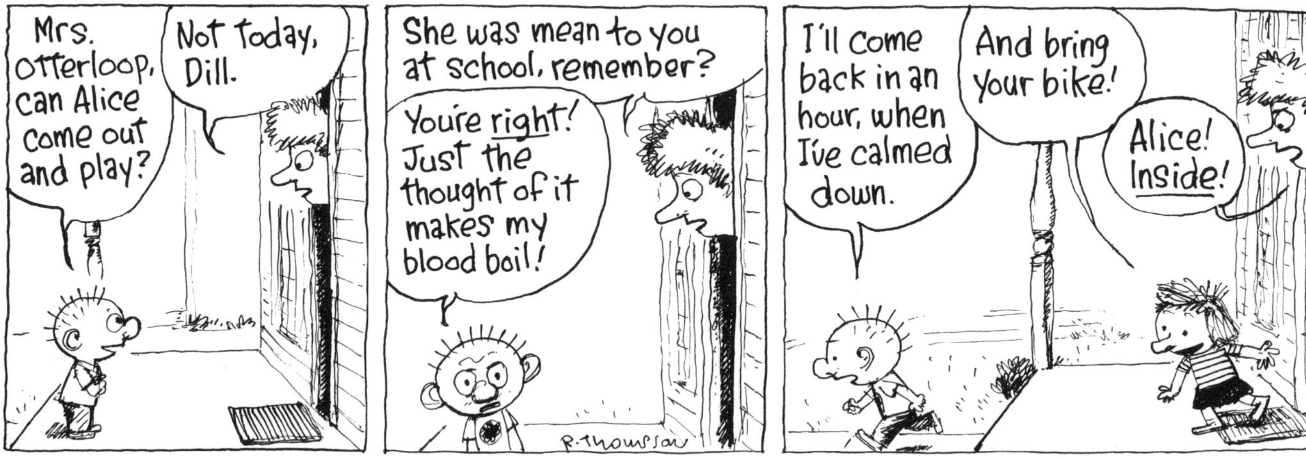
Mrs. Otterloop, can Alice come out and play?
Not today, Dill.
She was mean to you at school, remember?
You're right! Just the thought of it makes my blood boil!
I'll come back in an hour, when I've calmed down.
And bring your bike!
Alice! Inside!
R. Thompson

Good night, Alice.

Not yet!

No, I did the whole Bedtime Ritual. I did the Snuggy Song, the Rock-a-bye Dance, the Big Hugaboo and the Whoopsie Nighty-Night Pratfall.

But wait—

From now on I'd like to close out my Bedtime Ritual with a Topic of the Day, where we discuss some issue of national or personal concern.

Like what?

Why do goats eat tin cans?

CLICK

She turned out the light?

And she said I watch too many old TV cartoons.

You just needed a better topic, like "Why do pianos drop out of the clear blue sky?"

R. Thompson

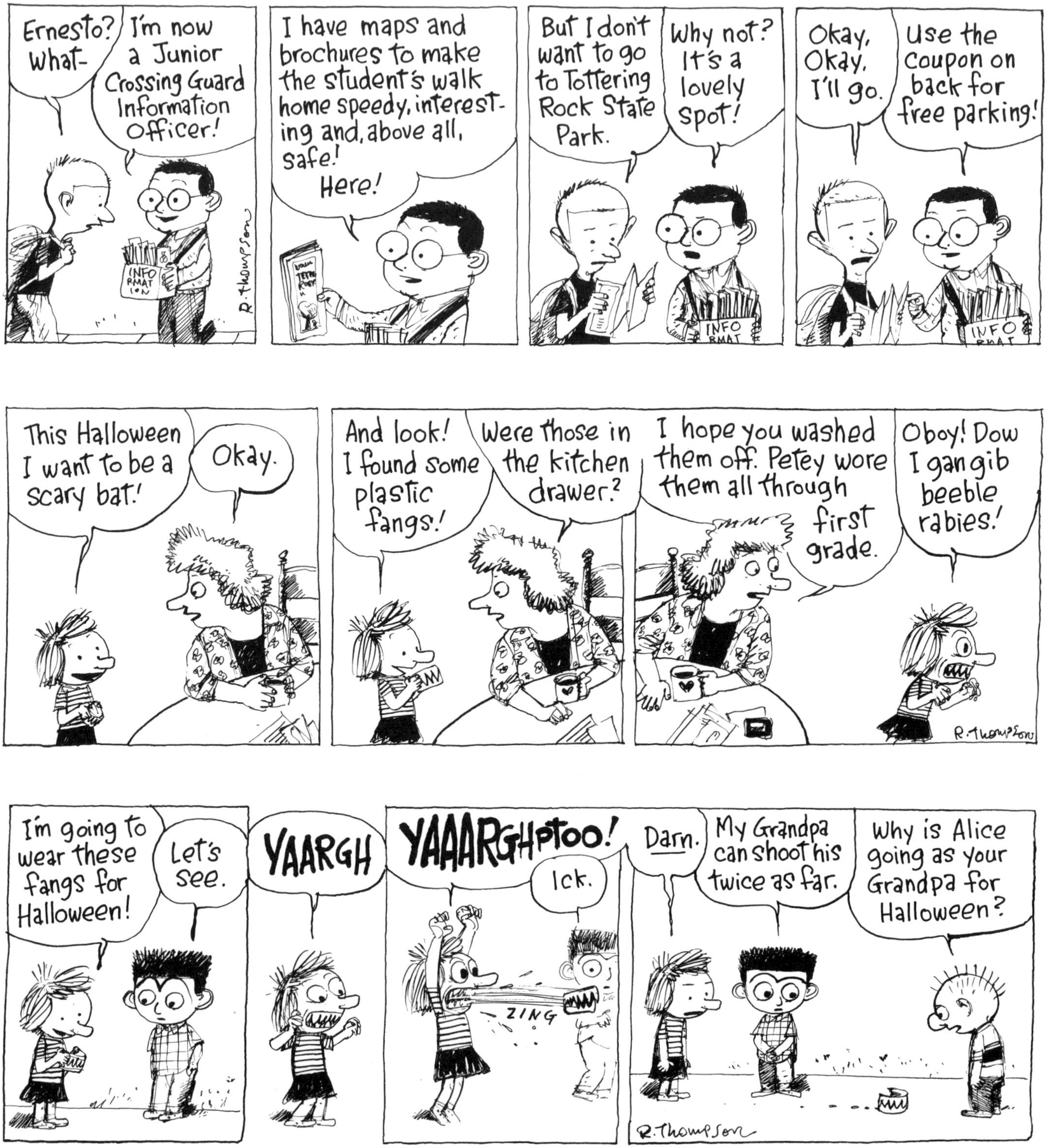
Ernesto? What-
I'm now a Junior Crossing Guard Information Officer!
I have maps and brochures to make the student's walk home speedy, interesting and, above all, safe!
Here!
But I don't want to go to Tottering Rock State Park.
Why not? It's a lovely spot!
Okay, Okay, I'll go.
Use the coupon on back for free parking!
INFO
This Halloween I want to be a scary bat!
Okay.
And look! I found some plastic fangs!
Were those in the kitchen drawer?
I hope you washed them off. Petey wore them all through first grade.
Oboy! Dow I gan gib beeble rabies!
I'm going to wear these fangs for Halloween!
Let's see.
YAARGH
YAAARGHPTOO!
Ick.
ZING
Darn.
My Grandpa can shoot his twice as far.
Why is Alice going as your Grandpa for Halloween?

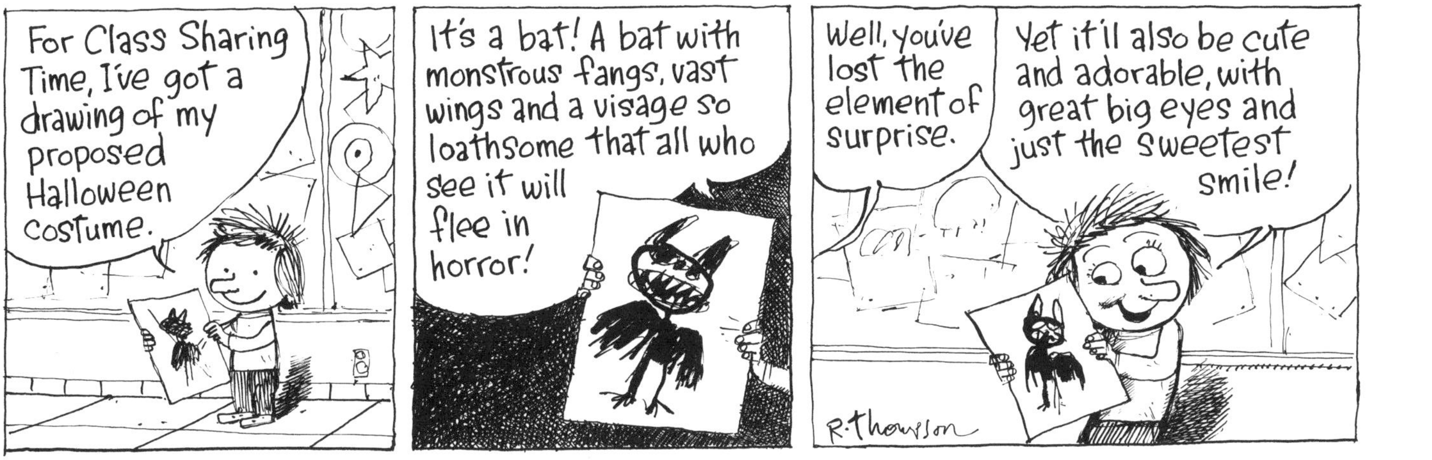
For Class Sharing Time, I've got a drawing of my proposed Halloween costume.
It's a bat! A bat with monstrous fangs, vast wings and a visage so loathsome that all who see it will flee in horror!
Well, you've lost the element of surprise.
Yet it'll also be cute and adorable, with great big eyes and just the sweetest smile!
R. Thompson

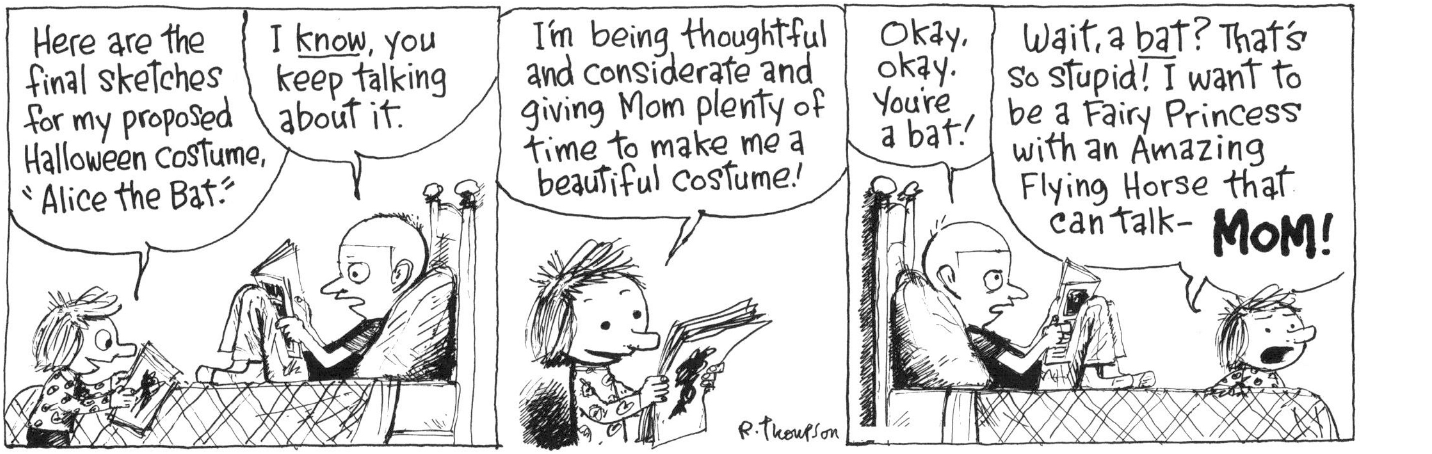
Here are the final sketches for my proposed Halloween costume, "Alice the Bat."
I know, you keep talking about it.
I'm being thoughtful and considerate and giving Mom plenty of time to make me a beautiful costume!
R. Thompson
Okay, okay. You're a bat!
Wait, a bat? That's so stupid! I want to be a Fairy Princess with an Amazing Flying Horse that can talk-
MOM!

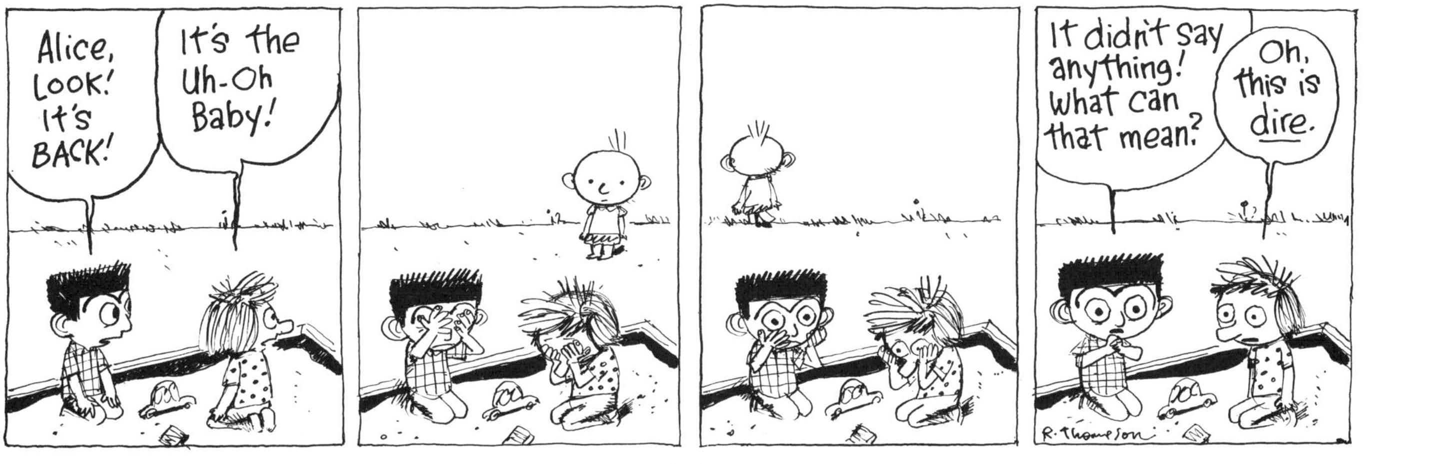
Alice, look! It's BACK!
It's the Uh-Oh Baby!
It didn't say anything! What can that mean?
Oh, this is dire.
R. Thompson

NEIGH! NEIGH!
WOOF WOOF!
VROOOOM NGEOWWW HONK HONK!
CRASH BOOM!
R. Thompson
MOMMY!!!
Did you play yourself into a corner again?
GET ME OUT OF HERE!
Could it be you have too many toys?
Don't even think that.

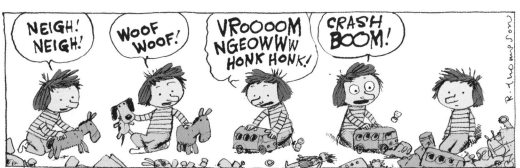

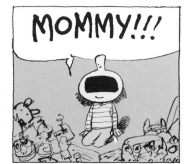

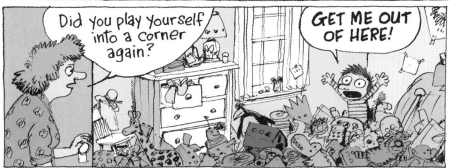

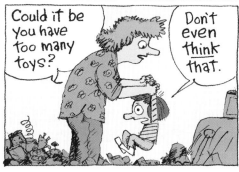

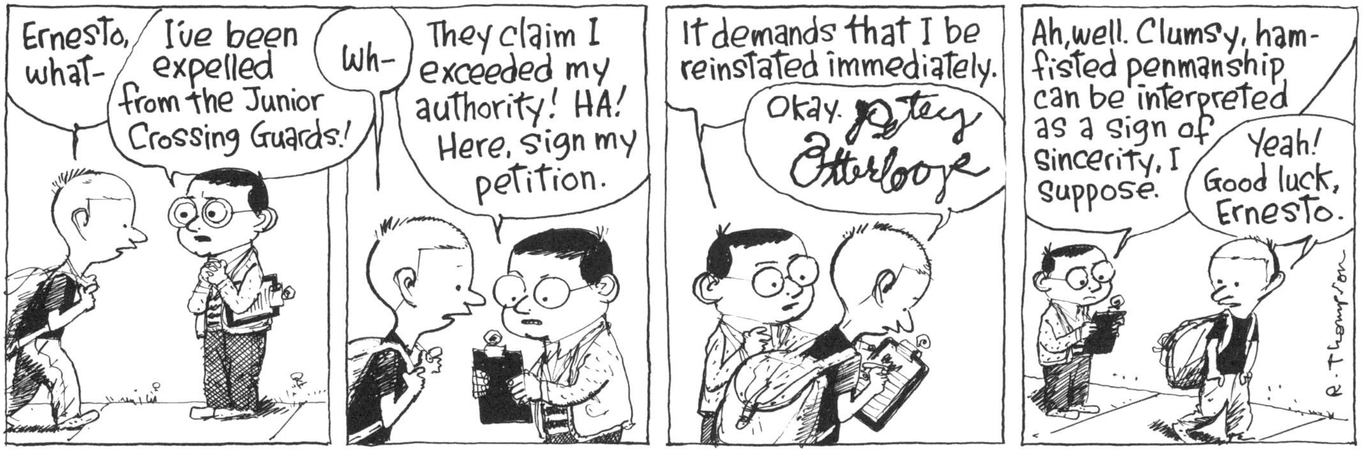
Ernesto, what-
I've been expelled from the Junior Crossing Guards!
Wh-
They claim I exceeded my authority! HA! Here, sign my petition.
It demands that I be reinstated immediately.
Okay. Petey Otterloop
Ah, well. Clumsy, ham-fisted penmanship can be interpreted as a sign of sincerity, I suppose.
Yeah! Good luck, Ernesto.
R. Thompson

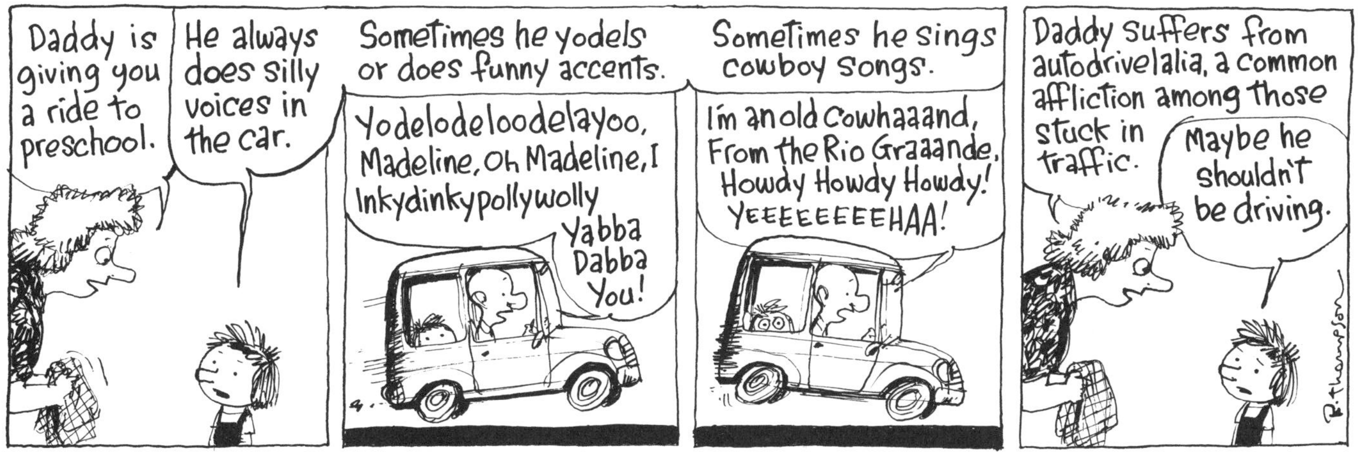
Daddy is giving you a ride to preschool.
He always does silly voices in the car.
Sometimes he yodels or does funny accents.
Yodelodeloodelayoo, Madeline, Oh Madeline, I Inkydinkypollywolly
Yabba Dabba You!
Sometimes he sings cowboy songs.
I'm an old Cowhaaand, From the Rio Graaande, Howdy Howdy Howdy! YEEEEEEEEHAA!
Daddy suffers from autodrivelalia, a common affliction among those stuck in traffic.
Maybe he shouldn't be driving.
R. Thompson

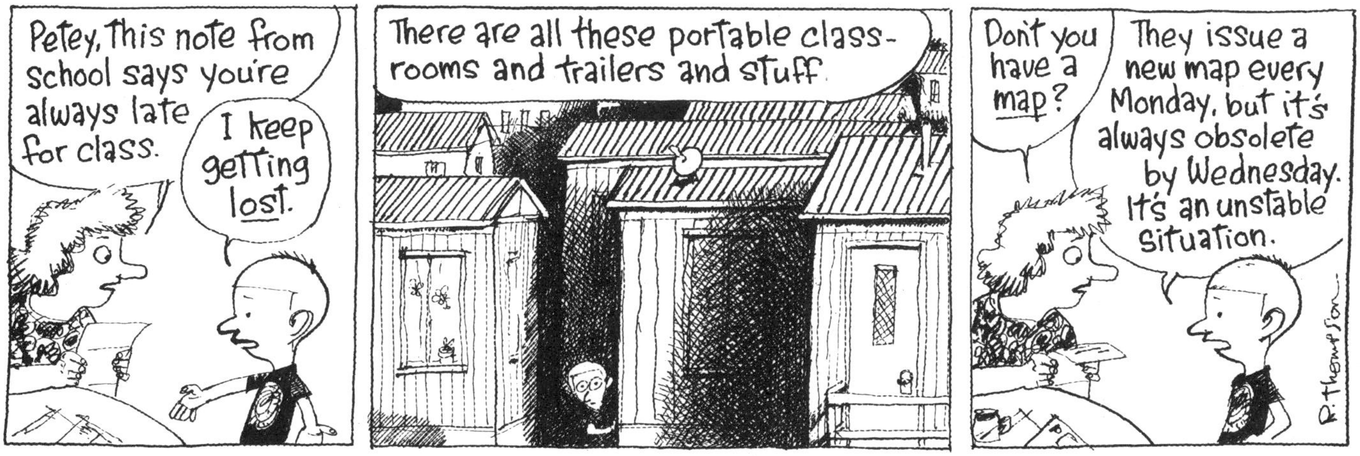
Petey, this note from school says you're always late for class.
I keep getting lost.
There are all these portable class-rooms and trailers and stuff.
Don't you have a map?
They issue a new map every Monday, but it's always obsolete by Wednesday. It's an unstable situation.
R. Thompson

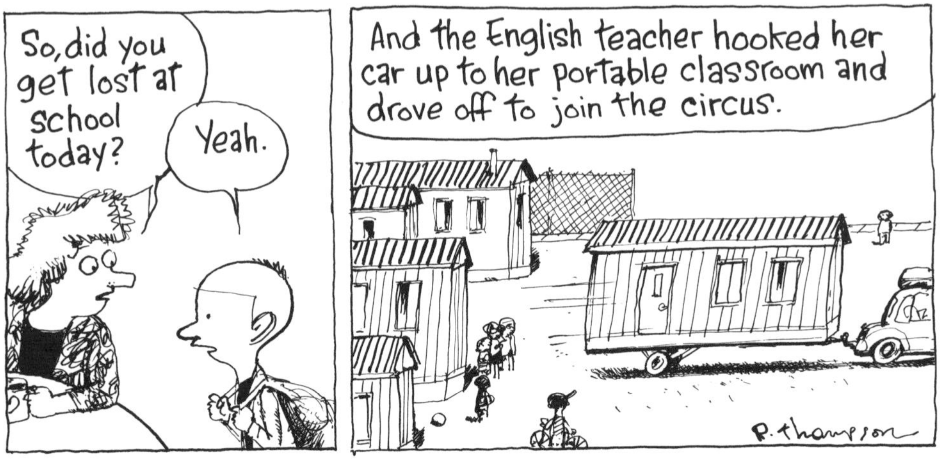
So, did you get lost at school today?
Yeah.
And the English teacher hooked her car up to her portable classroom and drove off to join the circus.
R. thompson
Why did she do that?
Word is the literacy rate among clowns is way down. I'm going to my room to read comic books now.

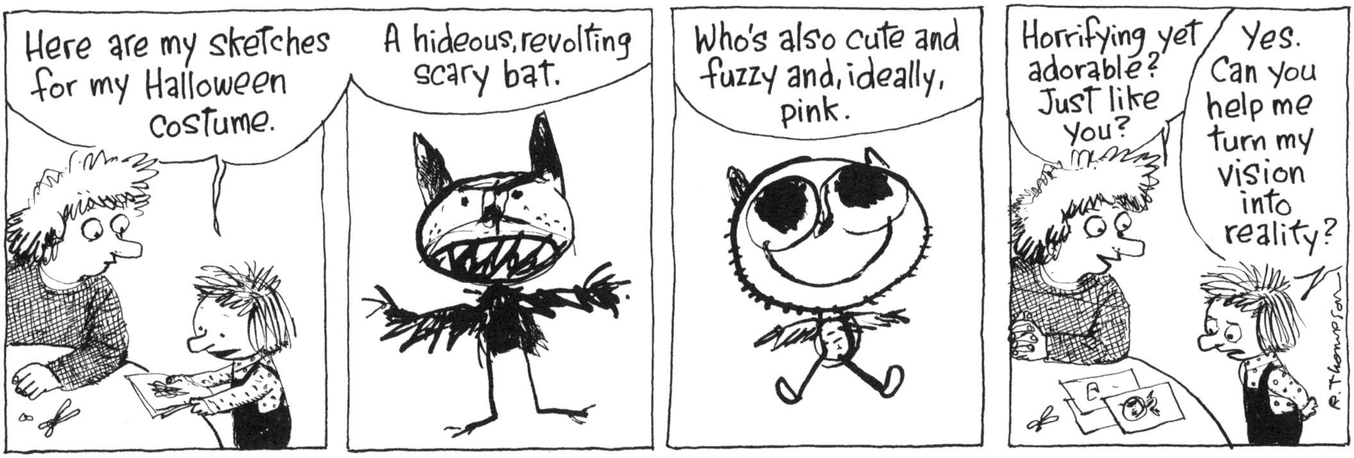
Here are my sketches for my Halloween costume.
A hideous, revolting scary bat.
Who's also cute and fuzzy and, ideally, pink.
Horrifying yet adorable? Just like you?
Yes. Can you help me turn my vision into reality?
R. thompson

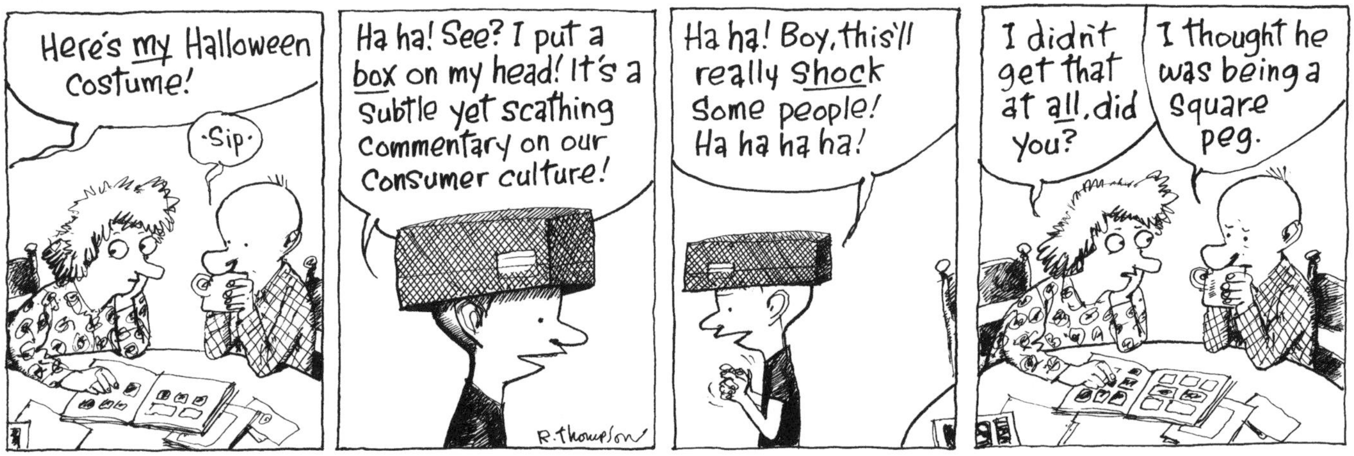
Here's my Halloween costume!
·Sip·
Ha ha! See? I put a box on my head! It's a subtle yet scathing commentary on our consumer culture!
R. thompson
Ha ha! Boy, this'll really shock some people! Ha ha ha ha!
I didn't get that at all, did you?
I thought he was being a square peg.

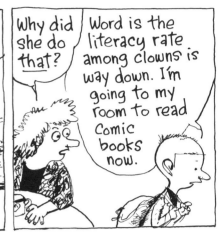

Petey! Dad says 'he'll take us to that superhero movie!

Ugh. No thanks.

But it's from a comic book!

Any translation of a comic book to film is a betrayal of the original's graphic nature.

Film is a <u>passive</u> medium. The story unfolds at a predetermined pace.

The comic book is an <u>active</u> medium.

You choose the pace at which your eye scans the page, pausing to admire a particularly fine panel, a well-chosen onomatopoeia, an intriguing whoopee cushion ad—

What I don't get in movies is when the actors get too close to each other and their eyeballs flicker back and forth while they're talking. Like this—

QUIT!

You'd think they'd get dizzy and throw up.

Like I've been reading this page for three weeks and I'm only half done!

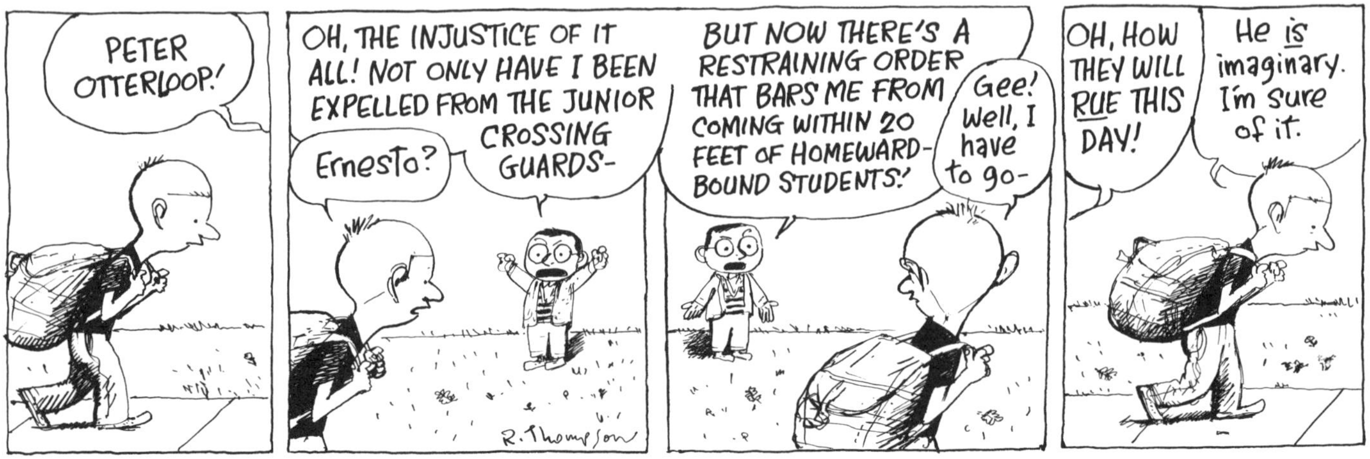
PETER OTTERLOOP!
Ernesto?
OH, THE INJUSTICE OF IT ALL! NOT ONLY HAVE I BEEN EXPELLED FROM THE JUNIOR CROSSING GUARDS-
BUT NOW THERE'S A RESTRAINING ORDER THAT BARS ME FROM COMING WITHIN 20 FEET OF HOMEWARD-BOUND STUDENTS!
Gee! Well, I have to go-
OH, HOW THEY WILL RUE THIS DAY!
He is imaginary. I'm sure of it.

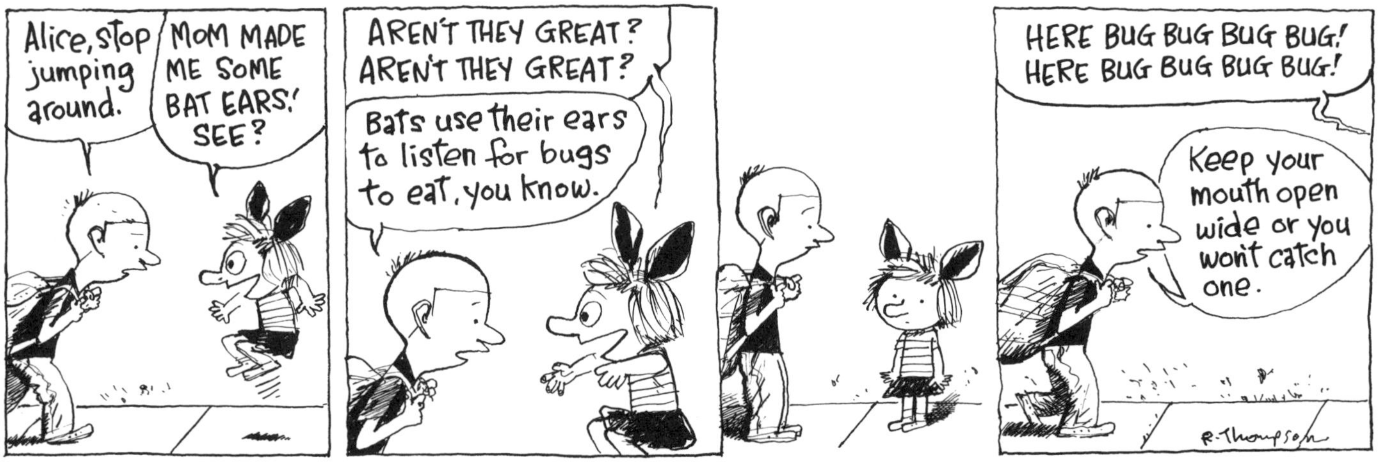
Alice, stop jumping around.
MOM MADE ME SOME BAT EARS! SEE?
AREN'T THEY GREAT? AREN'T THEY GREAT?
Bats use their ears to listen for bugs to eat, you know.
HERE BUG BUG BUG BUG! HERE BUG BUG BUG BUG!
Keep your mouth open wide or you won't catch one.

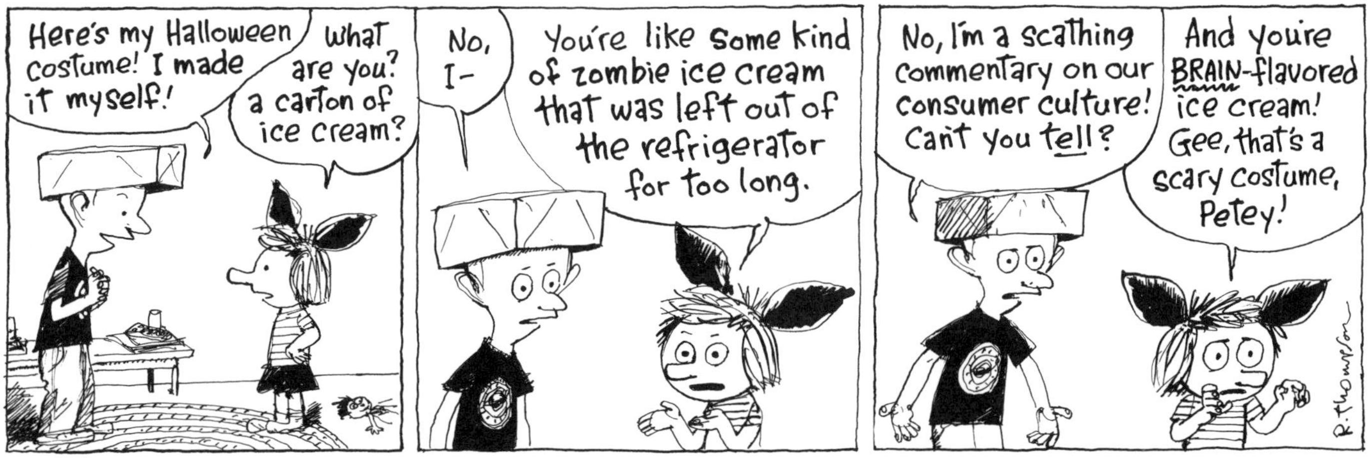
Here's my Halloween costume! I made it myself!
What are you? a carton of ice cream?
No, I-
You're like some kind of zombie ice cream that was left out of the refrigerator for too long.
No, I'm a scathing commentary on our consumer culture! Can't you tell?
And you're BRAIN-flavored ice cream! Gee, that's a scary costume, Petey!

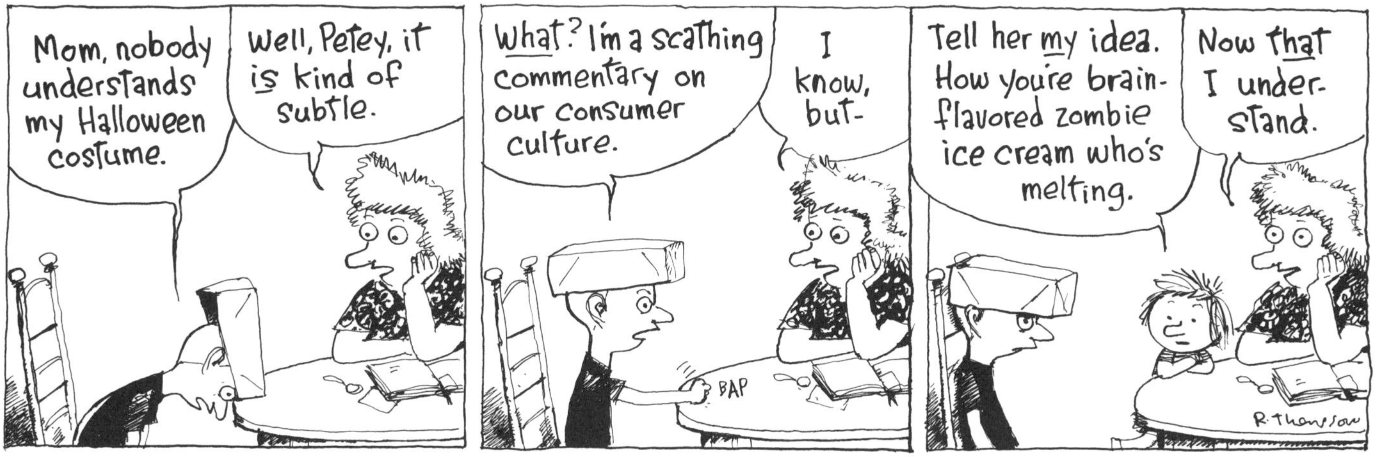
Mom, nobody understands my Halloween costume.
Well, Petey, it is kind of subtle.
What? I'm a scathing commentary on our consumer culture.
I know, but-
BAP
Tell her my idea. How you're brain-flavored zombie ice cream who's melting.
Now that I understand.
R. Thompson

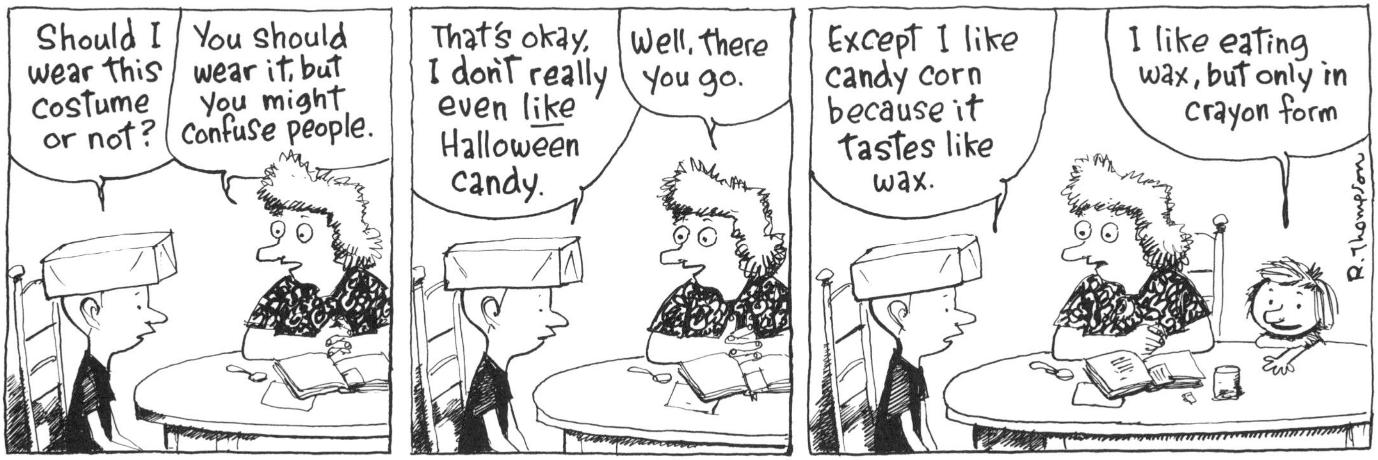
Should I wear this costume or not?
You should wear it, but you might confuse people.
That's okay, I don't really even like Halloween candy.
Well, there you go.
Except I like candy corn because it tastes like wax.
I like eating wax, but only in crayon form
R. Thompson

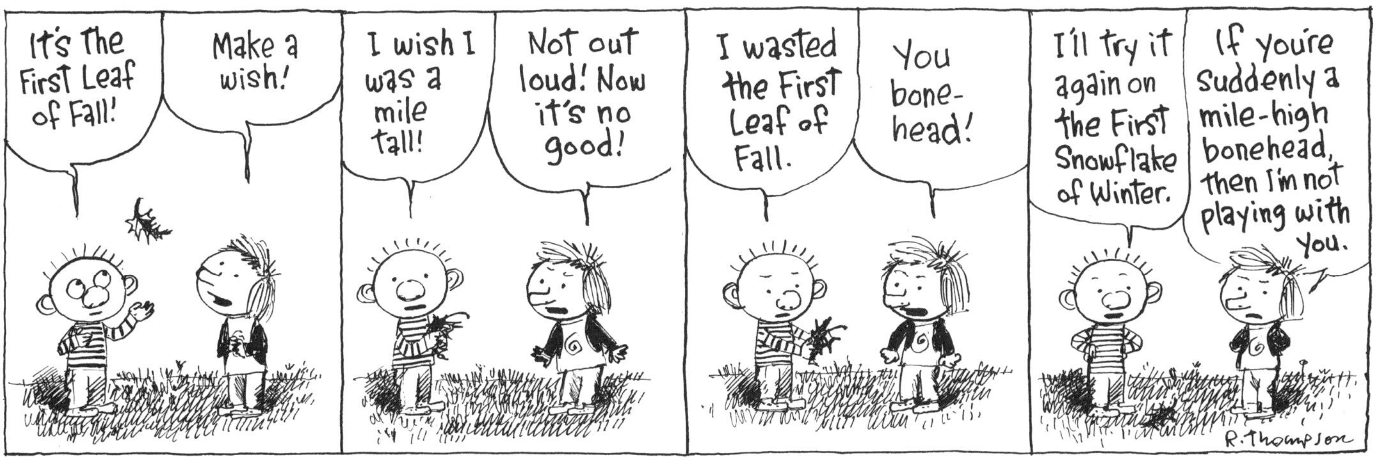
It's the First Leaf of Fall!
Make a wish!
I wish I was a mile tall!
Not out loud! Now it's no good!
I wasted the First Leaf of Fall.
You bone-head!
I'll try it again on the First Snowflake of Winter.
If you're suddenly a mile-high bonehead, then I'm not playing with you.
R. Thompson

Hello, Peter. We keep bumping into each other at these mad little Soirees.
Hi, um, Ernesto.
I've never been to this region of the lunchroom. It's quite remote.
I used to think you were imaginary. Ha-ha!
How many lunches are you eating today?
Just one. This bag is for the bologna sandwich, this one is for the yogurt, this one-
Interesting.
CHOMP CHEW CHEW CHOMP
It's so the food doesn't touch each other...
Well, I'm off to give a brief lecture-demonstration on mummification in ancient Egypt.
Wow! Good luck with that, Ernest-
O.
Petey, there are NO hallucinogens in bologna!
How about yogurt?
R. Thompson

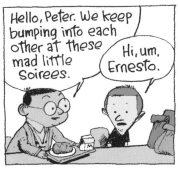

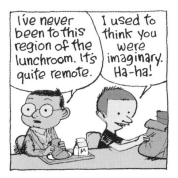

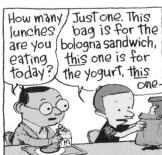

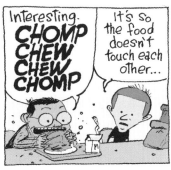

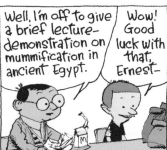

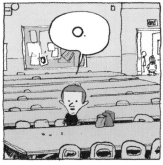

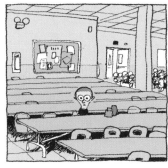

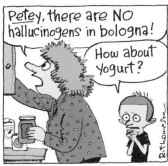

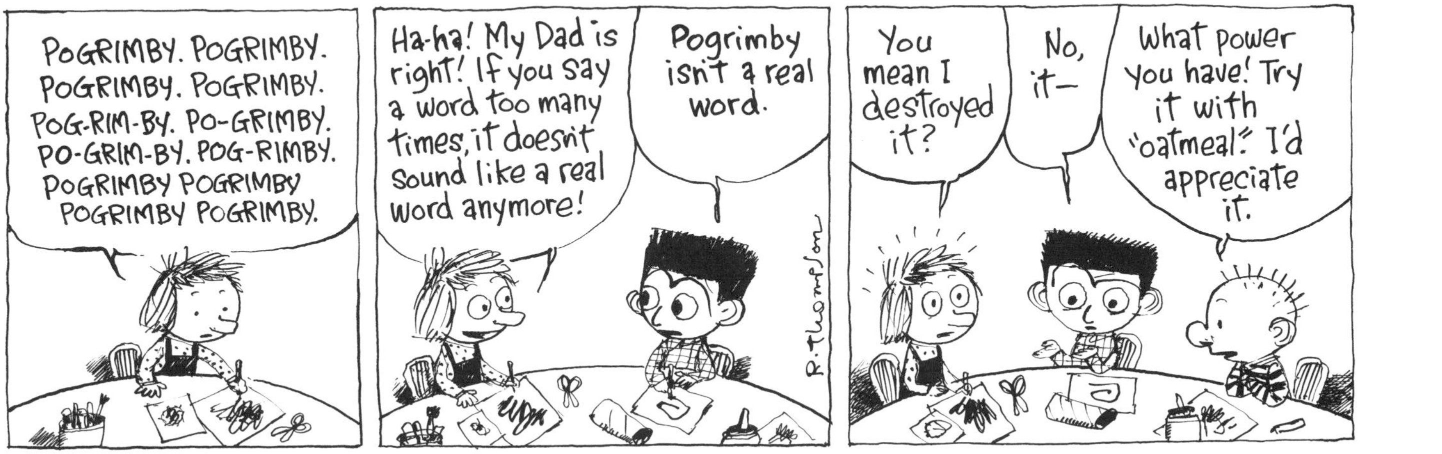
POGRIMBY. POGRIMBY. POGRIMBY. POGRIMBY. POG-RIM-BY. PO-GRIMBY. PO-GRIM-BY. POG-RIMBY. POGRIMBY POGRIMBY POGRIMBY POGRIMBY.
Ha-ha! My Dad is right! If you say a word too many times, it doesn't sound like a real word anymore!
Pogrimby isn't a real word.
You mean I destroyed it?
No, it–
What power you have! Try it with "oatmeal." I'd appreciate it.
R. Thompson

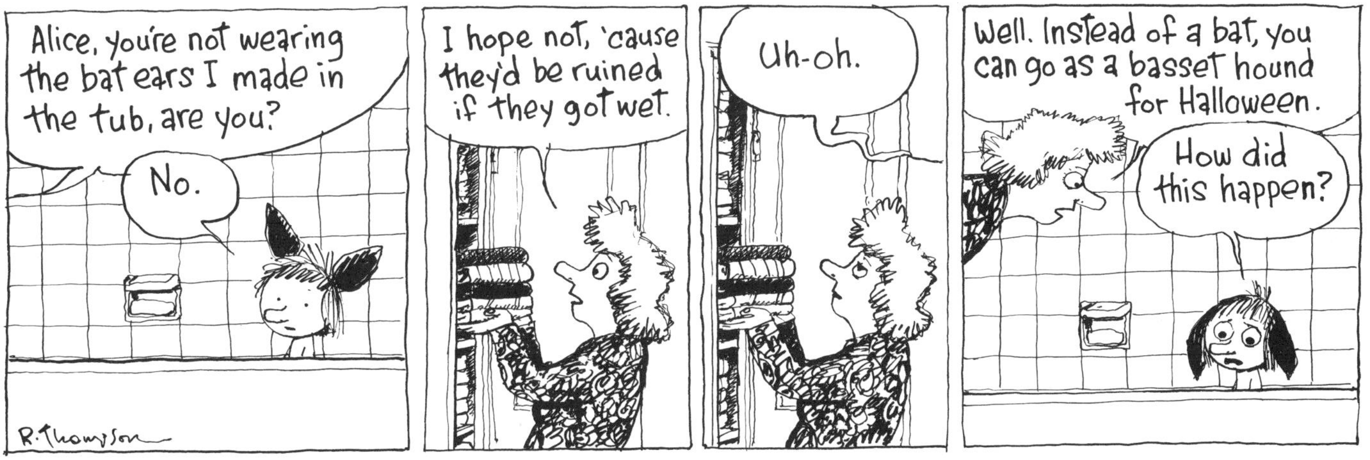
Alice, you're not wearing the bat ears I made in the tub, are you?
No.
R. Thompson
I hope not, 'cause they'd be ruined if they got wet.
Uh-oh.
Well. Instead of a bat, you can go as a basset hound for Halloween.
How did this happen?

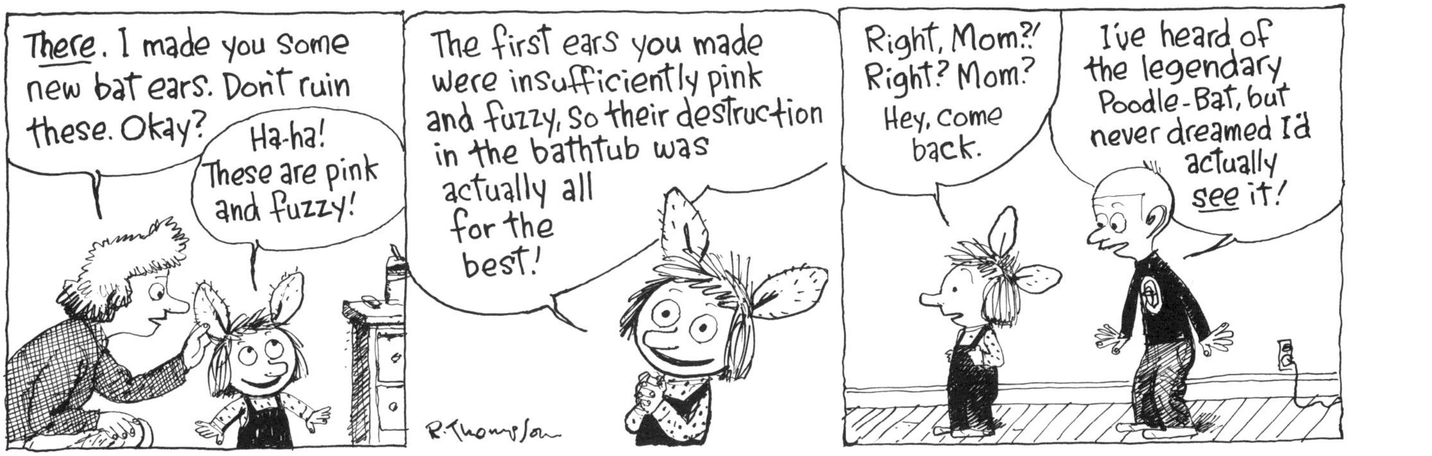
There. I made you some new bat ears. Don't ruin these. Okay?
Ha-ha! These are pink and fuzzy!
The first ears you made were insufficiently pink and fuzzy, so their destruction in the bathtub was actually all for the best!
R. Thompson
Right, Mom?! Right? Mom? Hey, come back.
I've heard of the legendary Poodle-Bat, but never dreamed I'd actually see it!

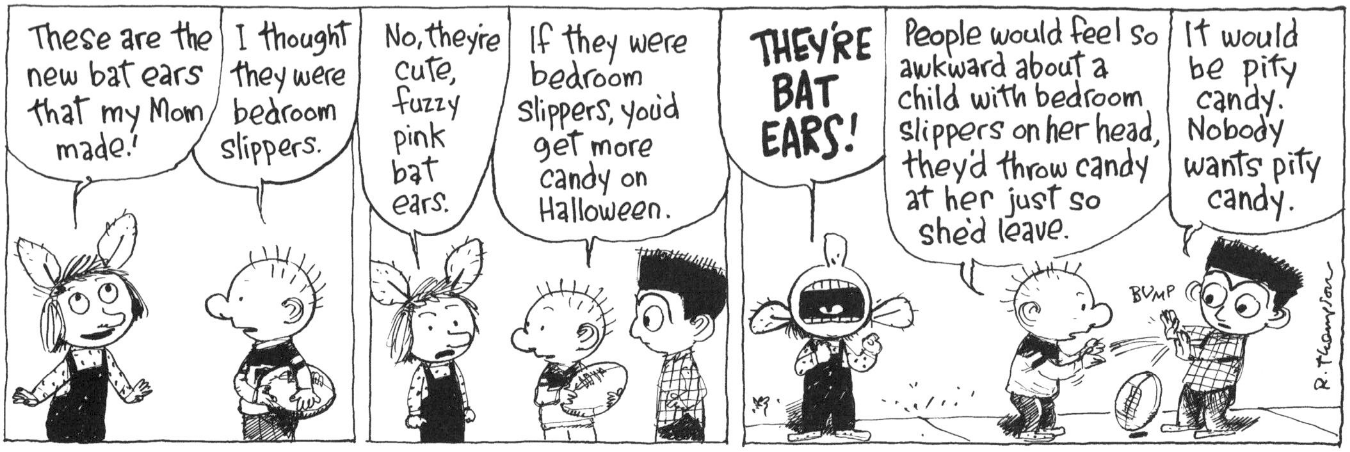
These are the new bat ears that my Mom made!
I thought they were bedroom slippers.
No, they're cute, fuzzy pink bat ears.
If they were bedroom slippers, you'd get more candy on Halloween.
THEY'RE BAT EARS!
People would feel so awkward about a child with bedroom slippers on her head, they'd throw candy at her just so she'd leave.
It would be pity candy. Nobody wants pity candy.
BUMP
R. Thompson

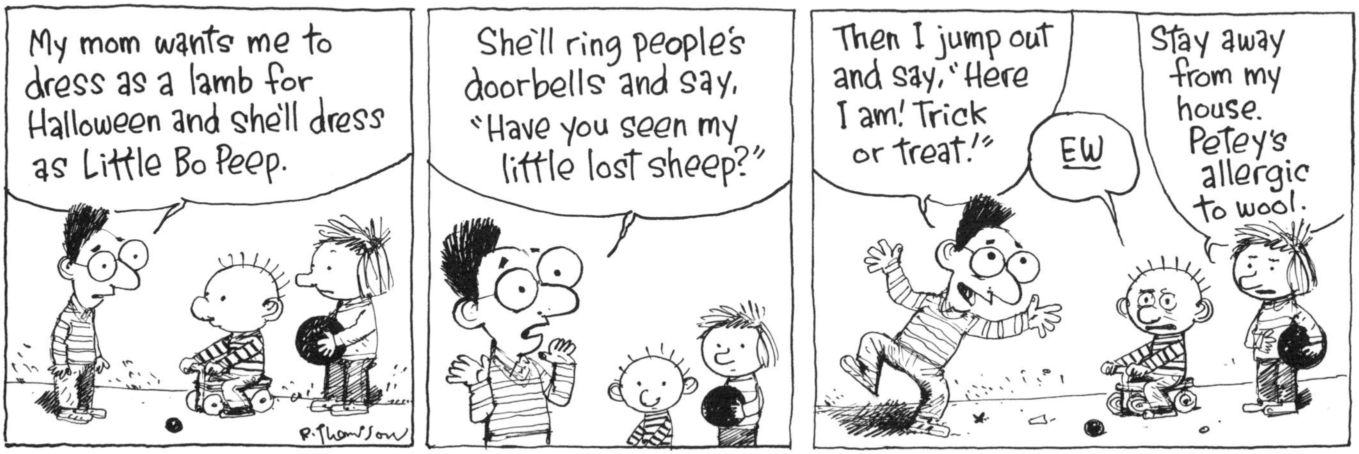
My mom wants me to dress as a lamb for Halloween and she'll dress as Little Bo Peep.
R. Thompson
She'll ring people's doorbells and say, "Have you seen my little lost sheep?"
Then I jump out and say, "Here I am! Trick or treat!"
EW
Stay away from my house. Petey's allergic to wool.

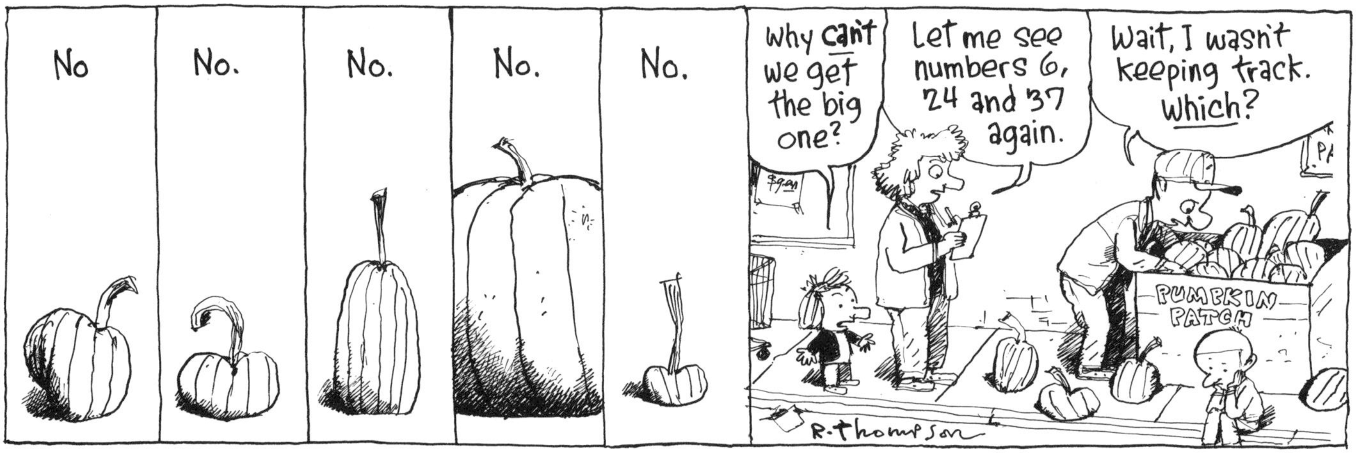
No
No.
No.
No.
No.
Why can't we get the big one?
Let me see numbers 6, 24 and 37 again.
Wait, I wasn't keeping track. Which?
PUMPKIN PATCH
R. Thompson

I'm tired. Where's Daddy?

He's down the block.

My feet hurt.

He's hiding behind a tree.

My bag's full. I want to go home.

He's going to jump out and scare us.

BOO!

AAGHK!

R. Thompson

YIKES.

UGHF

ALICE!

OW OW OW!

Well, jeez, I told her.

Daddy's outside trying to find all your candy. He's very, very sorry.

He should be. Look at the state I'm in. Tell him to leave the nougats.

All I got were nougats. How'd that happen?

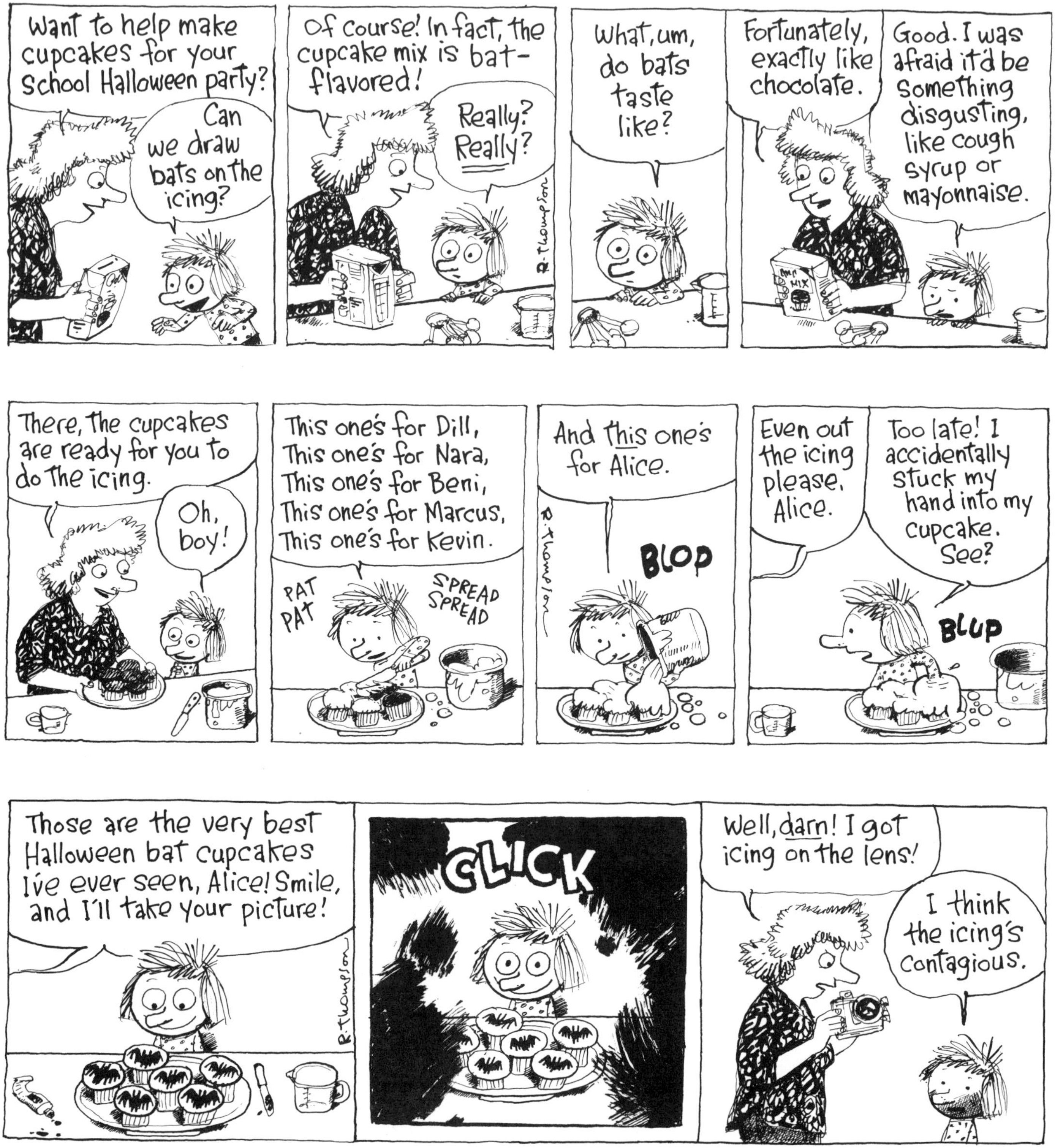
Want to help make cupcakes for your School Halloween party?
Can we draw bats on the icing?
Of course! In fact, the cupcake mix is bat-flavored!
Really? Really?
R. Thompson
What, um, do bats taste like?
Fortunately, exactly like chocolate.
Good. I was afraid it'd be something disgusting, like cough syrup or mayonnaise.
There, the cupcakes are ready for you to do the icing.
Oh, boy!
This one's for Dill, This one's for Nara, This one's for Beni, This one's for Marcus, This one's for Kevin.
PAT PAT
SPREAD SPREAD
R. Thompson
And this one's for Alice.
BLOP
Even out the icing please, Alice.
Too late! I accidentally stuck my hand into my cupcake. See?
BLUP
Those are the very best Halloween bat cupcakes I've ever seen, Alice! Smile, and I'll take your picture!
R. Thompson
CLICK
Well, darn! I got icing on the lens!
I think the icing's contagious.

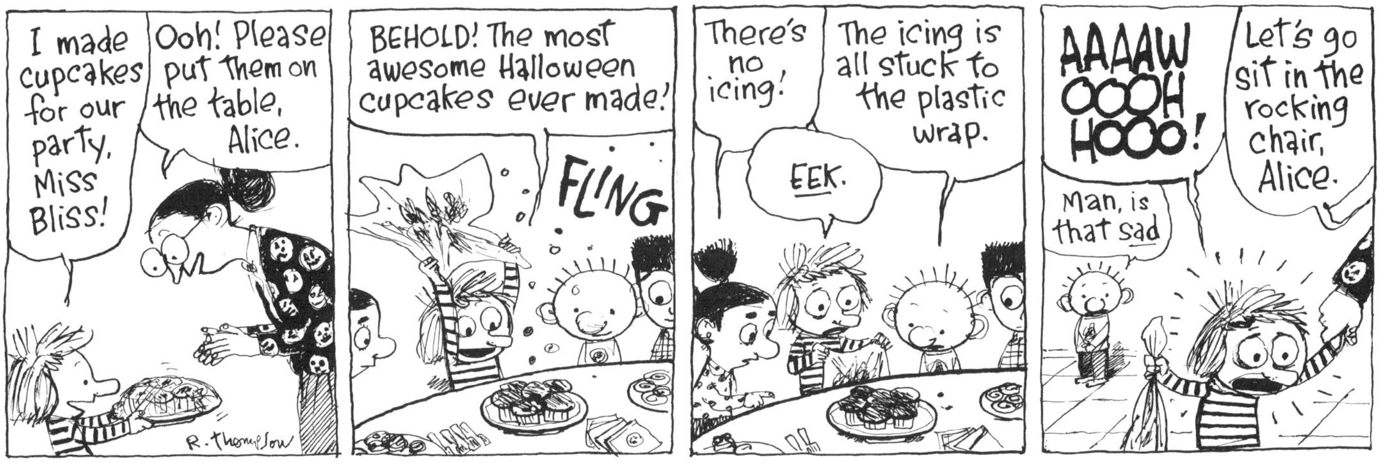
I made cupcakes for our party, Miss Bliss!
Ooh! Please put them on the table, Alice.
R. Thompson
BEHOLD! The most awesome Halloween cupcakes ever made!
FLING
There's no icing!
The icing is all stuck to the plastic wrap.
EEK.
AAAAW OOOH HOOO!
Let's go sit in the rocking chair, Alice.
Man, is that sad

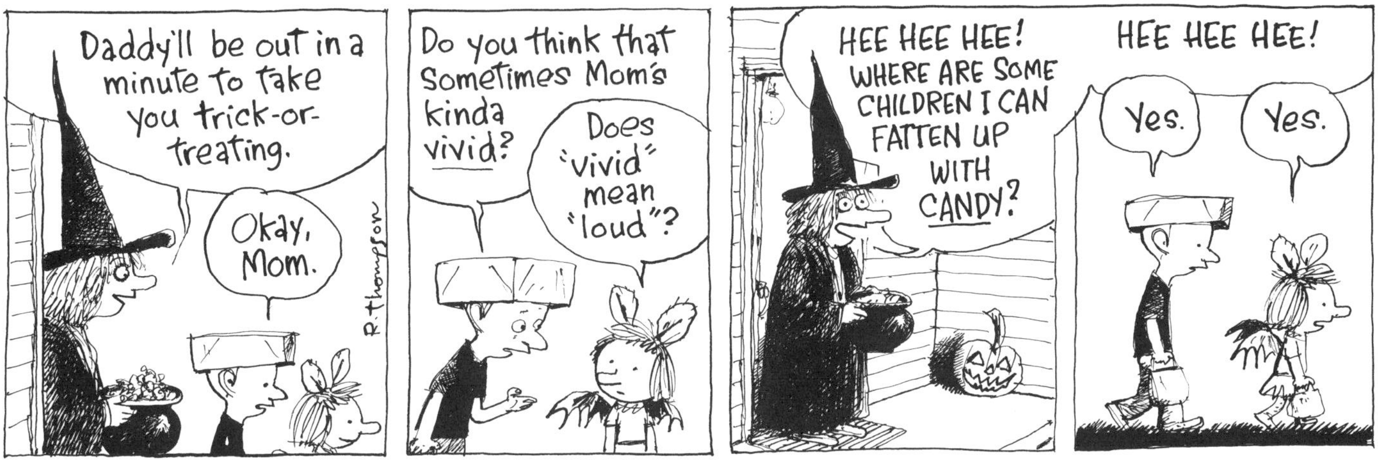
Daddy'll be out in a minute to take you trick-or-treating.
Okay, Mom.
R. Thompson
Do you think that sometimes Mom's kinda vivid?
Does "vivid" mean "loud"?
HEE HEE HEE! WHERE ARE SOME CHILDREN I CAN FATTEN UP WITH CANDY?
HEE HEE HEE!
Yes.
Yes.

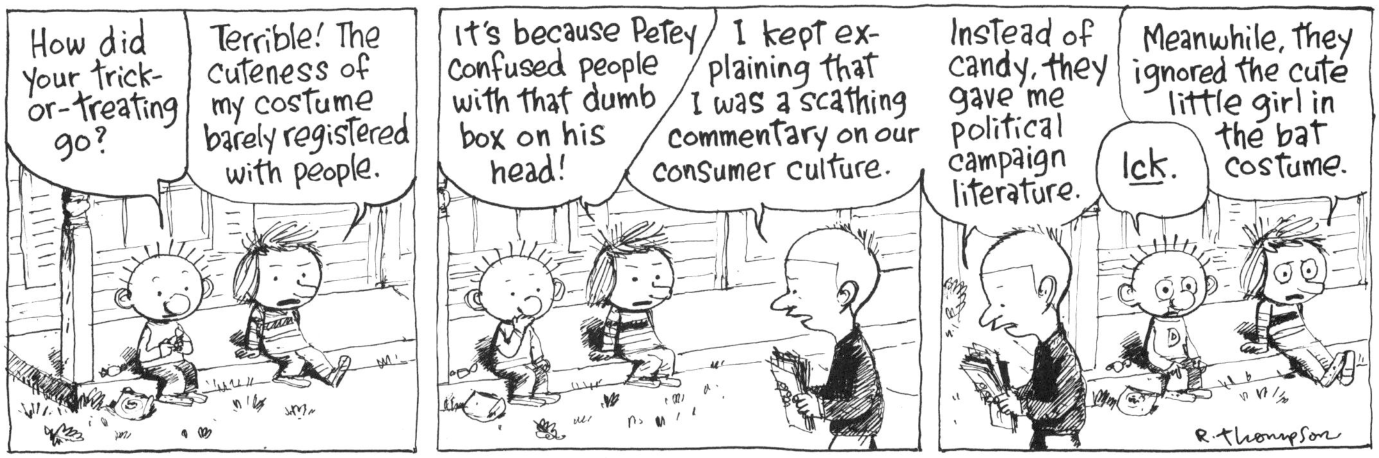
How did your trick-or-treating go?
Terrible! The cuteness of my costume barely registered with people.
It's because Petey confused people with that dumb box on his head!
I kept explaining that I was a scathing commentary on our consumer culture.
Instead of candy, they gave me political campaign literature.
Meanwhile, they ignored the cute little girl in the bat costume.
Ick.
R. Thompson

See, Alice, in the fall, Mother Nature goes from tree to tree and blasts every one of them with her Magic Bazooka.
KABLAM! The leaves are so stunned they change color then fall off.
Oh.
Who's Mother Nature?
She's like the Tooth Fairy, but with a wider range of interests.
KABLAM
R. Thompson

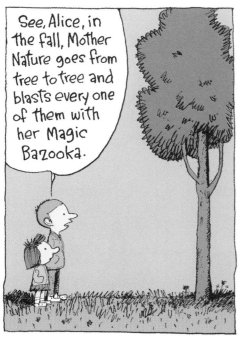

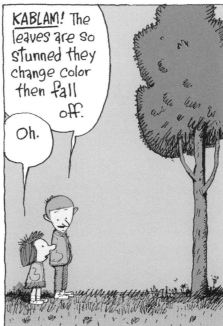

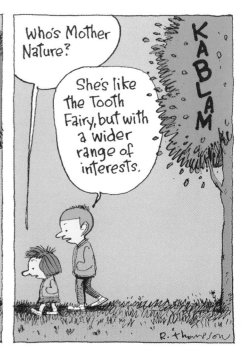

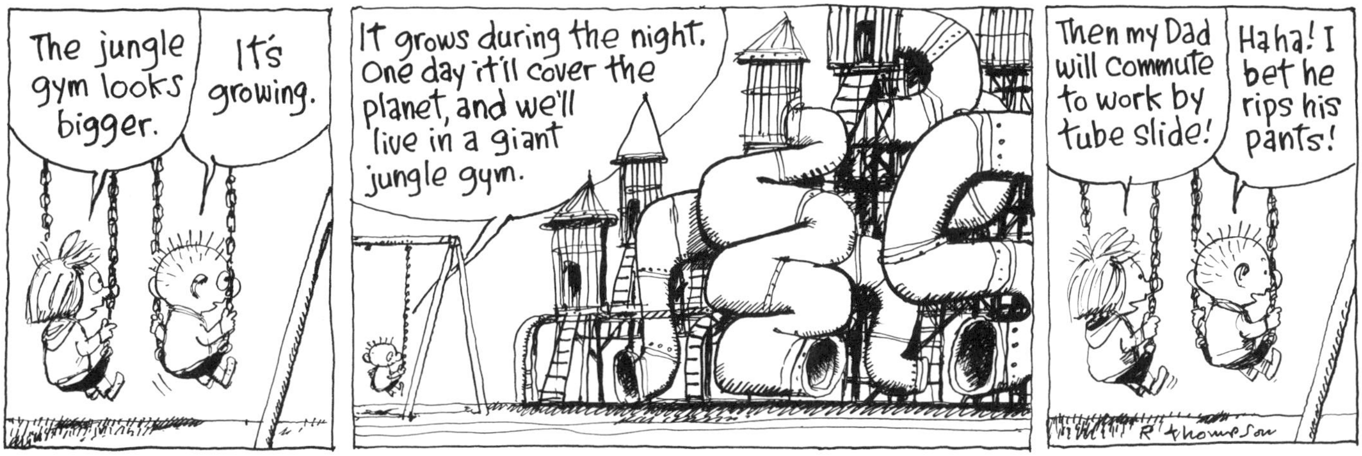
The jungle gym looks bigger.
It's growing.
It grows during the night. One day it'll cover the planet, and we'll live in a giant jungle gym.
Then my Dad will commute to work by tube slide!
Haha! I bet he rips his pants!

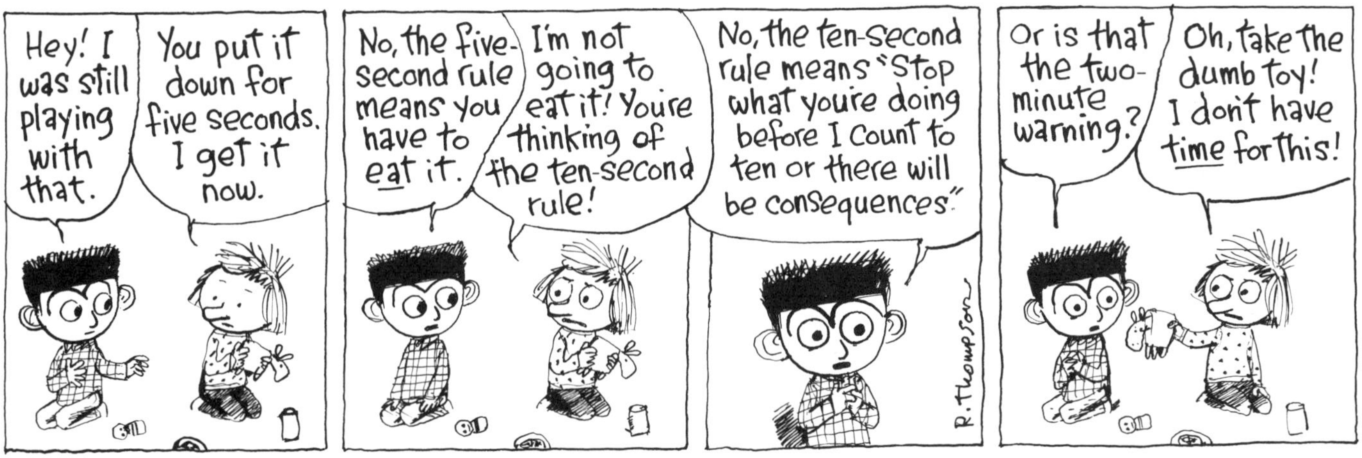
Hey! I was still playing with that.
You put it down for five seconds. I get it now.
No, the five-second rule means you have to eat it.
I'm not going to eat it! You're thinking of the ten-second rule!
No, the ten-second rule means "Stop what you're doing before I count to ten or there will be consequences."
Or is that the two-minute warning?
Oh, take the dumb toy! I don't have time for this!

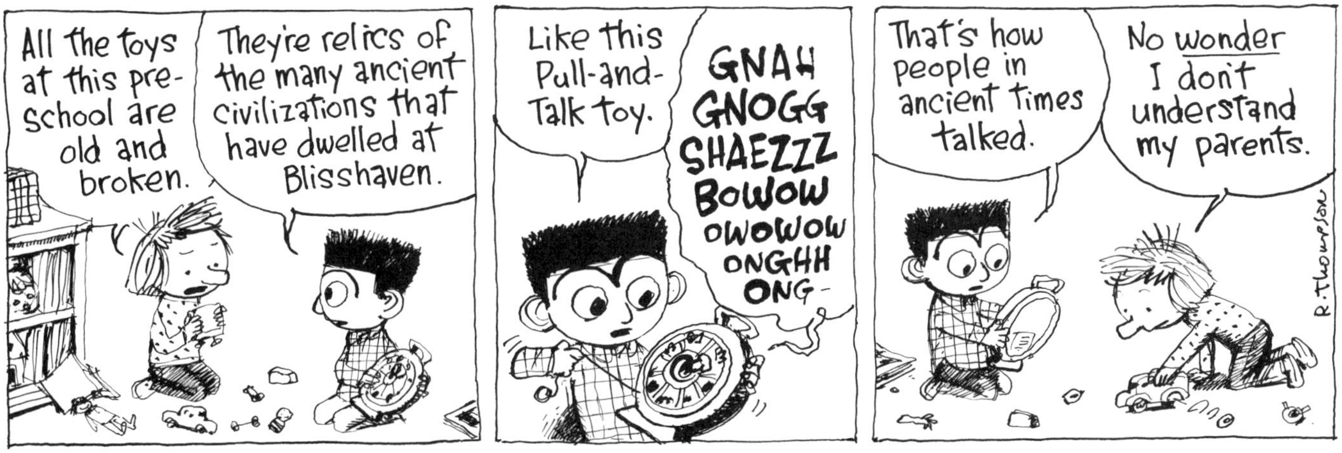
All the toys at this pre-school are old and broken.
They're relics of the many ancient civilizations that have dwelled at Blisshaven.
Like this Pull-and-Talk toy.
GNAH GNOGG SHAEZZZ BOWOW OWOWOW ONGHH ONG-
That's how people in ancient times talked.
No wonder I don't understand my parents.

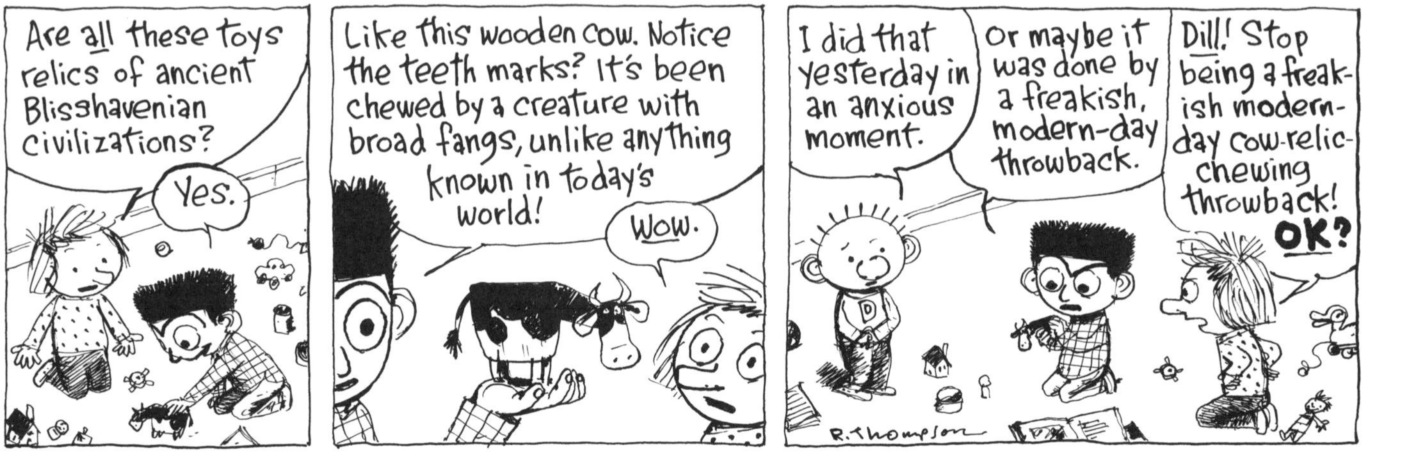
Are all these toys relics of ancient Blisshavenian civilizations?
Yes.
Like this wooden cow. Notice the teeth marks? It's been chewed by a creature with broad fangs, unlike anything known in today's world!
Wow.
I did that yesterday in an anxious moment.
Or maybe it was done by a freakish, modern-day throwback.
Dill! Stop being a freakish modern-day cow-relic-chewing throwback! OK?
R. Thompson

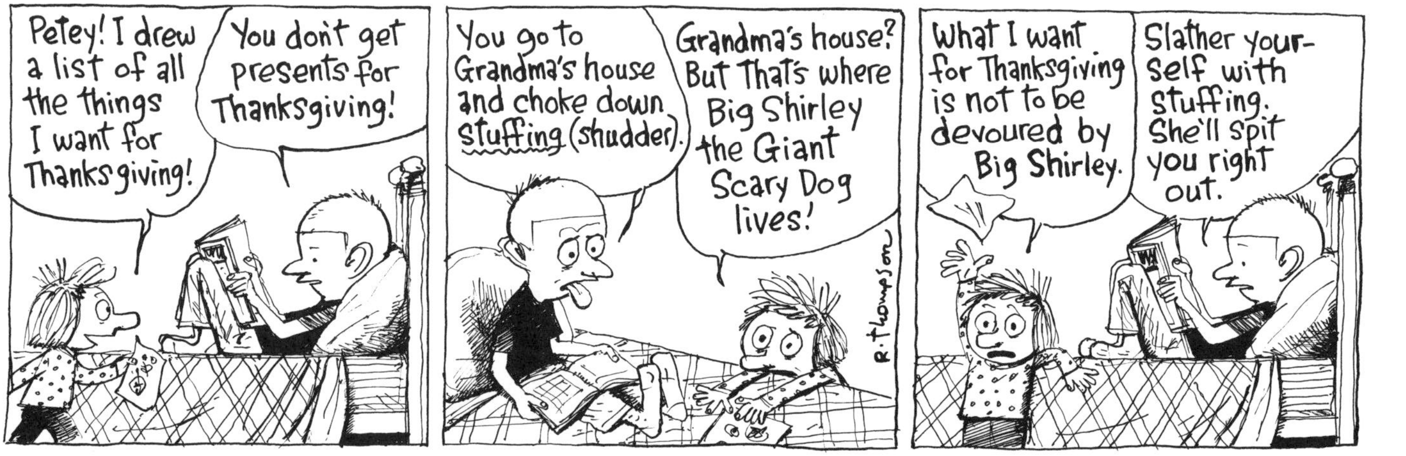
Petey! I drew a list of all the things I want for Thanksgiving!
You don't get presents for Thanksgiving!
You go to Grandma's house and choke down stuffing (shudder).
Grandma's house? But that's where Big Shirley the Giant Scary Dog lives!
R. Thompson
What I want for Thanksgiving is not to be devoured by Big Shirley.
Slather yourself with stuffing. She'll spit you right out.

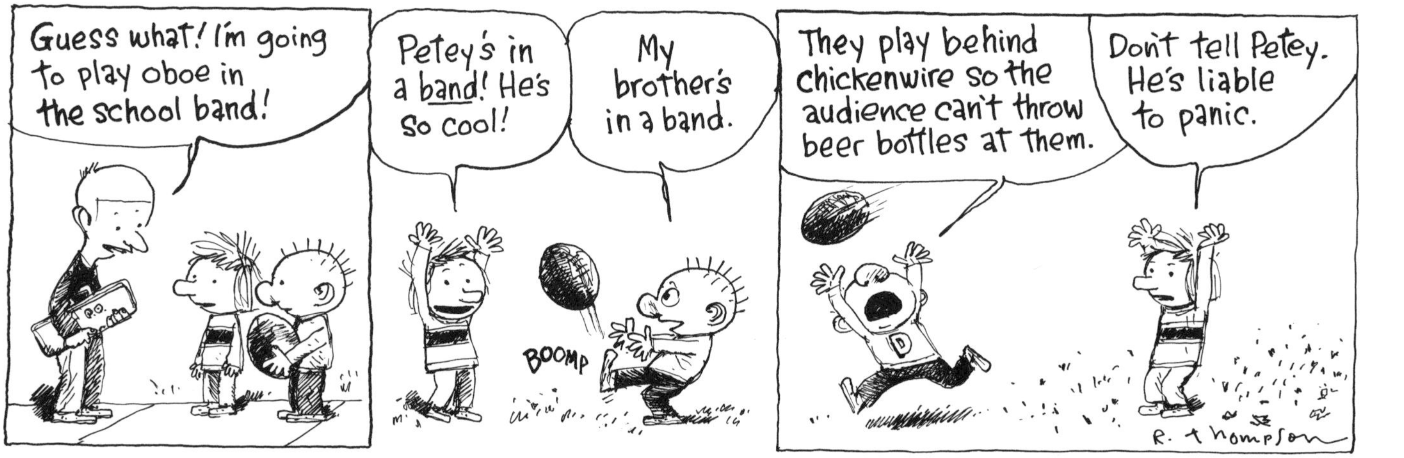
Guess what! I'm going to play oboe in the school band!
Petey's in a band! He's so cool!
My brother's in a band.
BOOMP
They play behind chickenwire so the audience can't throw beer bottles at them.
Don't tell Petey. He's liable to panic.
R. Thompson

My Mom's been scrapbooking everything I do. It's starting to get to me.

What's scrapbooking, Marcus?

She glues every little doodle I make onto archival paper, adds some decorations around it, then puts it in a big scrapbook.

She finishes a book every week. And each one has my name on it in big letters. We're up to MARCUS, VOLUME 23.

Lately the awful pressure to produce quality scrapbook-worthy work is making me a nervous wreck. Like this—

It's supposed to be a drawing of a dog eating pancakes and look. It doesn't remotely resemble a dog eating pancakes! What'll I do?

R. Thompson

This can't go into Marcus Volume 23!

Change the title to "Monkey Spinning Plates."

Oh, get a grip, man! It's almost recess!

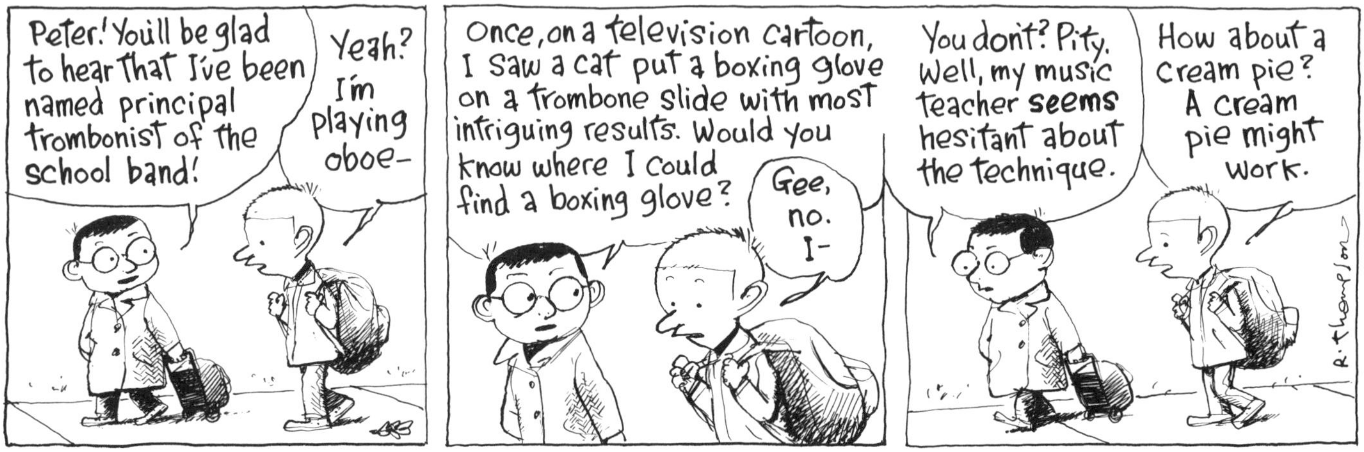
Peter! You'll be glad to hear that I've been named principal trombonist of the school band!
Yeah? I'm playing oboe-
Once, on a television cartoon, I saw a cat put a boxing glove on a trombone slide with most intriguing results. Would you know where I could find a boxing glove?
Gee, no. I-
You don't? Pity. Well, my music teacher **seems** hesitant about the technique.
How about a cream pie? A cream pie might work.
R. Thompson

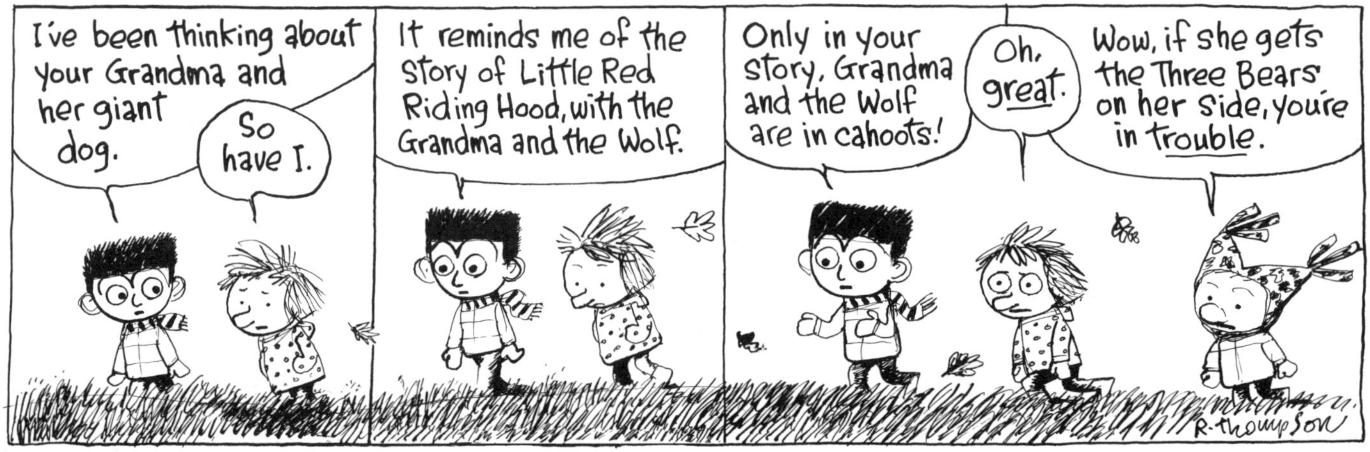
I've been thinking about your Grandma and her giant dog.
So have I.
It reminds me of the story of Little Red Riding Hood, with the Grandma and the Wolf.
Only in your story, Grandma and the Wolf are in cahoots!
Oh, great.
Wow, if she gets the Three Bears on her side, you're in trouble.
R. Thompson

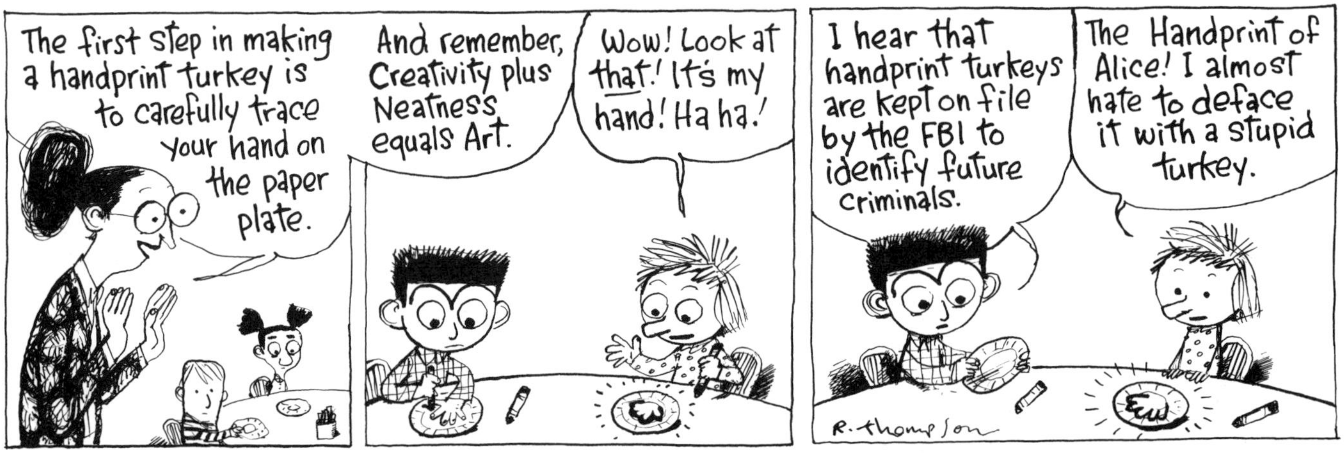
The first step in making a handprint turkey is to carefully trace your hand on the paper plate.
And remember, Creativity plus Neatness equals Art.
Wow! Look at that! It's my hand! Ha ha!
I hear that handprint turkeys are kept on file by the FBI to identify future criminals.
The Handprint of Alice! I almost hate to deface it with a stupid turkey.
R. Thompson

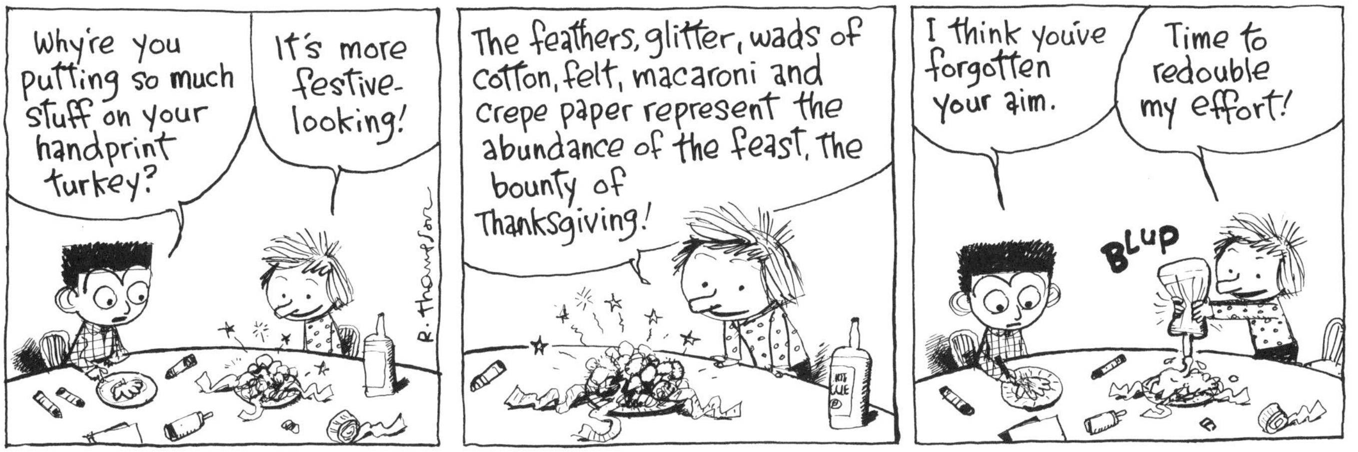
Why're you putting so much stuff on your handprint turkey?
It's more festive-looking!
The feathers, glitter, wads of cotton, felt, macaroni and crepe paper represent the abundance of the feast, the bounty of Thanksgiving!
I think you've forgotten your aim.
Time to redouble my effort!
BLUP

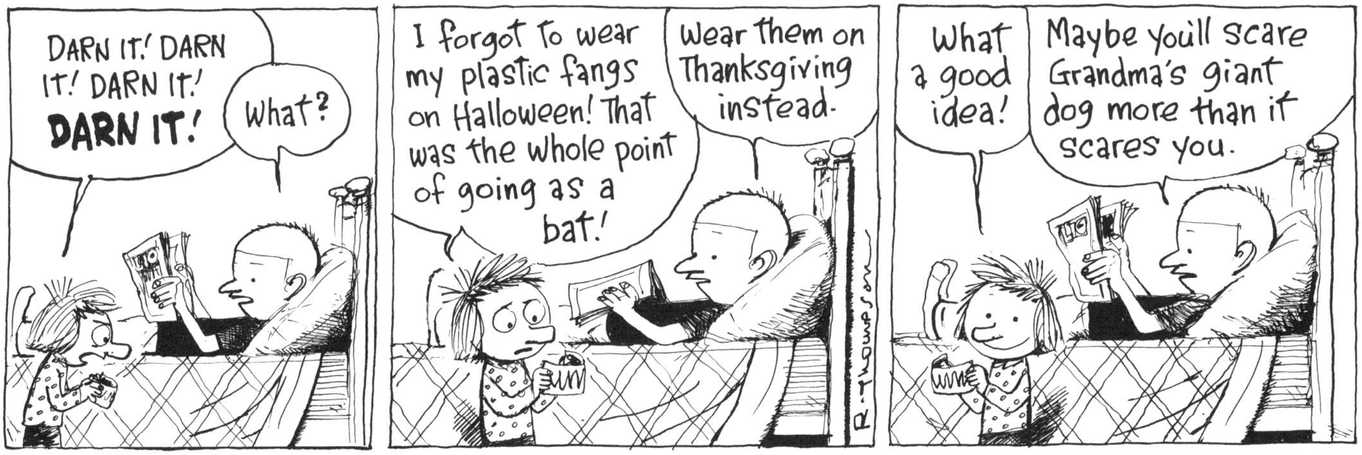
DARN IT! DARN IT! DARN IT! DARN IT!
What?
I forgot to wear my plastic fangs on Halloween! That was the whole point of going as a bat!
Wear them on Thanksgiving instead.
What a good idea!
Maybe you'll scare Grandma's giant dog more than it scares you.

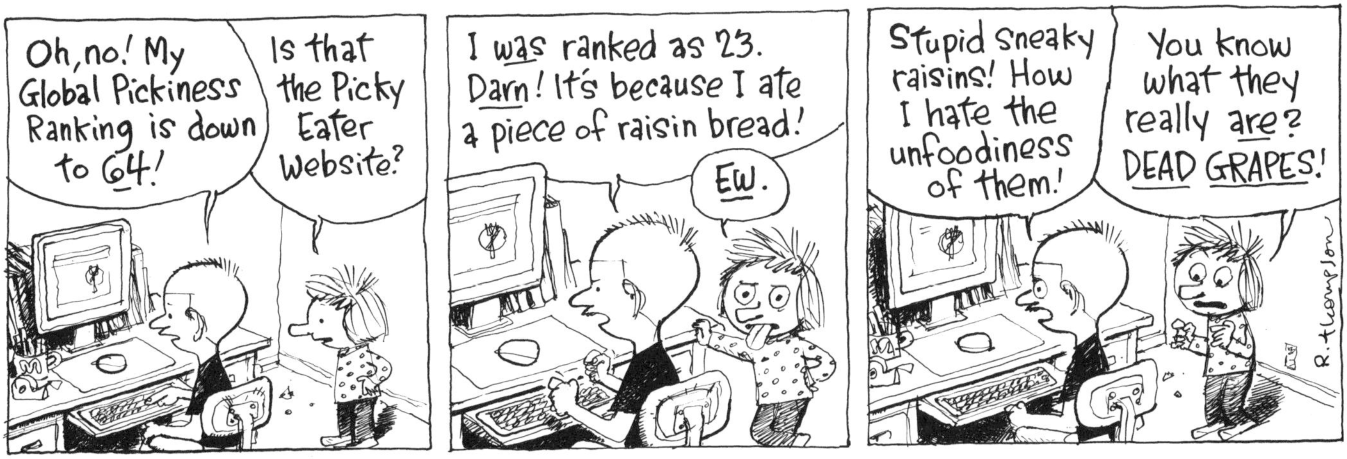
Oh, no! My Global Pickiness Ranking is down to 64!
Is that the Picky Eater Website?
I was ranked as 23. Darn! It's because I ate a piece of raisin bread!
EW.
Stupid sneaky raisins! How I hate the unfoodiness of them!
You know what they really are? DEAD GRAPES!

Mom turned off the TV and sent me outside to romp in the leaf pile.
There it is!
That's it?
We don't have many trees. Sorry.
What?
What are you doing?
I'm romping in the leaf pile!
Ah.
Mom sent me out to romp in the leaf pile.
You're too late. It's all gone.
Good. I hate romping.
My whole day, wasted.
Who knew that romping could have such an environmental impact?
R. Thompson

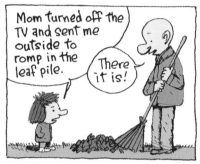

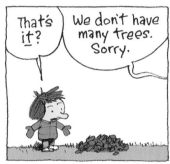

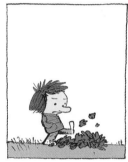

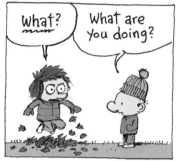

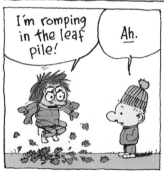

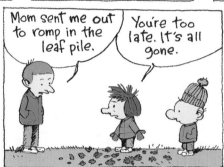

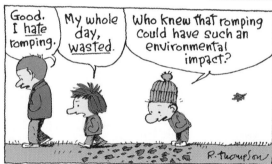

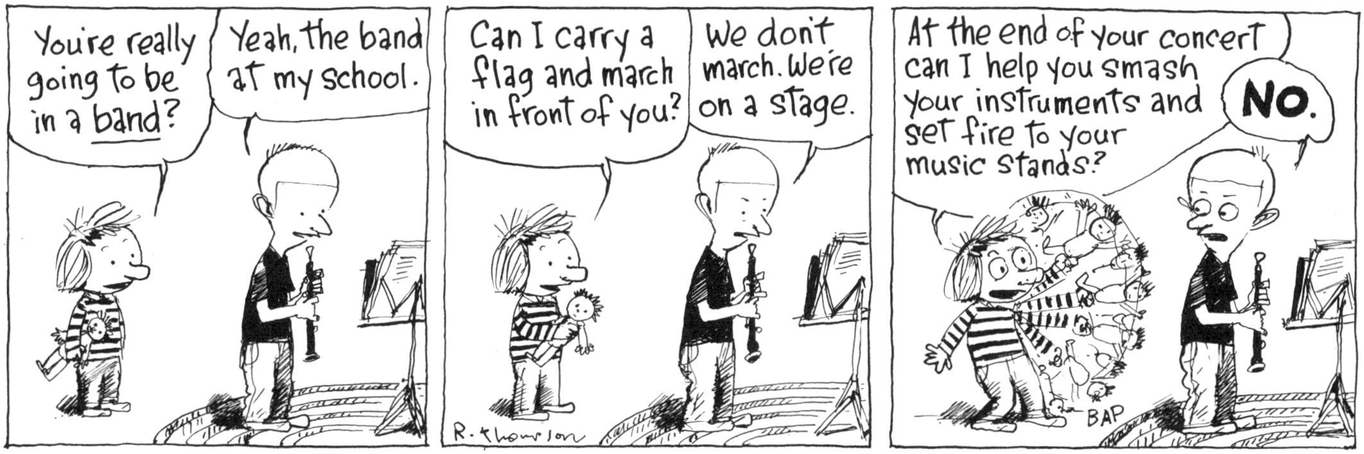
You're really going to be in a band?
Yeah, the band at my school.
Can I carry a flag and march in front of you?
We don't march. We're on a stage.
R. Thompson
At the end of your concert can I help you smash your instruments and set fire to your music stands?
NO.
BAP

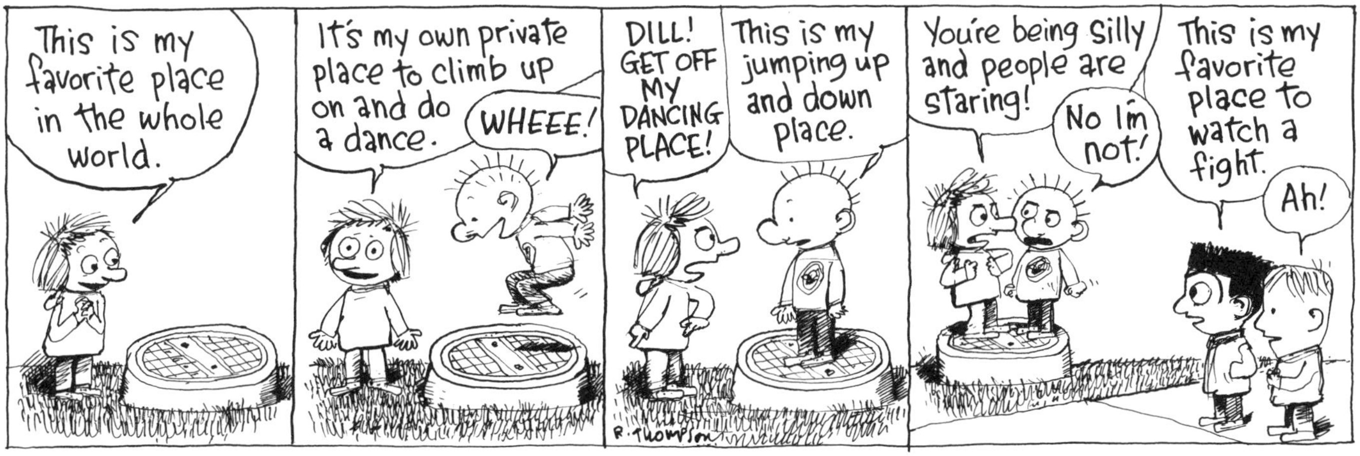
This is my favorite place in the whole world.
It's my own private place to climb up on and do a dance.
WHEEE!
DILL! GET OFF MY DANCING PLACE!
This is my jumping up and down place.
R. Thompson
You're being silly and people are staring!
No I'm not!
This is my favorite place to watch a fight.
Ah!

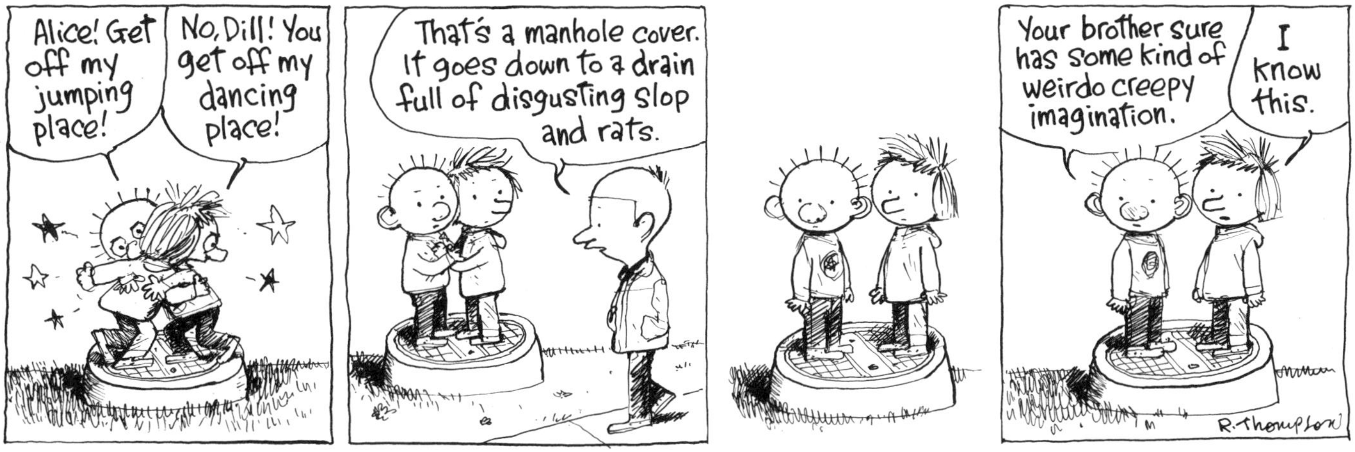
Alice! Get off my jumping place!
No, Dill! You get off my dancing place!
That's a manhole cover. It goes down to a drain full of disgusting slop and rats.
Your brother sure has some kind of weirdo creepy imagination.
I know this.
R. Thompson

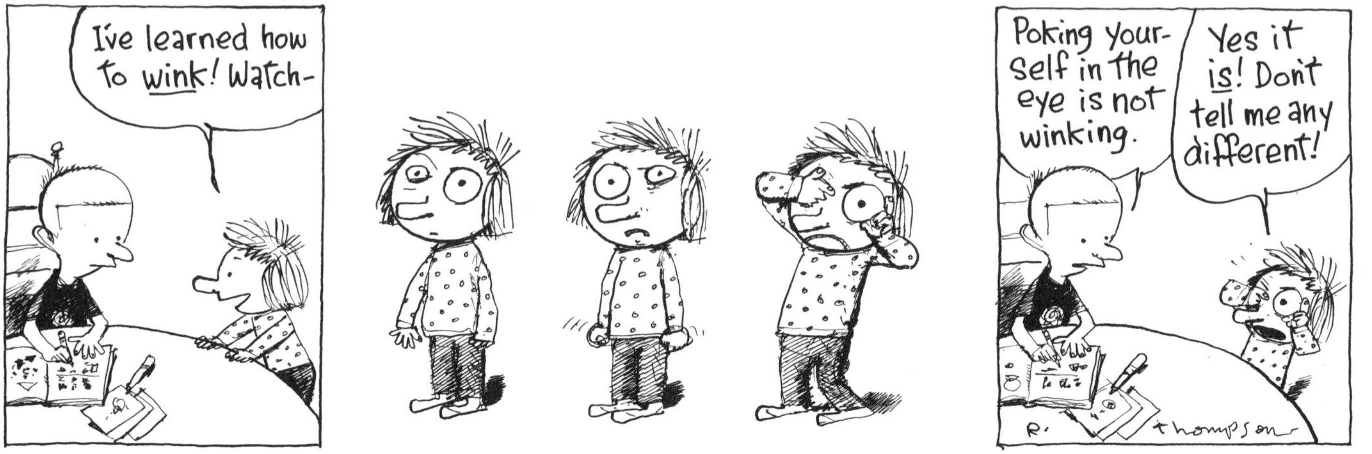
I've learned how to wink! Watch-
Poking yourself in the eye is not winking.
Yes it is! Don't tell me any different!

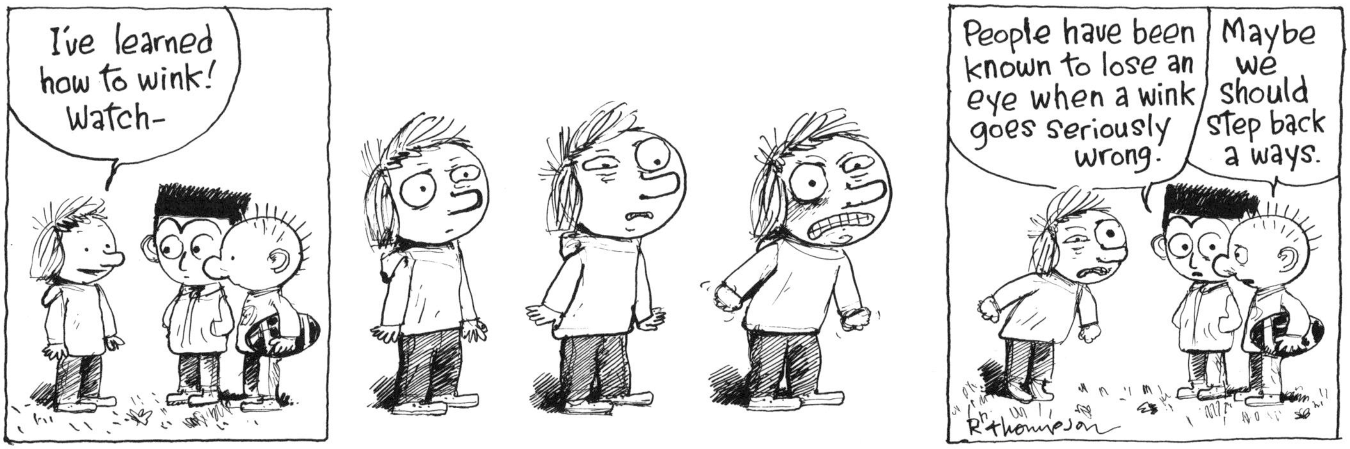
I've learned how to wink! Watch-
People have been known to lose an eye when a wink goes seriously wrong.
Maybe we should step back a ways.

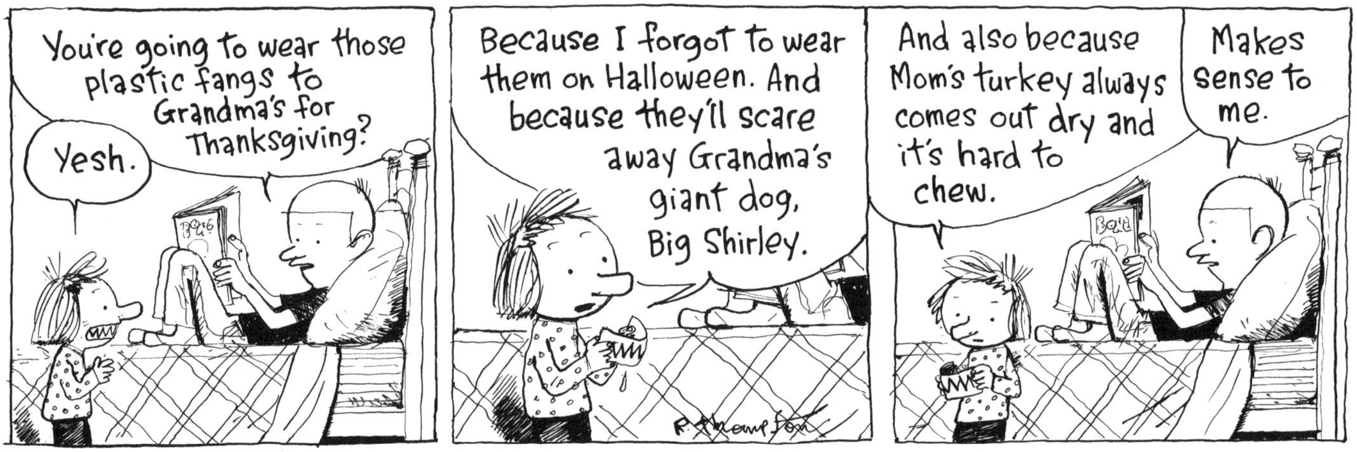
You're going to wear those plastic fangs to Grandma's for Thanksgiving?
Yesh.
Because I forgot to wear them on Halloween. And because they'll scare away Grandma's giant dog, Big Shirley.
And also because Mom's turkey always comes out dry and it's hard to chew.
Makes sense to me.

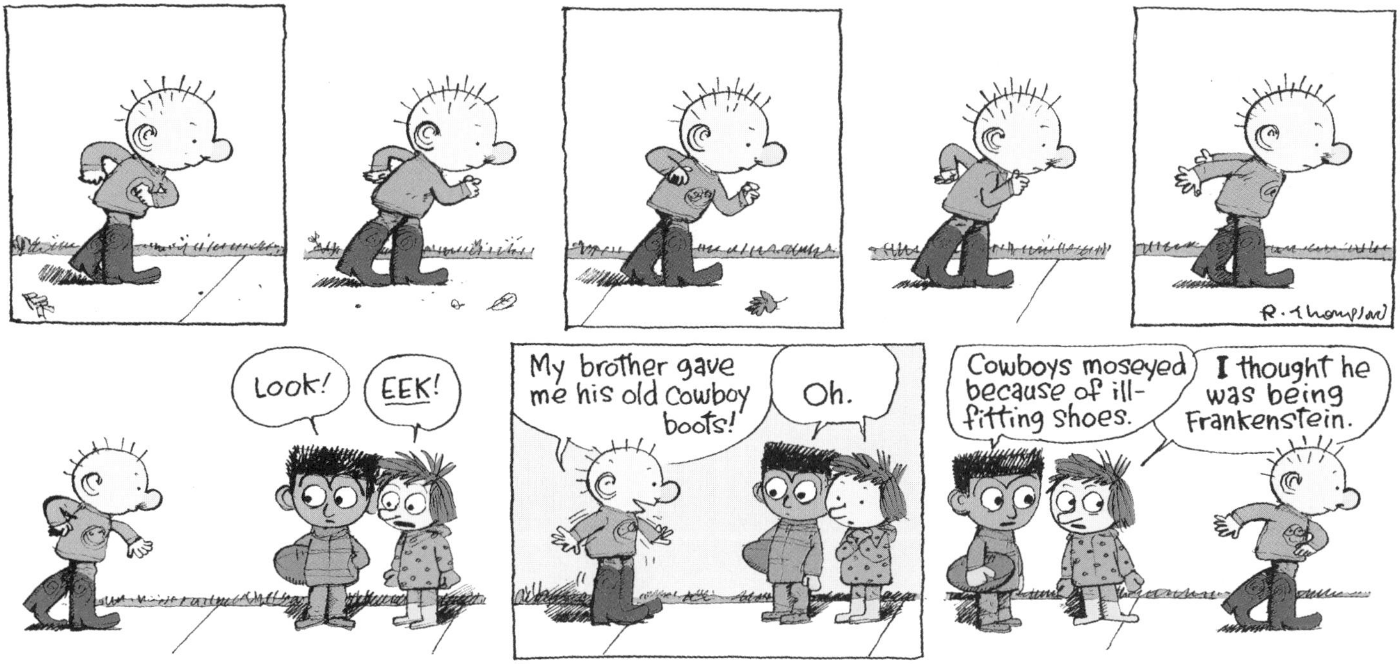
R. Thompson
Look!
EEK!
My brother gave me his old cowboy boots!
Oh.
Cowboys moseyed because of ill-fitting shoes.
I thought he was being Frankenstein.

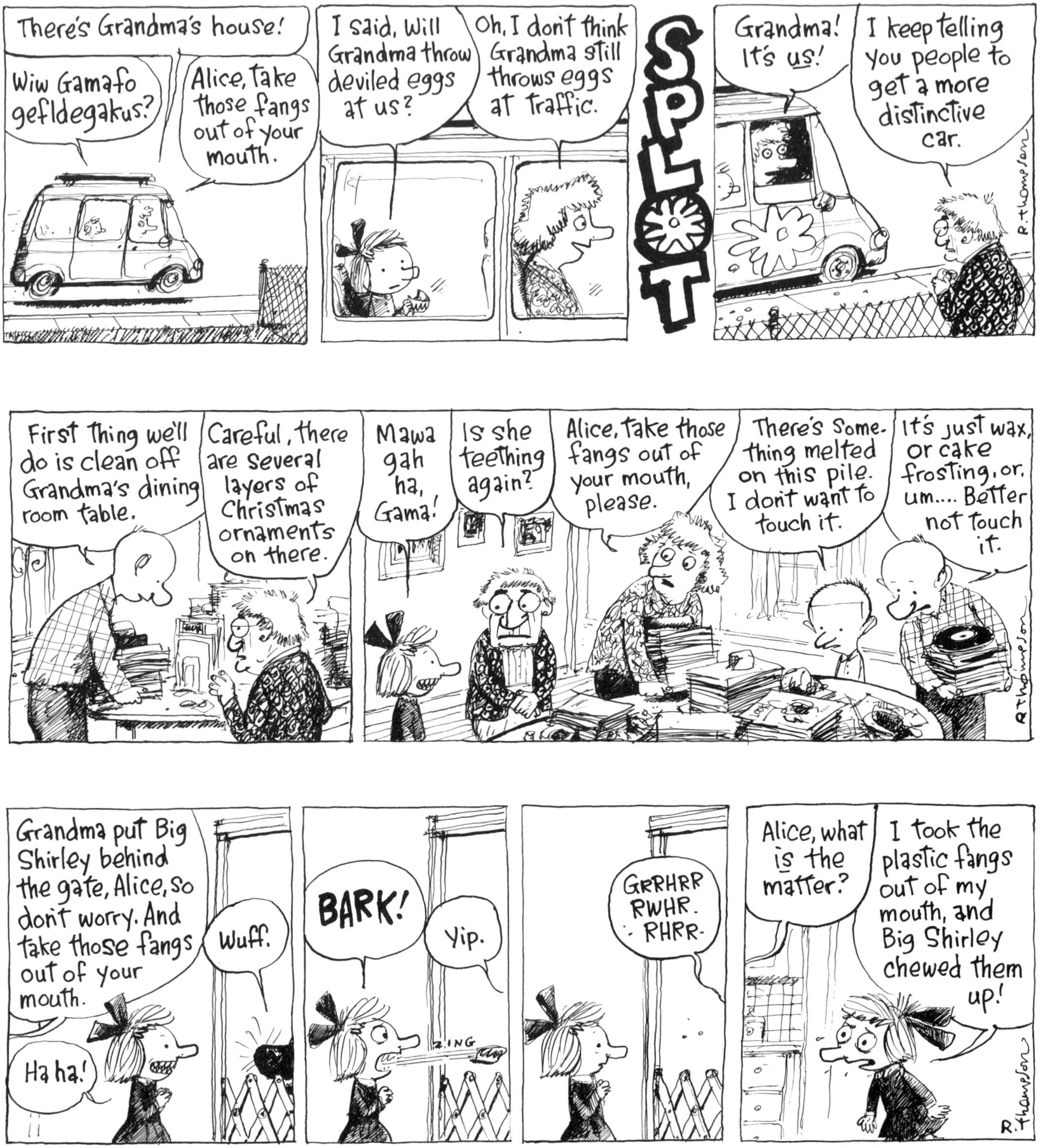
There's Grandma's house!
Wiw Gamafo gefldegakus?
Alice, take those fangs out of your mouth.
I said, Will Grandma throw deviled eggs at us?
Oh, I don't think Grandma still throws eggs at traffic.
SPLOT
Grandma! It's us!
I keep telling you people to get a more distinctive car.
R. thompson
First thing we'll do is clean off Grandma's dining room table.
Careful, there are several layers of Christmas ornaments on there.
Mawa gah ha, Gama!
Is she teething again?
Alice, take those fangs out of your mouth, please.
There's something melted on this pile. I don't want to touch it.
It's just wax, or cake frosting, or, um.... Better not touch it.
R. thompson
Grandma put Big Shirley behind the gate, Alice, so don't worry. And take those fangs out of your mouth.
Ha ha!
Wuff.
BARK!
Yip.
ZING
GRRHRR RWHR. RHRR.
Alice, what is the matter?
I took the plastic fangs out of my mouth, and Big Shirley chewed them up!
R. thompson

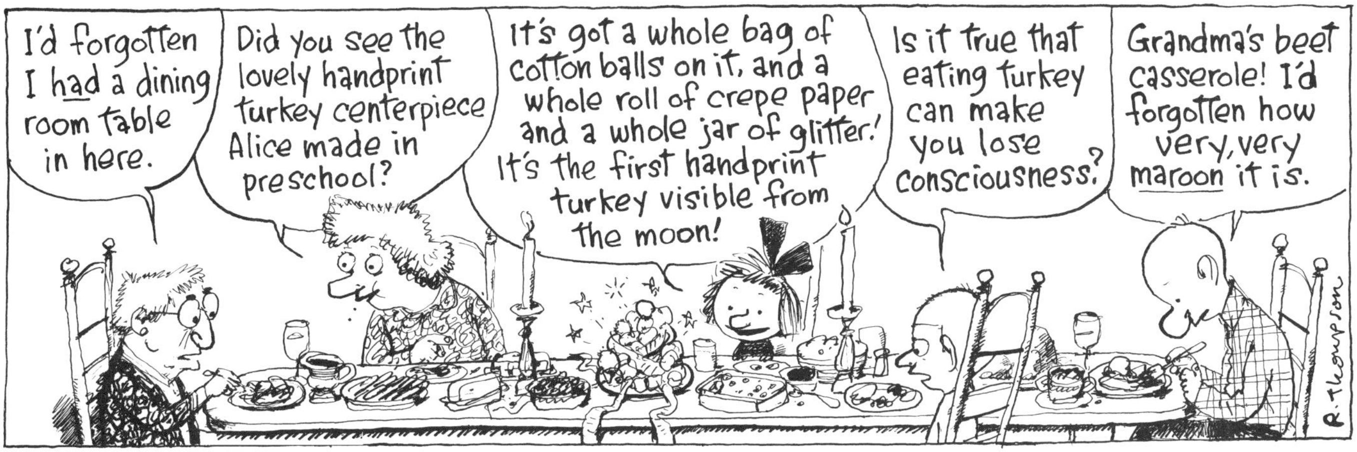
I'd forgotten I had a dining room table in here.
Did you see the lovely handprint turkey centerpiece Alice made in preschool?
It's got a whole bag of cotton balls on it, and a whole roll of crepe paper and a whole jar of glitter! It's the first handprint turkey visible from the moon!
Is it true that eating turkey can make you lose consciousness?
Grandma's beet casserole! I'd forgotten how very, very maroon it is.
R. Thompson

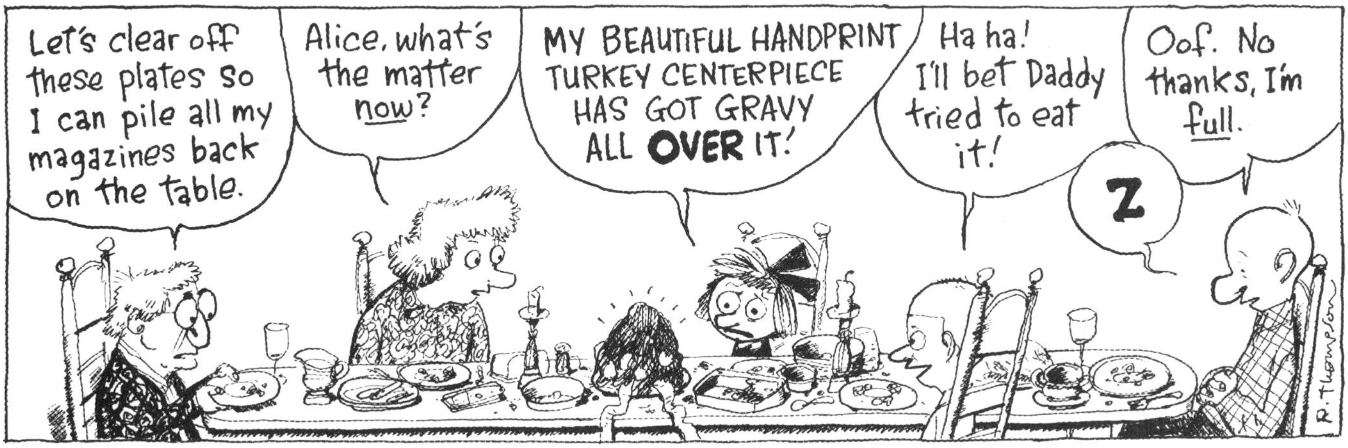
Let's clear off these plates so I can pile all my magazines back on the table.
Alice, what's the matter now?
MY BEAUTIFUL HANDPRINT TURKEY CENTERPIECE HAS GOT GRAVY ALL OVER IT!
Ha ha! I'll bet Daddy tried to eat it!
Z
Oof. No thanks, I'm full.
R. Thompson

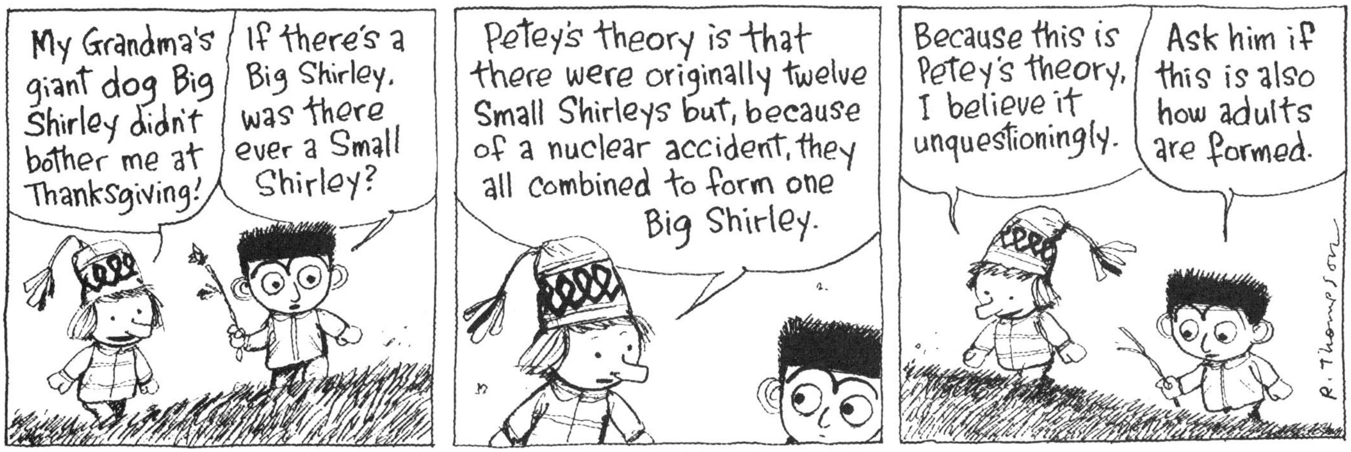
My Grandma's giant dog Big Shirley didn't bother me at Thanksgiving!
If there's a Big Shirley, was there ever a Small Shirley?
Petey's theory is that there were originally twelve Small Shirleys but, because of a nuclear accident, they all combined to form one Big Shirley.
Because this is Petey's theory, I believe it unquestioningly.
Ask him if this is also how adults are formed.
R. Thompson

Thanks for walking to the store with me, Alice-
Hold the bag for me, Daddy.
Why?
I always do a dance on this manhole cover!
Ha ha! That's very cute.
R. thompson
Almost finished?
Not yet.
Now?
No.
ALICE! LET'S GO!
OKAY!
Daddy has no appreciation for Art.
I know. I asked him to read the first 32 chapters of my Toad Zombies graphic novel and he practically ran away.

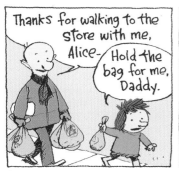

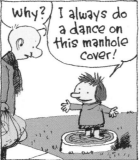

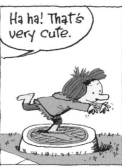

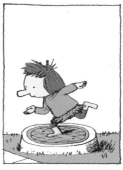

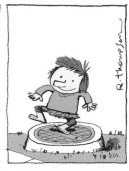

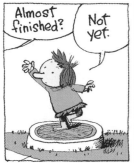

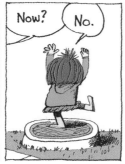

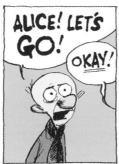

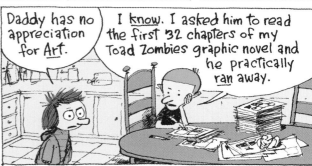

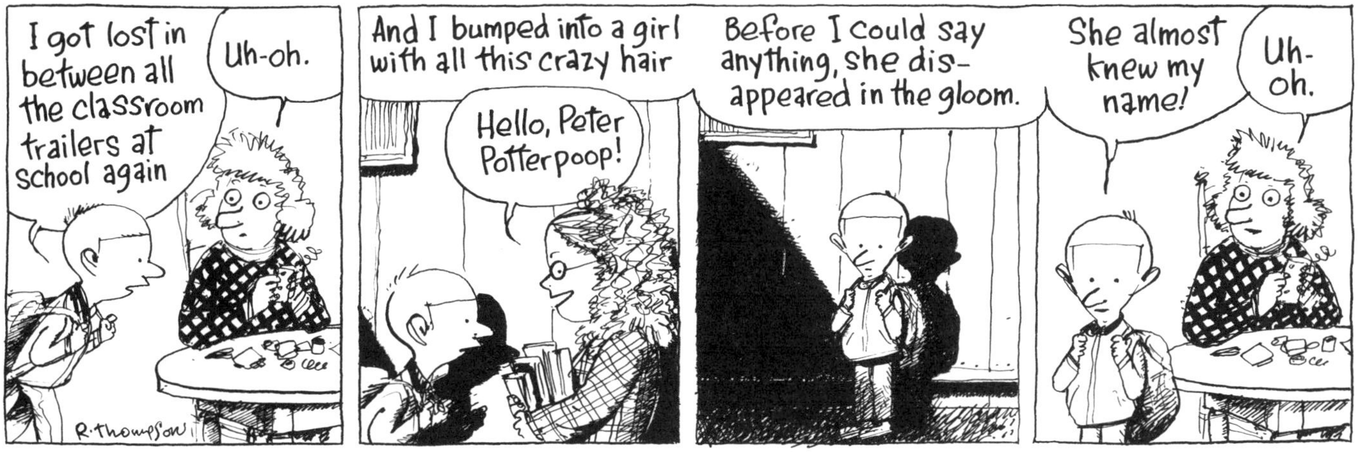
I got lost in between all the classroom trailers at school again
Uh-oh.
And I bumped into a girl with all this crazy hair
Hello, Peter Potterpoop!
Before I could say anything, she disappeared in the gloom.
She almost knew my name!
Uh-oh.

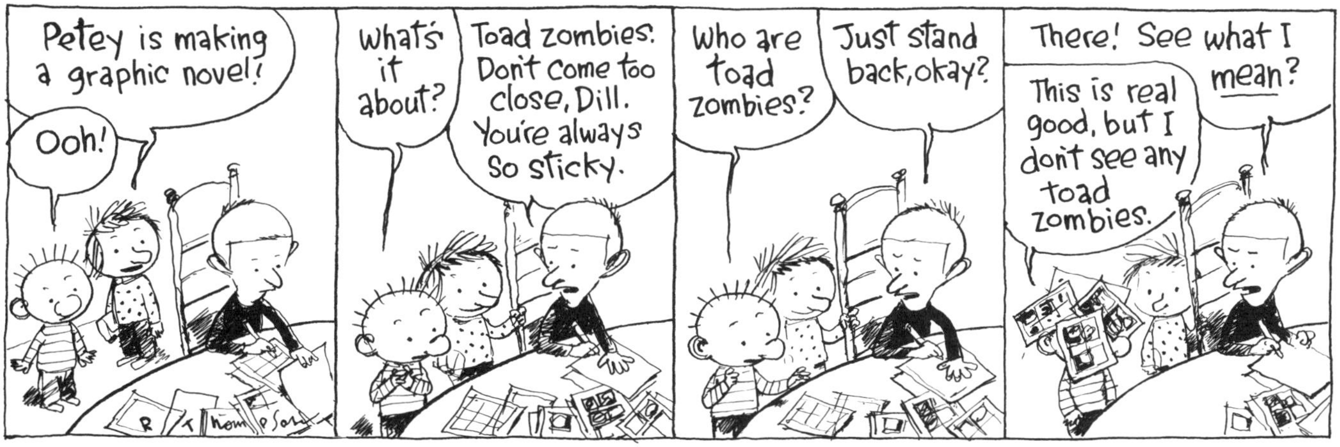
Petey is making a graphic novel!
Ooh!
What's it about?
Toad zombies. Don't come too close, Dill. You're always so sticky.
Who are toad zombies?
Just stand back, okay?
There! See what I mean?
This is real good, but I don't see any toad zombies.

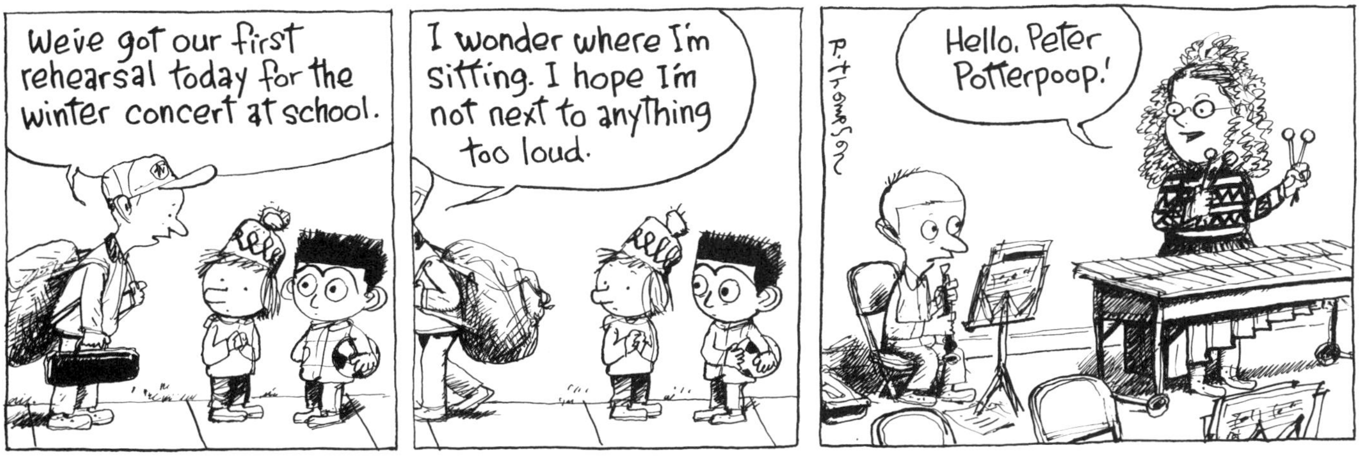
We've got our first rehearsal today for the winter concert at school.
I wonder where I'm sitting. I hope I'm not next to anything too loud.
Hello, Peter Potterpoop!

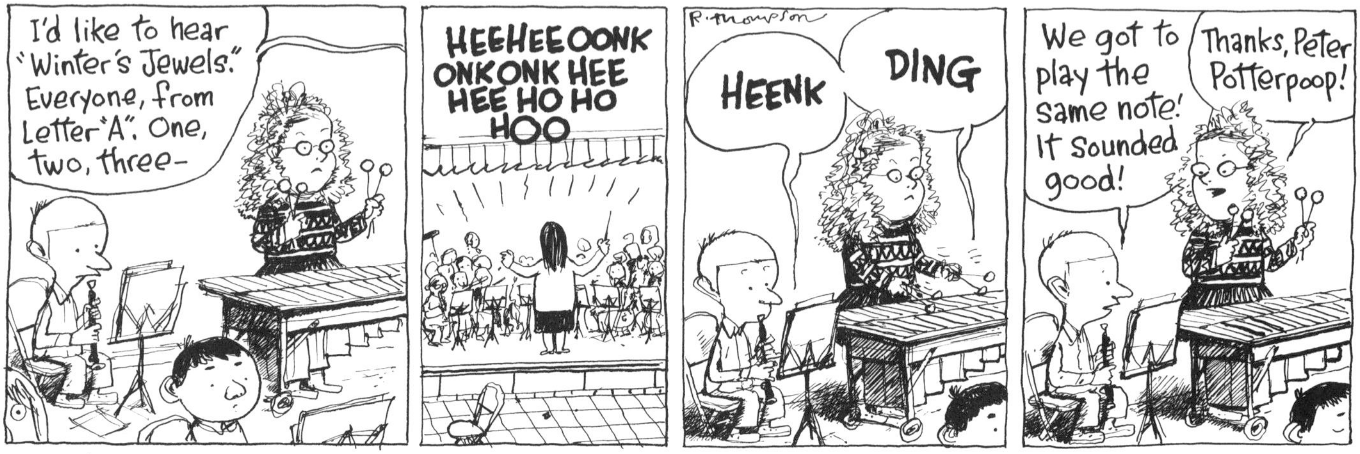
I'd like to hear "Winter's Jewels." Everyone, from Letter "A". One, two, three-
HEEHEEOONK ONKONK HEE HEE HO HO HOO
R. Thompson
HEENK
DING
We got to play the same note! It sounded good!
Thanks, Peter Potterpoop!

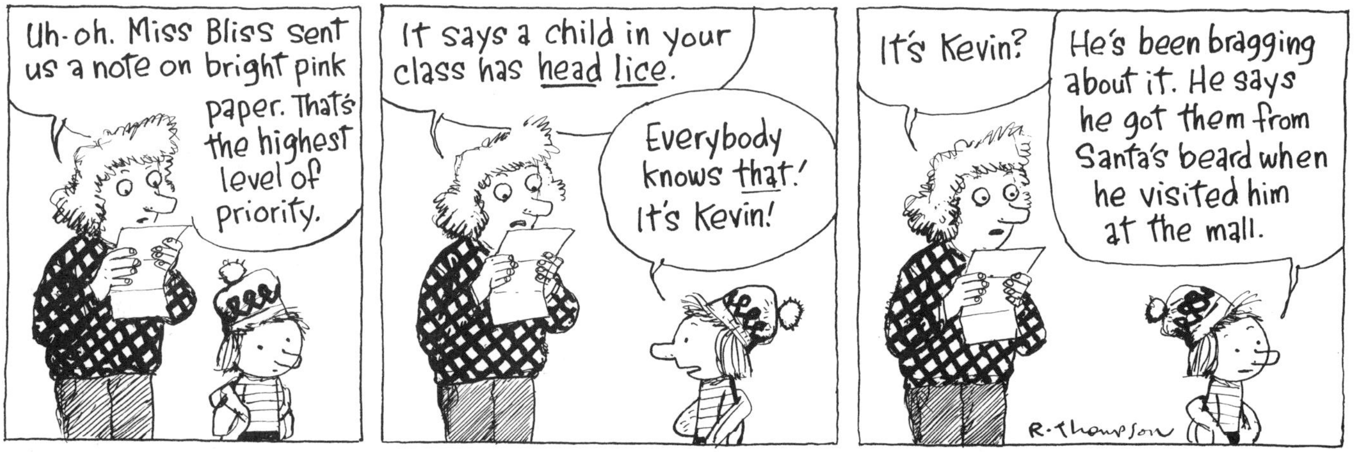
Uh-oh. Miss Bliss sent us a note on bright pink paper. That's the highest level of priority.
It says a child in your class has head lice.
Everybody knows that! It's Kevin!
It's Kevin?
He's been bragging about it. He says he got them from Santa's beard when he visited him at the mall.
R. Thompson

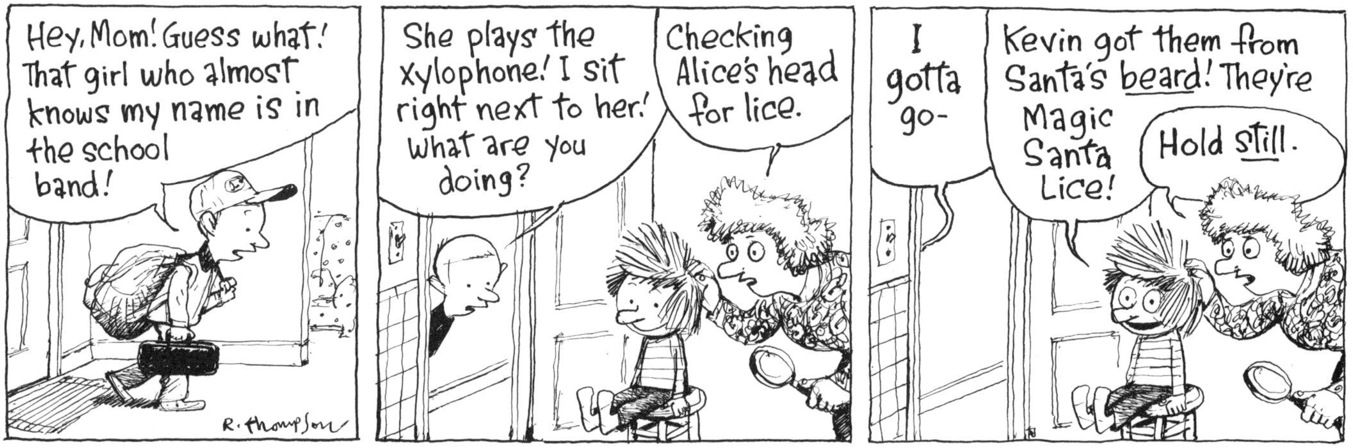
Hey, Mom! Guess what! That girl who almost knows my name is in the school band!
R. Thompson
She plays the xylophone! I sit right next to her! What are you doing?
Checking Alice's head for lice.
I gotta go-
Kevin got them from Santa's beard! They're Magic Santa Lice!
Hold still.

Look, Petey! I've been cutting and gluing things from Christmas catalogs.
By combining all my favorite toys, I've distilled my list for Santa into One Perfect Gift!
See? It's a robot pony princess that unfolds into a tricycle with a drum kit attachment and a lightbulb for baking pie!
You can't do that! You'll confuse Santa! His head will explode!
What?
Children everywhere will hate you if you make Santa's head explode.
Okay, forget it! I guess Santa's not such a genius after all.
And I'm sure he heard that.
No! NO! I DIDN'T MEAN IT! Where's the microphone? Is this it? SANTA IS A GENIUS! A GENIUS!
R. Thompson

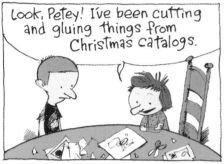

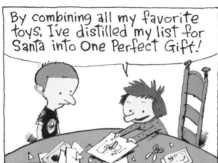

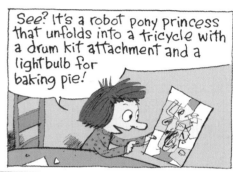

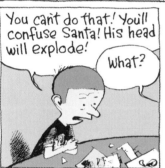

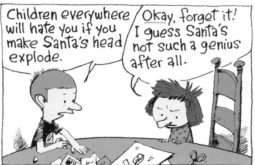

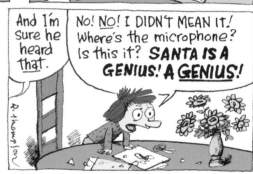

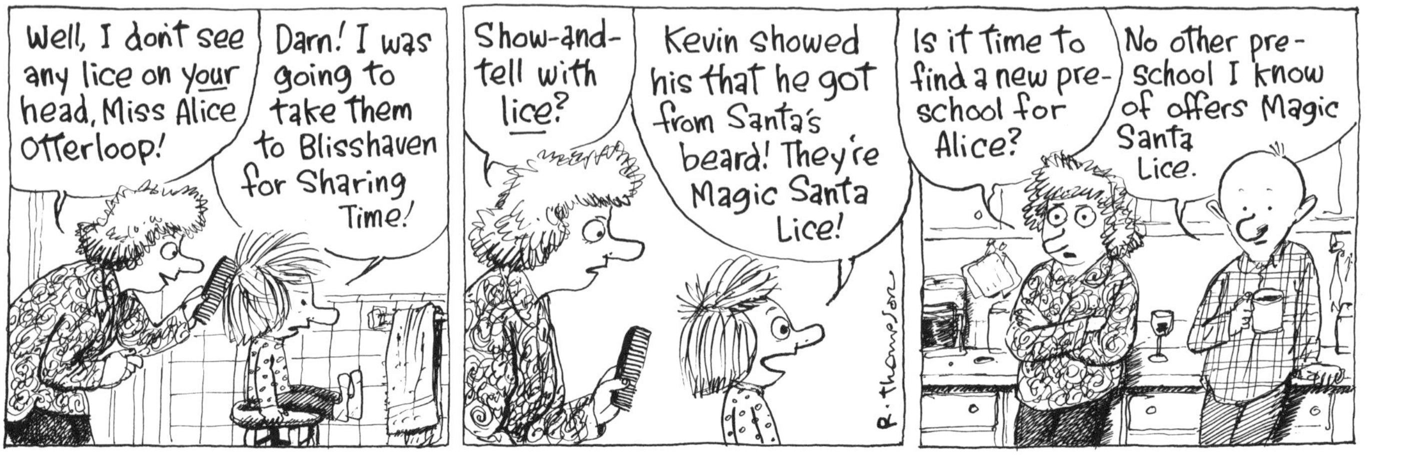
Well, I don't see any lice on your head, Miss Alice Otterloop!
Darn! I was going to take them to Blisshaven for Sharing Time!
Show-and-tell with lice?
Kevin showed his that he got from Santa's beard! They're Magic Santa Lice!
Is it time to find a new pre-school for Alice?
No other pre-school I know of offers Magic Santa Lice.
R. Thompson

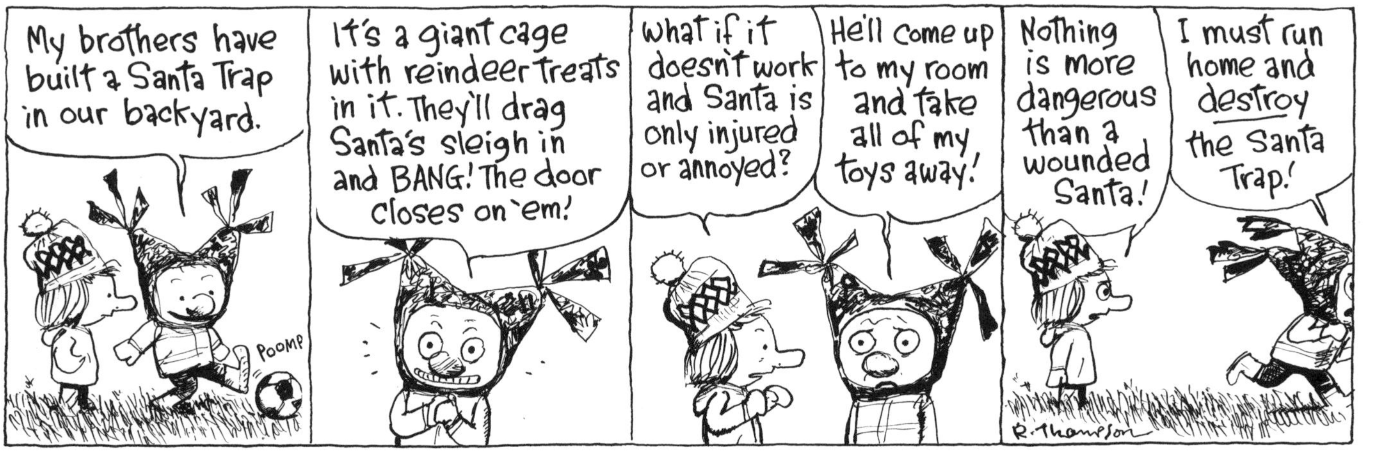
My brothers have built a Santa Trap in our backyard.
POOMP
It's a giant cage with reindeer treats in it. They'll drag Santa's sleigh in and BANG! The door closes on 'em!
What if it doesn't work and Santa is only injured or annoyed?
He'll come up to my room and take all of my toys away!
Nothing is more dangerous than a wounded Santa!
I must run home and destroy the Santa Trap!
R. Thompson

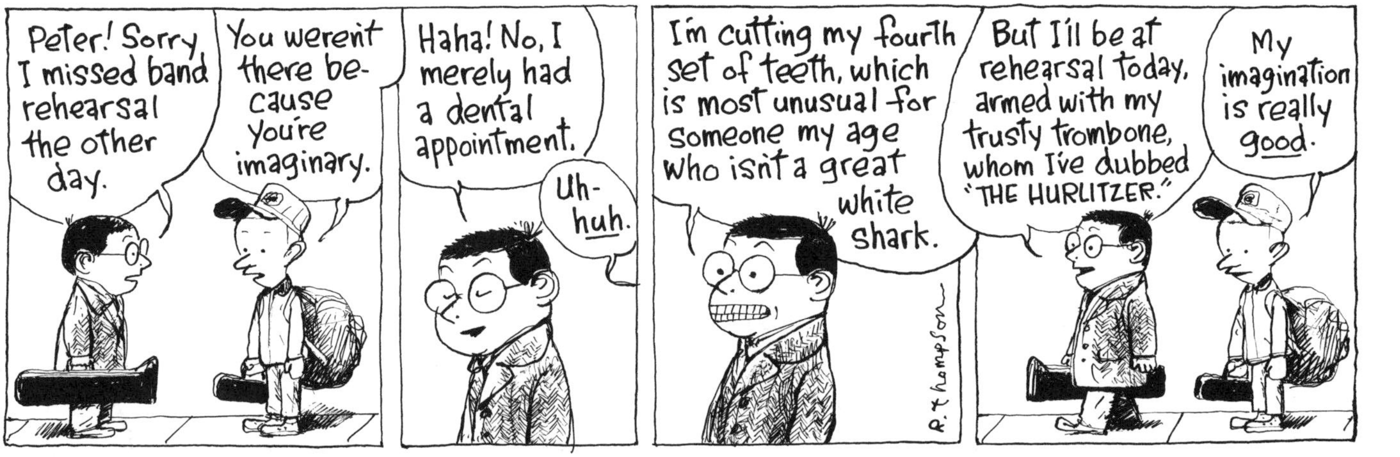
Peter! Sorry I missed band rehearsal the other day.
You weren't there because you're imaginary.
Haha! No, I merely had a dental appointment.
Uh-huh.
I'm cutting my fourth set of teeth, which is most unusual for someone my age who isn't a great white shark.
But I'll be at rehearsal today, armed with my trusty trombone, whom I've dubbed "THE HURLITZER."
My imagination is really good.
R. Thompson

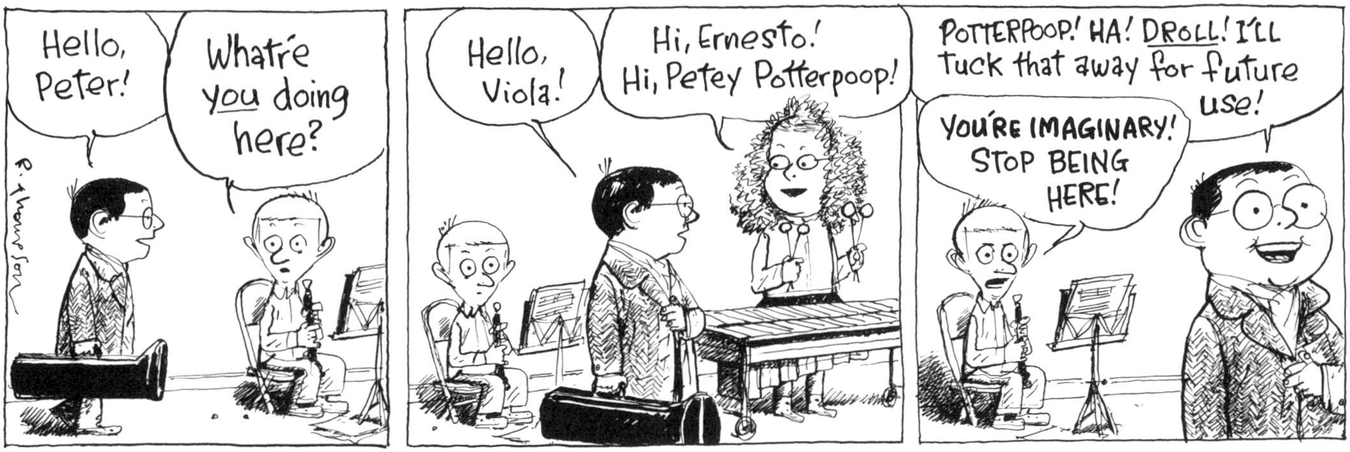
Hello, Peter!
Whatre you doing here?
Hello, Viola!
Hi, Ernesto! Hi, Petey Potterpoop!
YOU'RE IMAGINARY! STOP BEING HERE!
POTTERPOOP! HA! DROLL! I'LL tuck that away for future use!

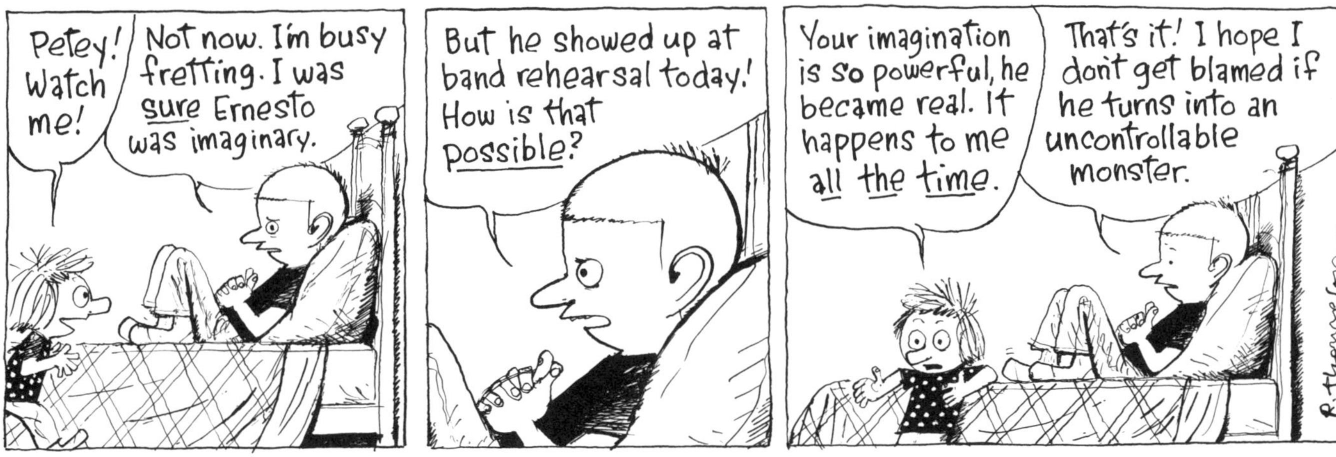
Petey! Watch me!
Not now. I'm busy fretting. I was sure Ernesto was imaginary.
But he showed up at band rehearsal today! How is that possible?
Your imagination is so powerful, he became real. It happens to me all the time.
That's it! I hope I don't get blamed if he turns into an uncontrollable monster.

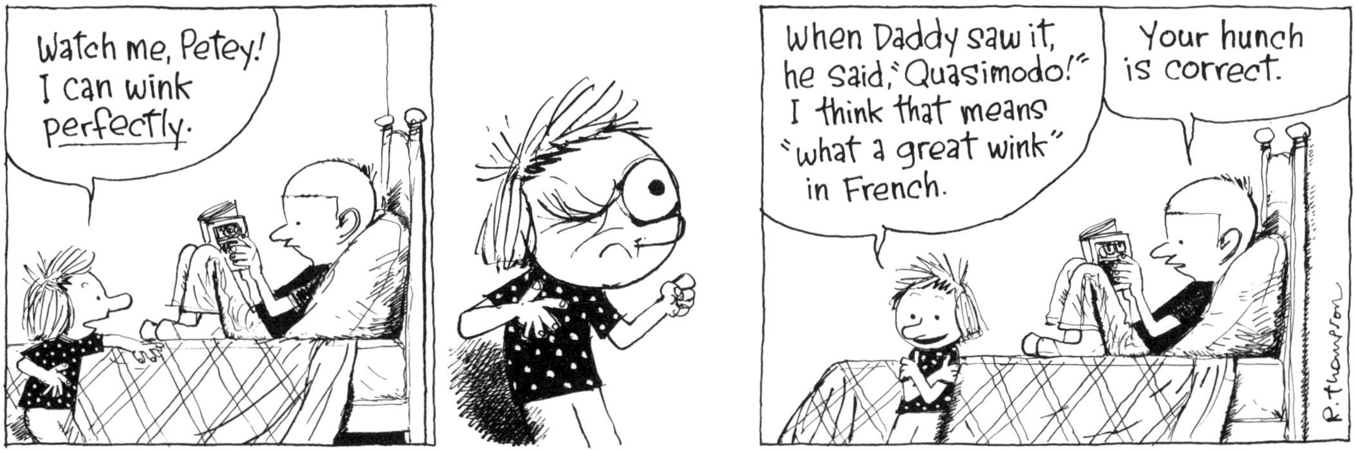
Watch me, Petey! I can wink perfectly.
When Daddy saw it, he said, "Quasimodo!" I think that means "what a great wink" in French.
Your hunch is correct.

"This isn't my usual cereal box!"

"It's almost the same."

"What do you mean almost? There's no picture of Happy the Hyena! I miss his cereal-crazed antics! Was he fired for being insufficiently cereal-crazed?"

"Alice, it's the store brand. It's two dollars cheaper than the Happy Hyena brand. And it is almost the same cereal."

"Well, we'll just see."

"UGH. This cereal has a strange texture. And the marshmallows are drab, misshapen and poorly distributed."

"Then I'll just fix you a big bowl of hot cereal! And look what we've got- INSTANT OATMEAL, EXTRA LUMPY, WITH RAISINS!"

"Ha ha! Actually this stuff is pretty darn good!"

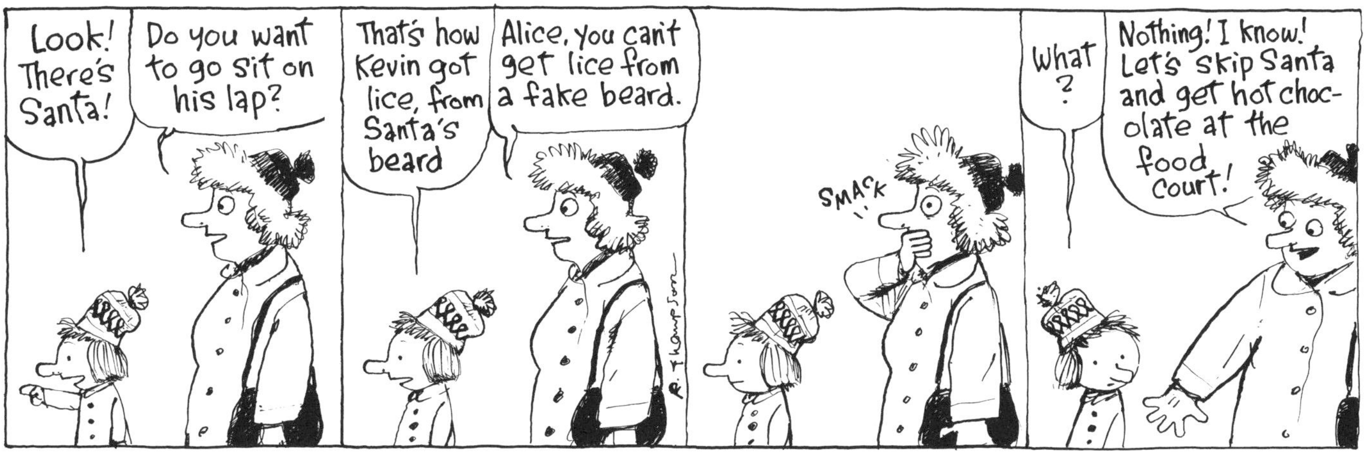
Look! There's Santa!
Do you want to go sit on his lap?
That's how Kevin got lice, from Santa's beard
Alice, you can't get lice from a fake beard.
SMACK
What?
Nothing! I know! Let's skip Santa and get hot chocolate at the food court!

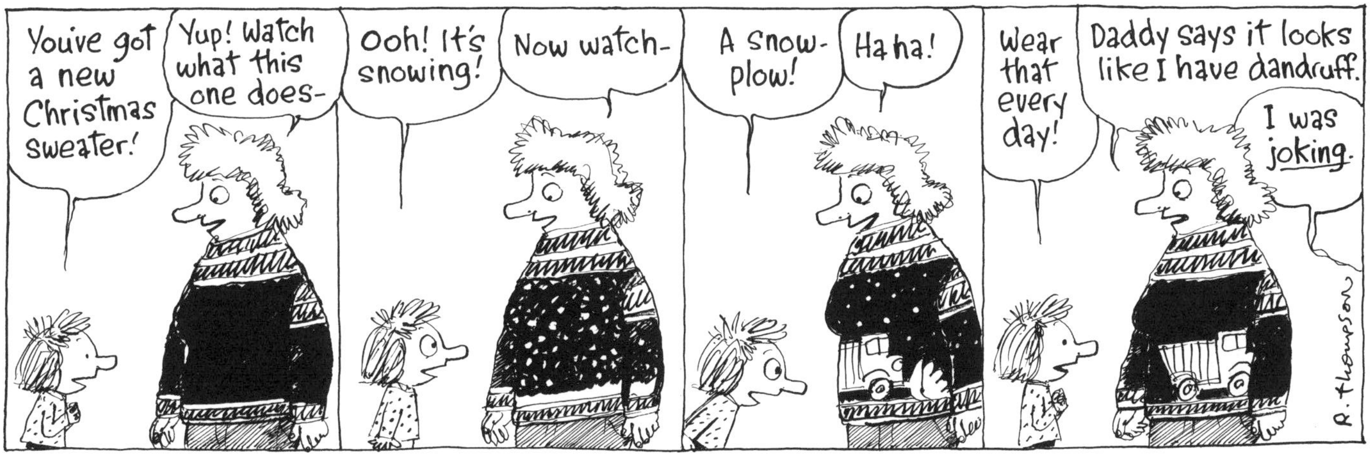
You've got a new Christmas sweater!
Yup! Watch what this one does-
Ooh! It's snowing!
Now watch-
A snow-plow!
Ha ha!
Wear that every day!
Daddy says it looks like I have dandruff.
I was joking.

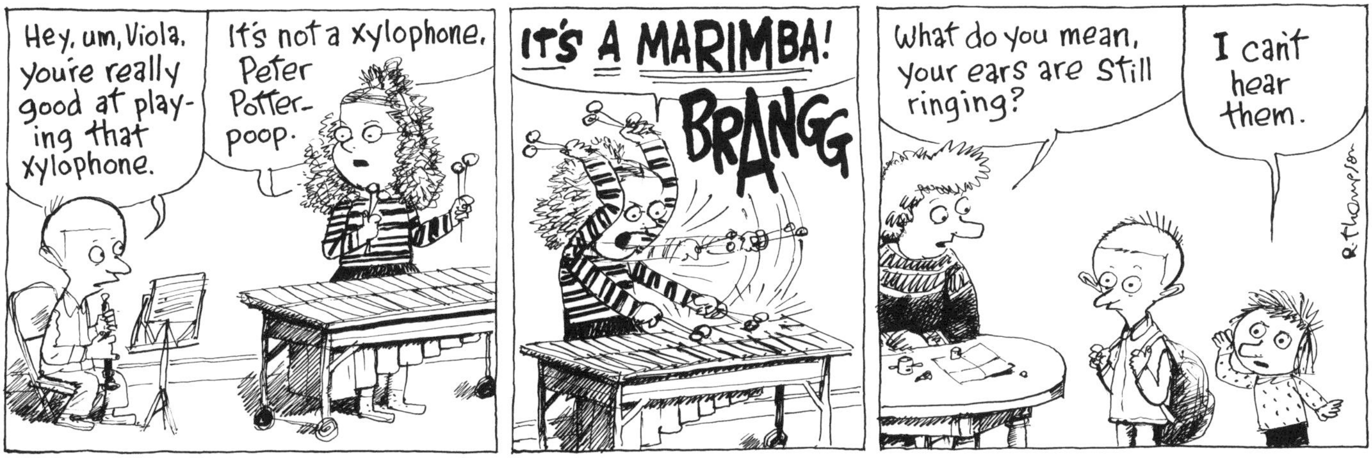
Hey, um, Viola, you're really good at play-ing that xylophone.
It's not a xylophone, Peter Potter-poop.
IT'S A MARIMBA!
BRANGG
What do you mean, your ears are still ringing?
I can't hear them.

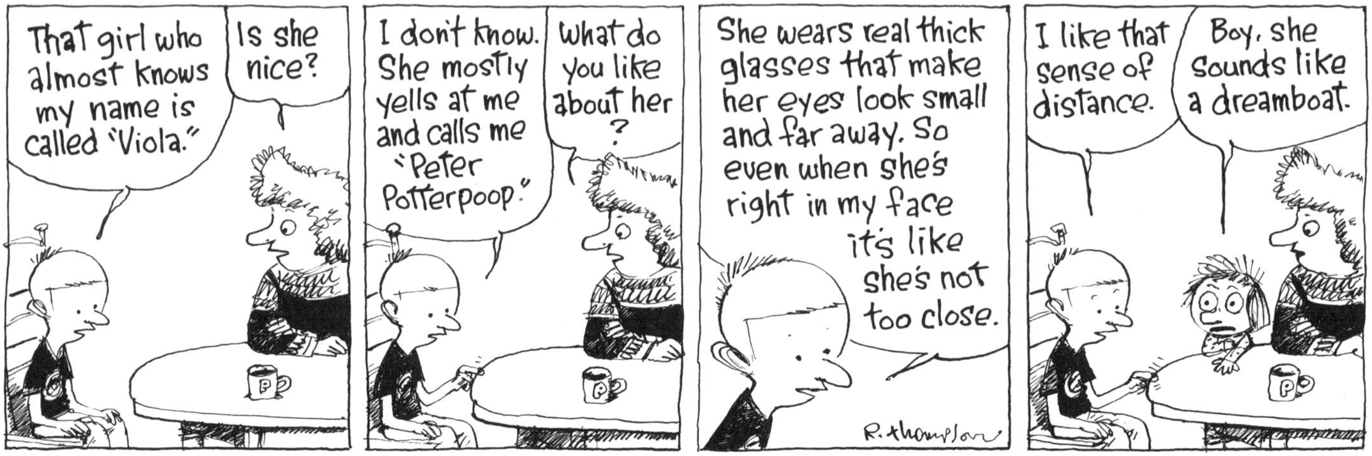
That girl who almost knows my name is called "Viola."
Is she nice?
I don't know. She mostly yells at me and calls me "Peter Potterpoop."
What do you like about her?
She wears real thick glasses that make her eyes look small and far away. So even when she's right in my face it's like she's not too close.
I like that sense of distance.
Boy, she sounds like a dreamboat.

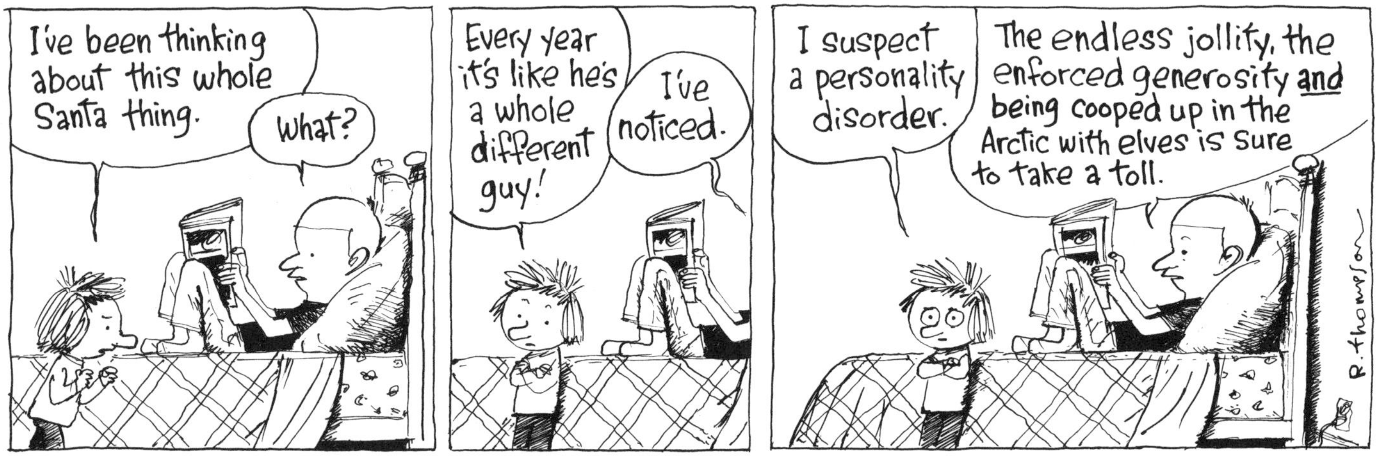
I've been thinking about this whole Santa thing.
What?
Every year it's like he's a whole different guy!
I've noticed.
I suspect a personality disorder.
The endless jollity, the enforced generosity and being cooped up in the Arctic with elves is sure to take a toll.

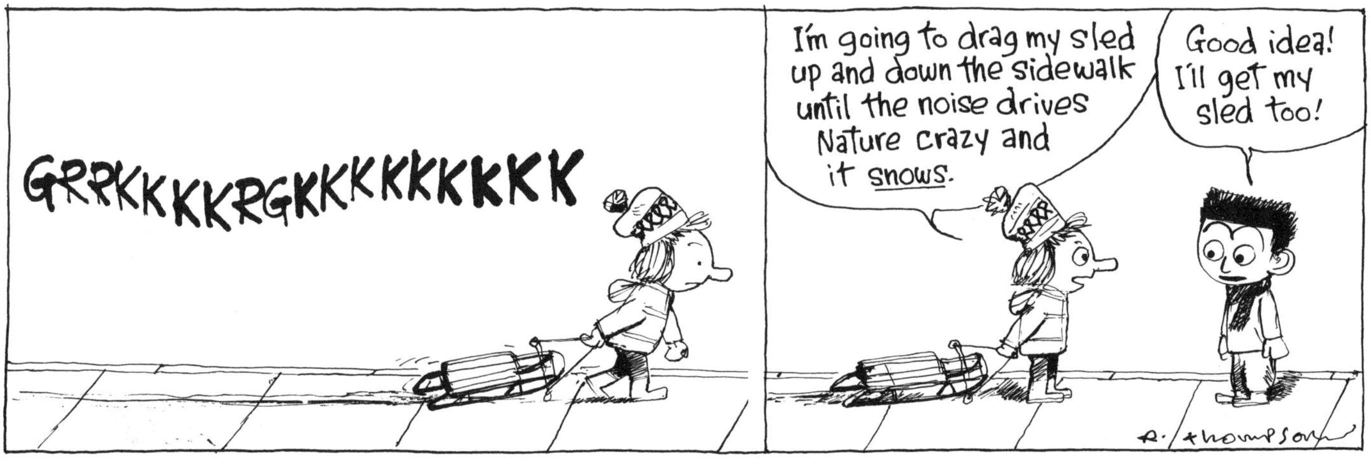
GRPKKKKRGKKKKKKKK
I'm going to drag my sled up and down the sidewalk until the noise drives Nature crazy and it snows.
Good idea! I'll get my sled too!